THE O'LEARY SERIES

INTRODUCTORY EDITION

Microsoft®
PowerPoint 2010:
A Case Approach

Timothy J. O'Leary
Professor Emeritus,
Arizona State University

Linda I. O'Leary

McGraw Hill

Connect
Learn
Succeed™

THE O'LEARY SERIES MICROSOFT® POWERPOINT 2010: A CASE APPROACH, INTRODUCTORY EDITION

Published by McGraw-Hill, a business unit of The McGraw-Hill Companies, Inc., 1221 Avenue of the Americas, New York, NY, 10020. Copyright © 2011 by The McGraw-Hill Companies, Inc. All rights reserved. No part of this publication may be reproduced or distributed in any form or by any means, or stored in a database or retrieval system, without the prior written consent of The McGraw-Hill Companies, Inc., including, but not limited to, in any network or other electronic storage or transmission, or broadcast for distance learning.

Some ancillaries, including electronic and print components, may not be available to customers outside the United States.

This book is printed on acid-free paper.

2 3 4 5 6 7 8 9 0 RMN/RMN 1 0 9 8 7 6 5 4 3 2 1

ISBN   978-0-07-733134-4
MHID   0-07-733134-6

Vice president/Editor in chief: *Elizabeth Haefele*
Vice president/Director of marketing: *John E. Biernat*
Senior sponsoring editor: *Scott Davidson*
Director of development: *Sarah Wood*
Developmental editor II: *Alaina Grayson*
Editorial coordinator: *Alan Palmer*
Marketing manager: *Tiffany Wendt*
Lead digital product manager: *Damian Moshak*
Digital developmental editor: *Kevin White*
Director, Editing/Design/Production: *Jess Ann Kosic*
Project manager: *Marlena Pechan*
Senior buyer: *Michael R. McCormick*
Senior designer: *Srdjan Savanovic*
Senior photo research coordinator: *Jeremy Cheshareck*
Photo researcher: *Evan Modesto*
Media project manager: *Cathy L. Tepper*
Cover design: *Evan Modesto*
Interior design: *Laurie Entringer*
Typeface: *10/12 New Aster LT STD*
Compositor: *Laserwords Private Limited*
Printer: *R. R. Donnelley*
Cover credit: © Kjpargeter/Dreamstime.com
Credits: The credits section for this book begins on page PPC.1 and is considered an extension of the copyright page.

Library of Congress Cataloging-in-Publication Data

O'Leary, Timothy J., 1947-
    Microsoft PowerPoint 2010 : a case approach / Timothy J. O'Leary, Linda I. O'Leary. —
Introductory ed.
        p. cm. — (The O'Leary series)
    Includes bibliographical references and index.
    ISBN-13: 978-0-07-733134-4 (alk. paper)
    ISBN-10: 0-07-733134-6 (alk. paper)
    1. Presentation graphics software. 2. Microsoft PowerPoint (Computer file) I. Title.
T385.O335346 2011
005.5'8--dc22

                                                                                        2010030103

The Internet addresses listed in the text were accurate at the time of publication. The inclusion of a Web site does not indicate an endorsement by the authors or McGraw-Hill, and McGraw-Hill does not guarantee the accuracy of the information presented at these sites.

www.mhhe.com

Brief Contents

Contents

Acknowledgments

We would like to extend our thanks to the professors who took time out of their busy schedules to provide us with the feedback necessary to develop the 2010 Edition of this text. The following professors offered valuable suggestions on revising the text:

Joan Albright
Greenville Technical College

Wilma Andrews
Virginia Commonwealth University

Robert M. Benavides
Collin College

Kim Cannon
Greenville Technical College

Paulette Comet
The Community College of Baltimore County

Michael Dunklebarger
Alamance Community College

Joel English
Centura College

Deb Fells
Mesa Community College

Tatyana Feofilaktova
ASA Institute

Sue Furnas
Collin College

Debbie Grande
The Community College of Rhode Island

Rachelle Hall
Glendale Community College

Katherine Herbert
Montclair State University

Terri Holly
Indian River State College

Mark W. Huber
University of Georgia

Joyce Kessel
Western International University

Hal P. Kingsley
Trocaire College

Diane Lending
James Madison University

Dr. Mo Manouchehripour
The Art Institute of Dallas

Sue McCrory
Missouri State University

Gary McFall
Purdue University

Margaret M. Menna
The Community College of Rhode Island

Philip H. Nielson
Salt Lake Community College

Craig Piercy
University of Georgia

Mark Renslow
Globe University/Minnesota School of Business

Ann Rowlette
Liberty University

Chakra Pani Sharma
ASA Institute

Eric Weinstein
Suffolk County Community College

Sheryl Wright
College of the Mainland

Laurie Zouharis
Suffolk University

We would like to thank those who took the time to help us develop the manuscript and ensure accuracy through painstaking edits: Brenda Nielsen of Mesa Community College–Red Mountain, Stephen J. Adams of Cleveland State University, Candice Spangler of Columbus State Community College, and Kate Scalzi.

Finally, we would like to thank team members from McGraw-Hill, whose renewed commitment, direction, and support have infused the team with the excitement of a new project. Leading the team from McGraw-Hill are Tiffany Wendt, Marketing Manager; and Developmental Editor Alaina Grayson.

The production staff is headed by Marlena Pechan, Project Manager, whose planning and attention to detail have made it possible for us to successfully meet a very challenging schedule; Srdjan Savanovic, Designer; Michael McCormick, Production Supervisor; Kevin White, Digital Developmental Editor; Jeremy Cheshareck, Photo Researcher; and Becky Komro, copyeditor—team members on whom we can depend to do a great job.

Christy Parrish spent 20 years developing, designing, and delivering corporate training programs. She has contributed to several books on Microsoft Office and other productivity software packages. As a freelance author, she also has written a magazine series and numerous online articles on a wide variety of topics. Christy is also a member of her community artists group and is recognized for her unique photographic skills that are on display at various galleries. She is married and has two sons that both share her love of writing and art.

Preface

The 20th century brought us the dawn of the digital information age and unprecedented changes in information technology. There is no indication that this rapid rate of change will be slowing—it may even be increasing. As we begin the 21st century, computer literacy is undoubtedly becoming a prerequisite in whatever career you choose.

The goal of the O'Leary Series is to provide you with the necessary skills to efficiently use these applications. Equally important is the goal to provide a foundation for students to readily and easily learn to use future versions of this software. This series does this by providing detailed step-by-step instructions combined with careful selection and presentation of essential concepts.

Times are changing, technology is changing, and this text is changing too. As students of today, you are different from those of yesterday. You put much effort toward the things that interest you and the things that are relevant to you. Your efforts directed at learning application programs and exploring the Web seem, at times, limitless.

On the other hand, students often can be shortsighted, thinking that learning the skills to use the application is the only objective. The mission of the series is to build upon and extend this interest by not only teaching the specific application skills but by introducing the concepts that are common to all applications, providing students with the confidence, knowledge, and ability to easily learn the next generation of applications.

Instructor's Resource Center

The online **Instructor's Resource Center** contains access to a Computerized Test Bank, an Instructor's Manual, Solutions, and PowerPoint Presentation Slides. Features of the Instructor's Resource are described below.

- **Instructor's Manual** The Instructor's Manual, authored by the primary contributor, contains lab objectives, concepts, outlines, lecture notes, and command summaries. Also included are answers to all end-of-chapter material, tips for covering difficult materials, additional exercises, and a schedule showing how much time is required to cover text material.

- **Computerized Test Bank** The test bank, authored by the primary contributor, contains hundreds of multiple choice, true/false, and discussion questions. Each question will be accompanied by the correct answer, the level of learning difficulty, and corresponding page references. Our flexible EZ Test software allows you to easily generate custom exams.

- **PowerPoint Presentation Slides** The presentation slides, authored by the primary contributor, include lab objectives, concepts, outlines, text figures, and speaker's notes. Also included are bullets to illustrate key terms and FAQs.

Online Learning Center/Website

Found at **www.mhhe.com/oleary,** this site provides additional learning and instructional tools to enhance the comprehension of the text. The OLC/Website is divided into these three areas:

- **Information Center** Contains core information about the text, supplements, and the authors.
- **Instructor Center** Offers the aforementioned instructional materials, downloads, and other relevant links for professors.
- **Student Center** Contains data files, chapter competencies, chapter concepts, self-quizzes, additional Web links, and more.

Simnet Assessment for Office Applications

Simnet Assessment for Office Applications provides a way for you to test students' software skills in a simulated environment. Simnet is available for Microsoft Office 2010 and provides flexibility for you in your applications course by offering:

Pretesting options
Post-testing options
Course placement testing
Diagnostic capabilities to reinforce skills
Web delivery of tests
Certification preparation exams
Learning verification reports

For more information on skills assessment software, please contact your local sales representative, or visit us at **www.mhhe.com.**

O'Leary Series

The O'Leary Application Series for Microsoft Office is available separately or packaged with *Computing Essentials*. The O'Leary Application Series offers a step-by-step case-based approach to learning computer applications and is available in both introductory and complete versions.

Computing Concepts

Computing Essentials 2012 offers a unique, visual orientation that gives students a basic understanding of computing concepts. *Computing Essentials* encourages "active" learning with exercises, explorations, visual illustrations, and screen shots. While combining the "active" learning style with current topics and technology, this text provides an accurate snapshot of computing trends. When bundled with software application lab manuals, students are given a complete representation of the fundamental issues surrounding the personal computing environment.

ABOUT THE AUTHORS

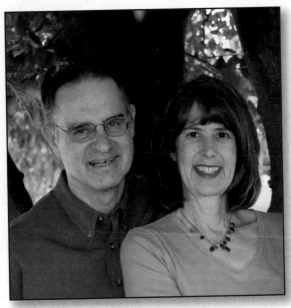

Tim and Linda O'Leary live in the American Southwest and spend much of their time engaging instructors and students in conversation about learning. In fact, they have been talking about learning for over 25 years. Something in those early conversations convinced them to write a book, to bring their interest in the learning process to the printed page. Today, they are as concerned as ever about learning, about technology, and about the challenges of presenting material in new ways, in terms of both content and method of delivery.

A powerful and creative team, Tim combines his 30 years of classroom teaching experience with Linda's background as a consultant and corporate trainer. Tim has taught courses at Stark Technical College in Canton, Ohio, and at Rochester Institute of Technology in upstate New York, and is currently a professor emeritus at Arizona State University in Tempe, Arizona. Linda offered her expertise at ASU for several years as an academic advisor. She also presented and developed materials for major corporations such as Motorola, Intel, Honeywell, and AT&T, as well as various community colleges in the Phoenix area.

Tim and Linda have talked to and taught numerous students, all of them with a desire to learn something about computers and applications that make their lives easier, more interesting, and more productive.

Each new edition of an O'Leary text, supplement, or learning aid has benefited from these students and their instructors who daily stand in front of them (or over their shoulders). The O'Leary Series is no exception.

Dedication

We dedicate this edition to our parents—Irene Perley Coats, Jean L. O'Leary, and Charles D. O'Leary—for all their support and love. We miss you.

Objectives

After completing the Introduction to Microsoft Office 2010, you should be able to:

1 Describe the Office 2010 applications.

2 Start an Office 2010 application.

3 Use the Ribbon, dialog boxes, and task panes.

4 Use menus, context menus, and shortcut keys.

5 Use Backstage view.

6 Open, close, and save files.

7 Navigate a document.

8 Enter, edit, and format text.

9 Select, copy, and move text.

10 Undo and redo changes.

11 Specify document properties.

12 Print a document.

13 Use Office 2010 Help.

14 Exit an Office 2010 application.

What Is Microsoft Office 2010?

Microsoft's Office 2010 is a comprehensive, integrated system of programs designed to solve a wide array of business needs. Although the programs can be used individually, they are designed to work together seamlessly, making it easy to connect people and organizations to information, business processes, and each other. The applications include tools used to create, discuss, communicate, and manage projects. If you share a lot of documents with other people, these features facilitate access to common documents. If you are away on business or do not have your PC with you, you can use Office 2010 Web applications, browser versions of Word, Excel, PowerPoint, and OneNote, to edit documents and collaborate with others.

Microsoft Office 2010 is packaged in several different combinations of programs or suites. The major programs and a brief description are provided in the following table.

Program	Description
Word 2010	Word processor program used to create text-based documents
Excel 2010	Spreadsheet program used to analyze numerical data
Access 2010	Database manager used to organize, manage, and display a database
PowerPoint 2010	Graphics presentation program used to create presentation materials
Outlook 2010	Desktop information manager and messaging client
InfoPath 2010	Used to create XML forms and documents
OneNote 2010	Note-taking and information organization tools
Publisher 2010	Tools to create and distribute publications for print, Web, and e-mail
Visio 2010	Diagramming and data visualization tools
SharePoint Designer 2010	Web site development and management for SharePoint servers
Project 2010	Project management tools

The four main components of Microsoft Office 2010—Word, Excel, Access, and PowerPoint—are the applications you will learn about in this series of labs. They are described in more detail in the following sections.

Word 2010

Word 2010 is a word processing software application whose purpose is to help you create text-based documents such as letters, memos, reports, e-mail messages, or any other type of correspondence. Word processors are one of the most flexible and widely used application software programs.

WORD 2010 FEATURES

The beauty of a word processor is that you can make changes or corrections as you are typing. Want to change a report from single spacing to double spacing? Alter the width of the margins? Delete some paragraphs and add others from yet another document? A word processor allows you to do all these things with ease.

Edit Content

Word 2010 excels in its ability to change or **edit** a document. Basic document editing involves correcting spelling, grammar, and sentence-structure errors and revising or updating existing text by inserting, deleting, and rearranging areas of text. For example, a document that lists prices can easily be updated to reflect new prices. A document that details procedures can be revised by deleting old procedures and inserting new ones. Many of these changes are made easily by cutting (removing) or copying (duplicating) selected text and then pasting (inserting) the cut or copied text in another location in the same or another document. Editing allows you to quickly revise a document, by changing only the parts that need to be modified.

To help you produce a perfect document, Word 2010 includes many additional editing support features. The AutoCorrect feature checks the spelling and grammar in a document as text is entered. Many common errors are corrected automatically for you. Others are identified and a correction suggested. A thesaurus can be used to display alternative words that have a meaning similar or opposite to a word you entered. The Find and Replace feature can be used to quickly locate specified text and replace it with other text throughout a document. In addition, Word 2010 includes a variety of tools that automate the process of many common tasks, such as creating tables, form letters, and columns.

Format Content

You also can easily control the appearance or **format** of the document. Perhaps the most noticeable formatting feature is the ability to apply different fonts (type styles and sizes) and text appearance changes such as bold, italics, and color to all or selected portions of the document. Additionally, you can add color shading behind individual pieces of text or entire paragraphs and pages to add emphasis. Other formatting features include changes to entire paragraphs, such as the line spacing and alignment of text between the margins. You also can format entire pages by displaying page numbers, changing margin settings, and applying backgrounds.

To make formatting even easier, Word 2010 includes Document Themes and Styles. Document Themes apply a consistent font, color, and line effect to an entire document. Styles apply the selected style design to a selection of text. Further, Word 2010 includes a variety of built-in preformatted content that helps you quickly produce modern-looking, professional documents. Among these are galleries of cover page designs, pull quotes, and header and footer designs. While selecting many of these design choices, a visual live preview is displayed, making it easy to see how the design would look in your document. In addition, you can select from a wide variety of templates to help you get started on creating many common types of documents such as flyers, calendars, faxes, newsletters, and memos.

Insert Illustrations

To further enhance your documents, you can insert many different types of graphic elements. These include drawing objects, SmartArt, charts, pictures, clip art, and screenshots. The drawing tools supplied with Word 2010 can be used to create your own drawings, or you can select from over 100 adjustable shapes and modify them to your needs. All drawings can be further enhanced with 3-D effects, shadows, colors, and textures. SmartArt graphics allow you to create a visual representation of your information. They include many different layouts such as a process or cycle that are designed to help you communicate an idea. Charts can be inserted to illustrate and compare data. Complex pictures can be inserted in documents by scanning your own, using supplied or purchased clip art, or downloading images from the World Wide Web. Additionally, you can produce fancy text effects using the WordArt tool. Finally, you can quickly capture and insert a picture, called a screenshot, from another application running on your computer into the current document.

Collaborate with Others

Group collaboration on projects is common in industry today. Word 2010 includes many features to help streamline how documents are developed and changed by group members. A discussion feature allows multiple people to insert remarks in the same document without having to route the document to each person or reconcile multiple reviewers' comments. You can easily consolidate all changes and comments from different reviewers in one simple step and accept or reject changes as needed.

Two documents you will produce in the first two Word 2010 labs, a letter and flyer, are shown here.

A letter containing a tabbed table, indented paragraphs, and text enhancements is quickly created using basic Word features

January 27, 2012

Dear Adventure Traveler:

Imagine camping under the stars in Africa, hiking and paddling your way through the rainforests of Costa Rica, or following in the footsteps of the ancient Inca as you backpack along the Inca trail to Machu Picchu. Turn these thoughts of adventure into memories you will cherish forever by joining Adventure Travel Tours on one of our four new adventure tours.

To tell you more about these exciting new adventu
area. These presentations will focus on the features and c
of the places you will visit and activities you can participate
Plan to attend one of the following presentations:

Date	Time	Locatio
February 5	8:00 p.m.	Renaissanc
February 19	7:30 p.m.	Airport Pla
March 8	8:00 p.m.	Crowne Co

In appreciation of your past patronage, we are ple
of the new tour packages. You must book the trip at least
this letter to qualify for the discount.

Our vacation tours are professionally developed s
everything in the price of your tour while giving you the be
these features:

➢ All accommodations and meals
➢ All entrance fees, excursions, transfers and tips
➢ Professional tour manager and local guides

We hope you will join us this year on another spec
Travel Tours each day is an adventure. For reservations, pl
Travel Tours directly at 1-800-555-0004.

Be

St
Ad

ADVENTURE TRAVEL TOURS

NEW ADVENTURES

Attention adventure travelers! Attend an Adventure Travel presentation to learn about some of the earth's greatest unspoiled habitats and find out how you can experience the adventure of a lifetime. This year Adventure Travel Tours is introducing four new tours that offer you a unique opportunity to combine many different outdoor activities while exploring the world.

Costa Rica Rivers and Rainforests

India Wildlife Adventure

Safari in Tanzania

Inca Trail to Machu Picchu

Presentation dates and times are January 5 at 7:00 p.m., February 3 at 7:30 p.m., and March 8 at 7:00 p.m. All presentations are held at convenient hotel locations. The hotels are located in downtown Los Angeles, in Santa Clara, and at the LAX airport.

Call Adventure Travel Tours at 1-800-555-0004 for presentation locations, a full color brochure, and itinerary information, costs, and trip dates. Student Name will gladly help with all of your questions.

A flyer incorporating many visual enhancements such as colored text, varied text styles, and graphic elements is both eye-catching and informative

Excel 2010 is an electronic spreadsheet, or **worksheet**, that is used to organize, manipulate, and graph numeric data. Once used almost exclusively by accountants, worksheets are now widely used by nearly every profession. Nearly any job that uses rows and columns of numbers can be performed using an electronic spreadsheet. Once requiring hours of labor and/or costly accountants' fees, data analysis is now available almost instantly using electronic spreadsheets and has become a routine business procedure. This powerful business tool has revolutionized the business world. Typical uses include the creation of budgets and financial planning for both business and personal situations. Marketing professionals record and evaluate sales trends. Teachers record grades and calculate final grades. Personal trainers record the progress of their clients.

EXCEL 2010 FEATURES

Excel 2010 includes many features that not only help you create a well-designed worksheet, but one that produces accurate results. The features include the ability to quickly edit and format data, perform calculations, create charts, and print the spreadsheet. Using Excel 2010, you can quickly analyze and manage data and communicate your findings to others. The program not only makes it faster to create worksheets, but it also produces professional-appearing results.

Enter and Edit Data

The Microsoft Excel 2010 spreadsheet program uses a workbook file that contains one or more worksheets. Each worksheet can be used to organize different types of related information. The worksheet consists of rows and columns that create a grid of cells. You enter numeric data or descriptive text into a cell. These entries can then be erased, moved, copied, or edited.

Format Data

Like text in a Word document, the design and appearance of entries in a worksheet can be enhanced in many ways. For instance, you can change the font style and size and add special effects such as bold, italic, borders, boxes, drop shadows, and shading to selected cells. You also can use cell styles to quickly apply predefined combinations of these formats to selections. Additionally, you can select from different document themes, predefined combinations of colors, fonts, and effects, to give your workbooks a consistent, professional appearance.

Unlike the Word application, Excel includes many formatting features that are designed specifically for numeric data. For example, numeric entries can be displayed with commas, dollar signs, or a set number of decimal places. Special formatting, such as color bars, can be applied automatically to ranges of cells to emphasize data based on a set of criteria you establish and to highlight trends.

Analyze Data

The power of a spreadsheet application is its ability to perform calculations from very simple sums to the most complex financial and mathematical formulas. Formulas can be entered that perform calculations using data contained in specified cells. The results of the calculations are displayed in the cell containing the formula. Predefined formulas, called functions, can be used to quickly perform complex calculations such as calculating loan payments or statistical analysis of data.

Analysis of data in a spreadsheet once was too expensive and time-consuming. Now, using electronic worksheets, you can use what-if or sensitivity analysis by changing the values in selected cells and immediately observing the effect on related cells in the worksheet. Other analysis tools such as Solver and Scenarios allow you to see the effects of possible alternative courses of action to help forecast future outcomes.

Chart Data

Using Excel, you also can produce a visual display of numeric data in the form of graphs or charts. As the values in the worksheet change, charts referencing those values automatically adjust to reflect the changes. You also can enhance the appearance of a chart by using different type styles and sizes, adding three-dimensional effects, and including text and objects such as lines and arrows. Two worksheets you will produce using Excel 2010 are shown below.

A worksheet showing the quarterly sales forecast containing a graphic, text enhancements, and a chart of the data is quickly created using basic Excel 2010 features

A large worksheet incorporating more complex formulas, visual enhancements such as colored text, varied text styles, and graphic elements is both informative and attractive

Access 2010 is a relational database management application that is used to create and analyze a database. A **database** is a collection of related data. **Tables** consist of columns (called **fields**) and rows (called **records**). Each row contains a record, which is all the information about one person, thing, or place. Each field is the smallest unit of information about a record.

In a relational database, the most widely used database structure, data is organized in linked tables. The tables are related or linked to one another by a common field. Relational databases allow you to create smaller and more manageable database tables, since you can combine and extract data between tables.

For example, a state's motor vehicle department database might have an address table. Each row (record) in the table would contain address information about one individual. Each column (field) would contain just one piece of information, for example, zip codes. The address table would be linked to other tables in the database by common fields. For example, the address table might be linked to a vehicle owner's table by name and linked to an outstanding citation table by license number (see example below).

Address Table

Name	License Number	Street Address	City	State	Zip
Aaron, Linda	FJ1987	10032 Park Lane	San Jose	CA	95127
Abar, John	D12372	1349 Oak St	Lakeville	CA	94128
Abell, Jack	LK3457	95874 State St	Stone	CA	95201

key fields linked

key fields linked

Owner's Table

Name	Plate Number
Abell, Jack	ABK241
Abrams, Sue	LMJ198
Abril, Pat	ZXA915

Outstanding Citation Table

License Number	Citation Code	Violation
T25476	00031	Speed
D98372	19001	Park
LK3457	89100	Speed

ACCESS 2010 FEATURES

Access 2010 is a powerful program with numerous easy-to-use features including the ability to quickly locate information; add, delete, modify, and sort records; analyze data; and produce professional-looking reports. Some of the basic Access 2010 features are described next.

Find Information

Once you enter data into the database table, you can quickly search the table to locate a specific record based on the data in a field. In a manual system, you can usually locate a record by knowing one key piece of information. For example, if the records are stored in a file cabinet alphabetically by last name, to quickly find a record, you must know the last name. In a computerized database, even if the records are sorted or organized by last name, you can still quickly locate a record using information in another field.

Add, Delete, and Modify Records

Using Access, it is also easy to add and delete records from the table. Once you locate a record, you can edit the contents of the fields to update the record or delete the record entirely from the table. You also can add new records to a table. When you enter a new record, it is automatically placed in the correct organizational location within the table. Creation of forms makes it easier to enter and edit data as well.

Sort and Filter Records

The capability to arrange or sort records in the table according to different fields can provide more meaningful information. You can organize records by name, department, pay, class, or any other category you need at a particular time. Sorting the records in different ways can provide information to different departments for different purposes.

Additionally, you can isolate and display a subset of records by specifying filter criteria. The criteria specify which records to display based on data in selected fields.

Analyze Data

Using Access, you can analyze the data in a table and perform calculations on different fields of data. Instead of pulling each record from a filing cabinet, recording the piece of data you want to use, and then performing the calculation on the recorded data, you can simply have the database program perform the calculation on all the values in the specified field. Additionally, you can ask questions or query the table to find only certain records that meet specific conditions to be used in the analysis. Information that was once costly and time-consuming to get is now quickly and readily available.

Generate Reports

Access includes many features that help you quickly produce reports ranging from simple listings to complex, professional-looking reports. You can create a simple report by asking for a listing of specified fields of data and restricting the listing to records meeting designated conditions. You can create a more complex professional report using the same restrictions or conditions as the simple report, but you can display the data in different layout styles, or with titles, headings, subtotals, or totals.

A database and a report that you will produce using Access 2010 are shown on the next page.

A relational database can be created and modified easily using basic Access 2010 features

Job Position Report
For Landis

Employee ID	First Name	Last Name	Position
12703	Jeff	Bader	Fitness Instructor
12389	Jennifer	Blackman	Sales Associate
05015	Scott	Briggs	Personal Trainer Director
12501	Elizabeth	DeLuca	Personal Trainer
12855	Kimberly	Fachet	Sales Associate
13484	Stephanie	Franklin	Food Service Server
12914	Alfonso	Gomez	Cleaning
22469	Ryan	Hogan	Personal Trainer
13303	Chris	Jensen	Greeter
13027	Kimberly	Kieken	Food Service Server
07650	Chris	Lamm	Sales Director
22085	Kristina	Lindau	Child Care Provider
13635	Juan	Martinez	Fitness Instructor
03225	Dan	Morgan	Food Service Director
99999	Student	Name	Human Resources Administrator
12420	Allison	Player	Maintenance
13005	Emily	Reilly	Assistant Manager
22297	Patricia	Rogondino	Greeter
07287	Anita	Roman	Child Care Director
12918	Carlos	Ruiz	Assistant Manager
00212	Chad	Schiff	Club Director
12583	Marie	Sullivan	Greeter
03890	Erona	Thi	Fitness Director
12380	Jessica	Thomas	Fitness Instructor

Saturday, December 01, 2012

Page 1 of 1

A professional-looking report can be quickly generated from information contained in a database

PowerPoint 2010 is a graphics presentation program designed to help you produce a high-quality presentation that is both interesting to the audience and effective in its ability to convey your message. A presentation can be as simple as overhead transparencies or as sophisticated as an on-screen electronic display. Graphics presentation programs can produce black-and-white or color overhead transparencies, 35 mm slides, onscreen electronic presentations called **slide shows**, Web pages for Web use, and support materials for both the speaker and the audience.

POWERPOINT 2010 FEATURES

Although creating an effective presentation is a complicated process, PowerPoint 2010 helps simplify this process by providing assistance in the content development phase, as well as in the layout and design phase. PowerPoint includes features such as text handling, outlining, graphing, drawing, animation, clip art, and multimedia support. In addition, the programs suggest layouts for different types of presentations and offer professionally designed templates to help you produce a presentation that is sure to keep your audience's attention. In addition, you can quickly produce the support materials to be used when making a presentation to an audience.

Develop, Enter, and Edit Content

The content development phase includes deciding on the topic of your presentation, the organization of the content, and the ultimate message you want to convey to the audience. As an aid in this phase, PowerPoint 2010 helps you organize your thoughts based on the type of presentation you are making by providing both content and design templates. Based on the type of presentation, such as selling a product or suggesting a strategy, the template provides guidance by suggesting content ideas and organizational tips. For example, if you are making a presentation on the progress of a sales campaign, the program would suggest that you enter text on the background of the sales campaign as the first page, called a **slide**; the current status of the campaign as the next slide; and accomplishments, schedule, issues and problems, and where you are heading on subsequent slides.

Design Layouts

The layout for each slide is the next important decision. Again, PowerPoint 2010 helps you by suggesting text layout features such as title placement, bullets, and columns. You also can incorporate graphs of data, tables, organizational charts, clip art, and other special text effects in the slides.

PowerPoint 2010 also includes professionally designed themes to further enhance the appearance of your slides. These themes include features that standardize the appearance of all the slides in your presentation. Professionally selected combinations of text and background colors, common typefaces and sizes, borders, and other art designs take the worry out of much of the design layout.

Deliver Presentations

After you have written and designed the slides, you can use the slides in an onscreen electronic presentation or a Web page for use on the Web. An onscreen presentation uses the computer to display the slides on an overhead projection screen. As you prepare this type of presentation, you can use the

WWW.MHHE.COM/OLEARY

rehearsal feature that allows you to practice and time your presentation. The length of time to display each slide can be set and your entire presentation can be completed within the allotted time. A presentation also can be modified to display on a Web site and run using a Web browser. Finally, you can package the presentation to a CD for distribution.

A presentation that you will produce using PowerPoint 2010 is shown below.

A presentation consists of a series of pages or "slides" presenting the information you want to convey in an organized and attractive manner

When running an on-screen presentation, each slide of the presentation is displayed full-screen on your computer monitor or projected onto a screen

As you follow the directions in the following hands-on section and in the application labs, you need to know the instructional conventions that are used. Hands-on instructions you are to perform appear as a sequence of numbered steps. Within each step, a series of bullets identifies the specific actions that must be performed. Step numbering begins over within each topic heading throughout the lab.

Three types of marginal notes appear throughout the labs. Another Method notes provide alternate ways of performing the same command. Having Trouble? notes provide advice or cautions for steps that may cause problems. Additional Information notes provide more information about a topic.

COMMANDS

Commands that are initiated using a command button and the mouse appear following the word "Click." The icon (and the icon name if the icon does not include text) is displayed following "Click." If there is another way to perform the same action, it appears in an Another Method margin note when the action is first introduced as shown in Example A.

When a feature has already been covered and you are more familiar with using the application, commands will appear as shown in Example B.

Example A

1

- Select the list of four tours.

- Open the Home tab.

- Click **B** Bold in the Font group.

Another Method

The keyboard shortcut is Ctrl + B.

Example B

1

- Select the list of four tours.

- Click **B** Bold in the Font group of the Home tab.

OR

1

- Bold the list of four tours.

Sometimes, clicking on an icon opens a drop-down list or a menu of commands. Commands that are to be selected follow the word "Select" and appear in black text. You can select an item by pointing to it using the mouse or by moving to it using the directional keys. When an option is selected, it appears highlighted; however, the action is not carried out. Commands that you are to complete appear following the word "Choose." You can choose a command by clicking on it using the mouse or by pressing the (Enter) key once it is selected. Initially these commands will appear as in Example A. Choosing a command carries out the associated action. As you become more familiar with the application, commands will appear as shown in Example B.

Example A

1

- Click **A ▾** Font Color in the Font group of the Home tab.
- Select Green.
- Choose Dark Blue.

Example B

1

- Click **A ▾** Font Color and choose Dark Blue.

FILE NAMES AND INFORMATION TO TYPE

Plain blue text identifies file names you need to select or enter. Information you are asked to type appears in blue and bold. (See Example C.)

Example C

1

- Open the document wd01_Flyer.
- Type **Adventure Travel presents four new trips**

Common Office 2010 Features

Now that you know a little about each of the applications in Microsoft Office 2010, you will take a look at some of the features that are common to all Office 2010 applications. In this hands-on section you will learn to use the common interface and application features to allow you to get a feel for how Office 2010 works. Although Word 2010 will be used to demonstrate how the features work, only features that are common to all the Office applications will be addressed.

COMMON INTERFACE FEATURES

All the Office 2010 applications have a common **user interface**, a set of graphical elements that are designed to help you interact with the program and provide instructions as to the actions you want to perform. These features include the use of the Ribbon, Quick Access Toolbar, task panes, menus, dialog boxes, and the File tab.

Starting an Office 2010 Application

To demonstrate the common features, you will start the Word 2010 application. There are several ways to start an Office 2010 application. The two most common methods are by clicking the ● Start button to see a menu of available programs or by clicking a desktop shortcut for the program if it is available.

1

- Click ● Start to display the Start menu.

- Choose Microsoft Word 2010.

OR

1

- Double-click the ▦ shortcut on the desktop.

2

- If necessary, click ▢ Maximize in the title bar to maximize the window.

Your screen should be similar to Figure 1

Figure 1

The Word 2010 program is started and displayed in a window on the desktop. All application windows display a title bar at the top of the window that includes the file name followed by the program name, in this case Microsoft Word. They also include the ⬚ Minimize, ⬚ Restore Down, and ⬚ Close buttons at the right end of the title bar. **Buttons** are graphical elements that perform the associated action when you click on them using the mouse. At the left end of the title bar is the ⬚ Window button. Clicking this button opens a menu of commands that allow you to size, move, and close the window just as the buttons on the right end of the title bar. To the right of the ⬚ Window button is the **Quick Access Toolbar** (QAT), which provides quick access to frequently used commands. By default, it includes the ⬚ Save, ⬚ Undo, and ⬚ Redo buttons, commands that Microsoft considers to be crucial. It is always available and is a customizable toolbar to which you can add your own favorite buttons.

Below the title bar is the **Ribbon**, which provides a centralized location of commands that are used to work in your document. The Ribbon has the same basic structure and is found in all Office 2010 applications. However, many of the commands found in the Ribbon vary with the specific applications. You will learn how to use the Ribbon shortly.

The large center area of the program window is the **document window** where open application files are displayed. When you first start Word 2010, a new blank Word document named Document1 (shown in the title bar) automatically opens, ready for you to start creating a new document. In Excel, a new, blank workbook named Book1 would be opened and in PowerPoint a new, blank presentation file named Presentation1 would be opened. In Access, however, a new blank database file is not opened automatically. Instead, you must create and name a new database file or open an existing database file.

The **cursor**, also called the **insertion point**, is the blinking vertical bar that marks your location in the document and indicates where text you type will appear. Across all Office applications, the mouse pointer appears as I I-beam when it is used to position the insertion point when entering text and as a ⬚ when it can be used to select items. There are many other mouse pointer shapes that are both common to and specific to the different applications.

On the right of the document window is a vertical scroll bar. A **scroll bar** is used with a mouse to bring additional information into view in a window. The vertical scroll bar is used to move up or down. A horizontal scroll bar is also displayed when needed and moves side to side in the window. The scroll bar is a common feature to all Windows and Office 2010 applications; however, it may not appear in all applications until needed.

At the bottom of the application window is another common feature called the **status bar**. It displays information about the open file and features that help you view the file. It displays different information depending upon the application you are using. For example, the Word status bar displays information about the number of pages and words in the document, whereas the Excel status bar displays the mode of operation and the count, average, and sum of values in selected cells. All Office 2010 applications include **View buttons** that are used to change how the information in the document window is displayed. The View buttons are different for each application. Finally, a **Zoom Slider**, located at the far right end of the status bar, is used to change the amount of information displayed in the document window by "zooming in" to get a close-up view or "zooming out" to see more of the document at a reduced view.

Displaying ScreenTips

You are probably wondering how you would know what action the different buttons perform. To help you identify buttons, the Office applications display ScreenTips when you point to them.

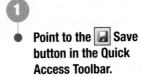

1

● Point to the Save button in the Quick Access Toolbar.

Your screen should be similar to Figure 2

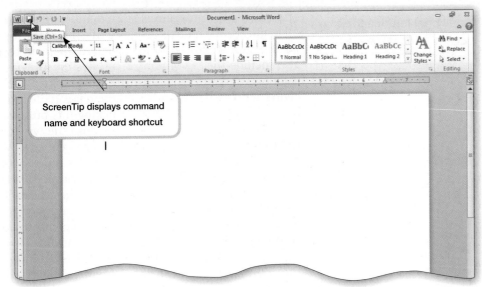

> ScreenTip displays command name and keyboard shortcut

Figure 2

A **ScreenTip**, also called a **tooltip**, appears displaying the command name and the keyboard shortcut, Ctrl + S. A **keyboard shortcut** is a combination of keys that can be used to execute a command in place of clicking the button. In this case, if you hold down the Ctrl key while typing the letter S, you will access the command to save a file. ScreenTips also often include a brief description of the action a command performs.

Using Menus

Notice the small button at the end of the Quick Access Toolbar. Clicking this button opens a menu of commands that perform tasks associated with the Quick Access Toolbar.

1

● Point to the button at the end of the Quick Access Toolbar to display the ScreenTip.

● Click to open the menu.

Your screen should be similar to Figure 3

> Click to open menu

> Menu of commands for Quick Access Toolbar

> Check indicates feature is on

Figure 3

The first 11 items in the menu allow you to quickly add a command button to or remove a command button from the Quick Access Toolbar. Those commands that are already displayed in the Quick Access Toolbar are preceded with a checkmark. The last two commands allow you to access other command features to customize the Quick Access Toolbar or change its location.

Once a menu is open, you can select a command from the menu by pointing to it. As you do the selected command appears highlighted. Like buttons, resting the mouse pointer over the menu command options will display a ScreenTip. Then to choose a selected command, you click on it. Choosing a command performs the action associated with the command or button. You will use several of these features next.

2

Point to the commands in the Quick Access Toolbar menu to select (highlight) them and see the ScreenTips.

Click on the Open command to choose it and add it to the Quick Access Toolbar.

Your screen should be similar to Figure 4

Figure 4

The command button to open a document has been added to the Quick Access Toolbar. Next, you will remove this button and then you will change the location of the Quick Access Toolbar. Another way to access some commands is to use a context menu. A **context menu**, also called a **shortcut menu**, is opened by right-clicking on an item on the screen. This menu is context sensitive, meaning it displays only those commands relevant to the item or screen location. For example, right-clicking on the Quick Access Toolbar will display the commands associated with using the Quick Access Toolbar and the Ribbon. You will use this method to remove the Open button and move the Quick Access Toolbar.

3

● Point to the ⬚ Open button on the Quick Access Toolbar and right-click.

● Click on the Remove from Quick Access Toolbar command to choose it.

● Right-click on any button in the Quick Access Toolbar again and choose the Show Quick Access Toolbar Below the Ribbon option.

Another Method

You also can type the underlined letter of a command to choose it or press Enter to choose a selected command.

Your screen should be similar to Figure 5

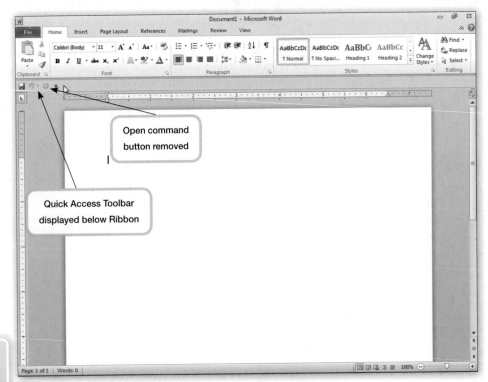

Open command button removed

Quick Access Toolbar displayed below Ribbon

Figure 5

The Quick Access Toolbar is now displayed full size below the Ribbon. This is useful if you have many buttons on the toolbar; however, it takes up document viewing space. You will return it to its compact size.

4

● Display the Quick Access Toolbar menu.

● Choose Show Above the Ribbon.

Your screen should be similar to Figure 6

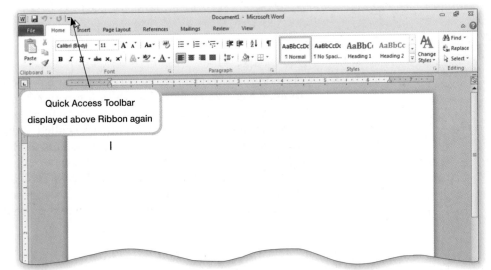

Quick Access Toolbar displayed above Ribbon again

Figure 6

The Quick Access Toolbar is displayed above the Ribbon again.

Using the Ribbon

The Ribbon has three basic parts: tabs, groups, and commands (see Figure 7). **Tabs** are used to divide the Ribbon into major activity areas. Each tab is then organized into **groups** that contain related items. The related items are **commands** that consist of command buttons, a box to enter information, or a menu. Clicking on a command button performs the associated action or displays a list of additional options.

The Ribbon tabs, commands, and features vary with the different Office applications. For example, the Word Ribbon displays tabs and commands used to create a text document, whereas the Excel Ribbon displays tabs and commands used to create an electronic worksheet. Although the Ribbon commands are application specific, many are also common to all Office 2010 applications. In all applications, the Ribbon also can be customized by changing the built-in tabs or creating your own tabs and groups to personalize your workspace and provide faster access to the commands you use most.

Opening Tabs

The Word application displays the File tab and seven Ribbon tabs. The Home tab (shown in Figure 6), consisting of five groups, appears highlighted, indicating it is the open or active tab. This tab is available in all the Office 2010 applications and because it contains commands that are most frequently used when you first start an application or open a file, it is initially the open tab. In Word, the commands in the Home tab help you perform actions related to creating the text content of your document. In the other Office 2010 applications, the Home tab contains commands related to creating the associated type of document, such as a worksheet, presentation, or database. To open another tab you click on the tab name.

Click on the Insert tab.

Your screen should be similar to Figure 7

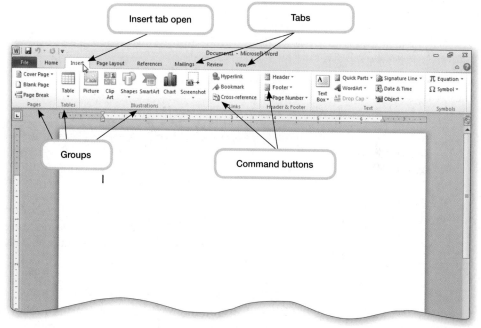

Figure 7

This Insert tab is now open and is the active tab. It contains seven groups whose commands have to do with inserting items into a document. As you use the Office applications, you will see that the Ribbon contains many of the same tabs, groups, and commands across the applications. For example, the Insert tab is available in all applications except Access. Others, such as the References tab in Word, are specific to the application. You also will see that many of the groups and commands in the common tabs, such as the Clipboard group of commands in the Home tab, contain all or many of the same commands across applications. Other groups in the common tabs contain commands that are specific to the application.

To save space, some tabs, called **contextual tabs** or **on-demand tabs**, are displayed only as needed. For example, when you are working with a picture, the Picture Tools tab appears. The contextual nature of this feature keeps the work area uncluttered when the feature is not needed and provides ready access to it when it is needed.

2

● Click on each of the other tabs, ending with the View tab, to see their groups and commands.

Additional Information

If you have a mouse with a scroll wheel, pointing to the tab area of the ribbon and using the scroll wheel will scroll the tabs.

Your screen should be similar to Figure 8

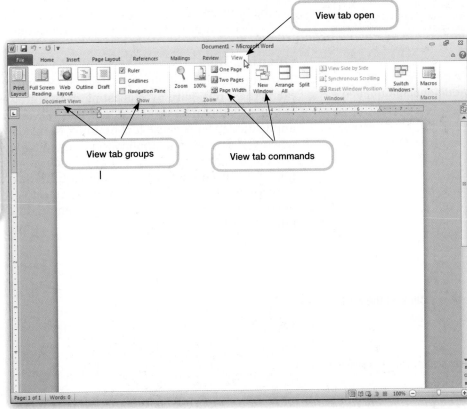

Figure 8

Each tab relates to a type of activity; for example, the View tab commands perform activities related to viewing the document. Within each tab, similar commands are grouped together to make it easy to find the commands you want to use.

Displaying Enhanced ScreenTips

Although command buttons display graphic representations of the action they perform, often the graphic is not descriptive enough. As you have learned, pointing to a button displays the name of the button and the keyboard shortcut in a ScreenTip. To further help explain what a button does, many buttons in the Ribbon display **Enhanced ScreenTips**. For example, the Paste button in the Clipboard group of the Home tab is a two-part button. Clicking on the upper part will immediately perform an action, whereas clicking on the lower part will display additional options. You will use this feature next to see the Enhanced ScreenTips.

1

- **Click on the Home tab to open it.**

- **Point to the upper part of the [paste icon] Paste button in the Clipboard group.**

- **Point to the lower part of the [Paste] button in the Clipboard group.**

- **Point to [Format Painter icon] Format Painter in the Clipboard group.**

Your screen should be similar to Figure 9

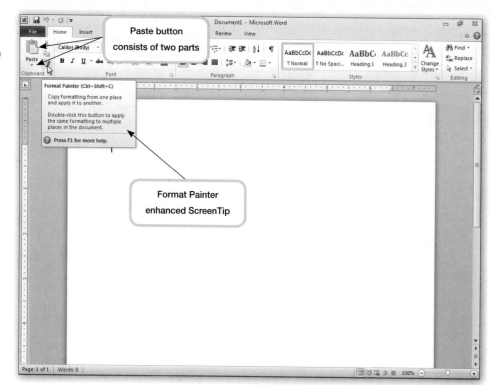

Figure 9

Additional Information

Not all commands have keyboard shortcuts.

Additional Information

You will learn about using Help shortly.

Because the [Paste icon] button is divided into two parts, both parts display separate Enhanced ScreenTips containing the button name; the keyboard shortcut key combination, Ctrl + V; and a brief description of what action will be performed when you click on that part of the button. Pointing to [icon] Format Painter displays an Enhanced ScreenTip that provides more detailed information about the command. Enhanced ScreenTips may even display information such as procedures or illustrations. You can find out what the feature does without having to look it up using Office Help, a built-in reference source. If a feature has a Help article, you can automatically access it by pressing F1 while the Enhanced ScreenTip is displayed.

Using Command Buttons

Clicking on most command buttons immediately performs the associated action. Many command buttons, however, include an arrow as part of the button that affects how the button works. If a button includes an arrow that is separated from the graphic with a line when you point to the button (as in [icon] Bullets), clicking the button performs the associated default action and clicking the arrow displays a menu of options. If a button displays an arrow that is not separated from the graphic with a line when you point to it (as in [icon] Line Spacing), clicking the button immediately displays a menu of options. To see an example of a drop-down menu, you will open the [icon] Bullets menu.

1

Click in the Bullets button.

Your screen should be similar to Figure 10

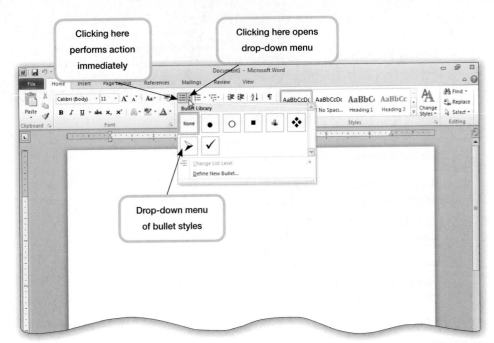

Figure 10

A drop-down menu of different bullet styles is displayed. The drop-down menu will disappear when you make a selection or click on any other area of the window.

2

Click outside the Bullet menu to clear it.

Click 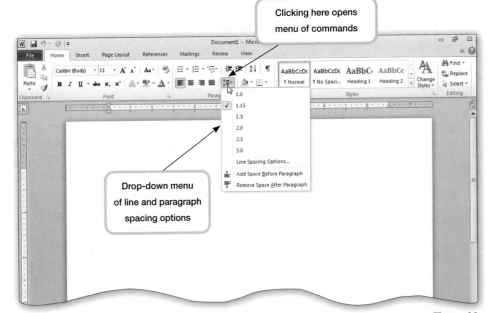 Line and Paragraph Spacing.

Your screen should be similar to Figure 11

Figure 11

Another Method

You also can open tabs and choose Ribbon commands using the access key shortcuts. Press Alt or F10 to display the access key letters in KeyTips over each available feature. Then type the letter for the feature you want to use.

The menu of options opened automatically when you clicked Line and Paragraph Spacing.

Using the Dialog Box Launcher

Because there is not enough space, only the most used commands are displayed in the Ribbon. If more commands are available, a ▣ button, called the **dialog box launcher**, is displayed in the lower-right corner of the group. Clicking ▣ opens a dialog box or task pane of additional options.

1

● Click outside the Line and Paragraph Spacing menu to clear it.

● Point to the ▣ of the Paragraph group to see the ScreenTip.

● Click ▣ of the Paragraph group.

Your screen should be similar to Figure 12

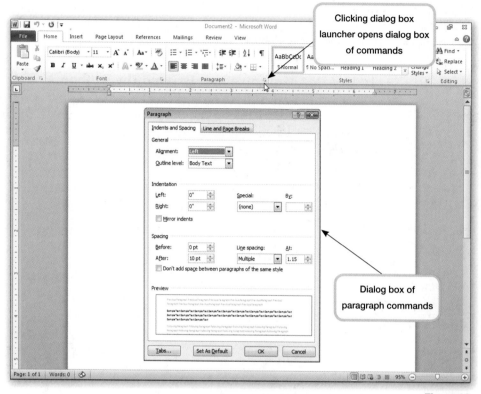

Figure 12

The Paragraph dialog box appears. It provides access to the more advanced paragraph settings options. Selecting options from the dialog box and clicking [OK] will close the dialog box and apply the options as specified. To cancel the dialog box, you can click [Cancel] or ☒ Close in the dialog box title bar.

2

● Click ☒ to close the dialog box.

● Click ▣ in the Clipboard group.

Your screen should be similar to Figure 13

Figure 13

A task pane is open that contains features associated with the Clipboard. Unlike a dialog box, a task pane is a separate window that can be sized and moved. Generally, task panes are attached or docked to one edge of the application window. Also, task panes remain open until you close them. This allows you to make multiple selections from the task pane while continuing to work on other areas of your document.

● **Click** ✕ **Close in the upper-right corner of the task pane to close it.**

Minimize and Expand the Ribbon

Sometimes you may not want to see the entire Ribbon so that more space is available in the document area. You can minimize the Ribbon by double-clicking the active tab.

● **Double-click the Home tab.**

Your screen should be similar to Figure 14

Figure 14

Now, the only part of the Ribbon that is visible is the tab area. Then, to expand the Ribbon, simply double click on the tab you want to make active. Another way to hide and redisplay the Ribbon is to click ⌃ Minimize the Ribbon or ⌄ Expand the Ribbon located at the far right end of the Ribbon tabs. You will unhide it using this feature.

● **Click** ⌄ **Expand the Ribbon.**

The full Ribbon reappears and the tab that was active when you minimized the Ribbon is active again.

Using Backstage View

To the left of the Home tab in the Ribbon is the File tab. Unlike the other tabs that display a Ribbon of commands, the File tab opens Backstage view. **Backstage view** contains commands that allow you to work *with* your document, unlike the Ribbon that allows you to work *in* your document.

Backstage view contains commands that apply to the entire document. For example, you will find commands to open, save, print, and manage your files and set your program options. This tab is common to all the Office 2010 applications, although the menu options may vary slightly.

1

● **Click the File tab to open Backstage view.**

Your screen should be similar to Figure 15

Command buttons

Tabs

Command buttons

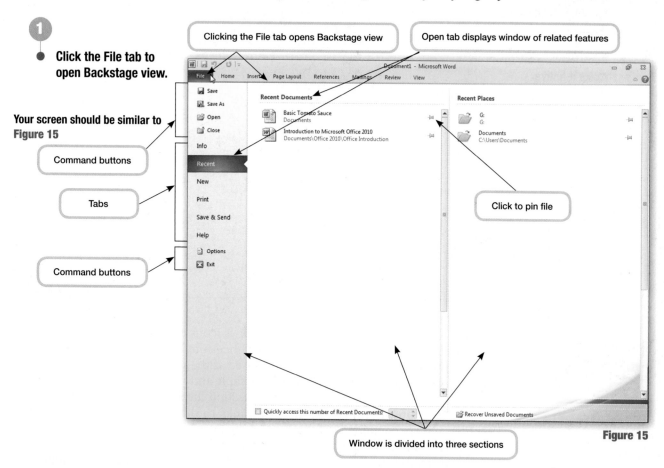

Clicking the File tab opens Backstage view

Open tab displays window of related features

Click to pin file

Window is divided into three sections

Figure 15

Another Method

You also can use the directional keys to move up, down, left, or right within Backstage view and press Enter to choose a selected command or tab.

Additional Information

A list of recent files also may appear above the Info tab if this option is selected.

Additional Information

Clicking [ ] next to a file name pins the file and permanently keeps the file name in the recently used list until it is unpinned.

The document window is hidden and the Backstage view window is open. The Backstage view window completely covers the document window and is divided into sections or panes. In all Office 2010 applications, the first (left) section always displays command buttons and tabs. You can select a tab or a button by pointing to it. As you do, the selected tab or button appears highlighted. Then to choose a selected tab or button, you click on it. Choosing a command button either opens a dialog box or immediately performs the associated action. Clicking a tab opens the tab and displays the related commands and features.

When you first open Backstage view and you have not yet opened a document or started to create a new document, the Recent tab is open. It displays a list of links to recently opened Word files in the second section, making it easy to quickly locate and resume using a file. The third section displays a list of folder locations that have been recently visited. In Excel, PowerPoint, and Access, the recently opened file list displays files for the associated application. The list of files and folders changes as you work to reflect only the most recent files and folder locations. The most recently used files and folder locations appear at the top of the list.

Next, you will try out some of these features by selecting and opening different tabs and command buttons.

2

● Point to all the tabs and commands in the Backstage view menu.

● Click the New tab to make it active.

Additional Information

The open tab is identified with a dark blue background.

Your screen should be similar to Figure 16

New tab displays links to template files that are used to create new documents

Preview of selected file

Icons representing folders containing template files on the Office.com Web site

Figure 16

Additional Information

When you start the Word 2010 application, the Blank document template is automatically opened.

The second section of the New tab displays icons representing links to available templates on your computer or on the Office.com Web site. A **template** is a professionally designed document that is used as the basis for a new document. The Blank document icon is selected by default and is used to create a new Word document file from scratch. The third section displays a preview of the selected file. Icons in the Office.com area are links to different categories of template files that are contained in folders. Clicking on a folder icon opens the folder and displays file icons. Double-clicking on a file icon opens the file in Word. Again, the available templates are specific to the Office application you are using.

3

● Click the Info tab.

Your screen should be similar to Figure 17

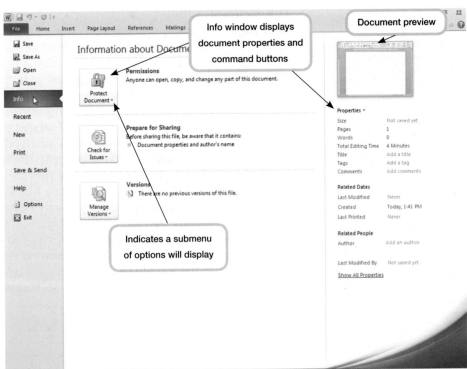

Info window displays document properties and command buttons

Document preview

Indicates a submenu of options will display

Figure 17

WWW.MHHE.COM/OLEARY

The Info tab displays information about your current document. The three buttons in the second section are used to define permissions, check for issues related to distribution, and manage document versions for the current document. A description of these buttons and the current document settings is shown to the right of the button. Notice that the buttons display a ⬇. This indicates that a menu of commands will be displayed when you click the button. The third section displays a preview picture of the current document and a list of the settings, called **properties**, associated with the document. The current properties displayed in the Info window show the initial or **default** properties associated with a new blank document.

Additional Information

You will learn more about document properties shortly.

4

● Click to open the menu.

● Point to Restrict Permission by People.

Your screen should be similar to Figure 18

Figure 18

The Protect Document drop-down menu displays five commands. The highlighted command displays a submenu of additional commands. Next, you will clear the Protect Document menu and close Backstage view.

5

● Click again to clear the submenu.

● Click the Home tab to close Backstage view and open the Home tab again.

Another Method

You also can press Esc, click on the File tab or any other Ribbon tab, or click on the document preview in the Info screen to close the Backstage view window.

COMMON APPLICATION FEATURES

So far you have learned about using the Office 2010 user interface features. Next, you will learn about application features that are used to work in and modify documents and are the same or similar in all Office 2010 applications. These include how to open, close, and save files; navigate, scroll, and zoom a document; enter, select, edit, and format text; and document, preview, and print a file. To do this, you will open a Word document file and make a few changes to it. Then you will save and print the revised document. Once you have gained an understanding of the basic concepts of the common features using Word, you will be able to easily apply them in the other Office applications.

Opening a File

In all Office 2010 applications, you either need to create a new file using the blank document file or open an existing file. Opening a file retrieves a file that is stored on your computer hard drive or an external storage device and places it in RAM (random access memory) of your computer so it can be read and modified. There are two main methods that can be used to open an existing file. One is to select the file to be opened from the list of recently opened documents. If you have not recently opened the file you want to use, then you use the Open command in Backstage view.

- Click the **File tab** to open Backstage view.

- Click [Open].

Your screen should be similar to Figure 19

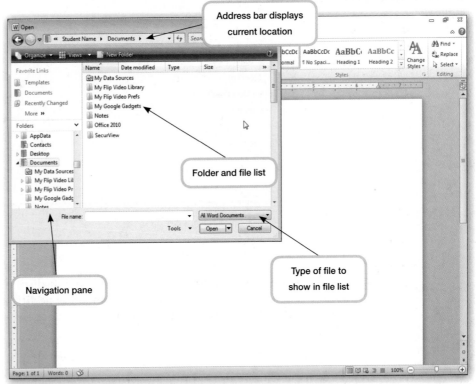

Figure 19

Additional Information

The Open dialog box is common to all programs using the Windows operating system. Your dialog box may look slightly different depending on the version of Windows on your computer.

The Open dialog box is displayed in which you specify the location where the file you want to open is stored and the file name. The location consists of identifying the hard drive of your computer or an external storage device or a remote computer followed by folders and subfolders within that location. The Address bar displays the default folder as the location to open the file. The file list displays folder names as well as the names of any Word documents in the current location. Only Word documents are listed because All Word Documents is the specified file type in the File Type list box. In Excel and PowerPoint, only files of that application's file type would be displayed.

Additional Information

By default, the Open dialog box only lists files created in the application. You will learn about the different file types shortly.

Another Method

You also can navigate by clicking the Back or Forward buttons to the left of the Address bar to return to locations that were previously visited during this session.

First you need to change the location to where your data files for completing these labs are stored. The file location may be on a different drive, in an external storage device, or in a folder or subfolder. There are several methods that can be used to locate files. One is to use the Address bar to specify another location by either typing the complete folder name or path or by opening the drop-down list of previously accessed locations and clicking a new location. Another is to use the Favorite Links list in the Navigation pane, which provides shortcut links to specific folders on your computer. A third is to use the Folders list in the navigation pane to navigate through the hierarchical structure of drives and folders on your computer. Clicking a link or folder from the list displays files at that location in the file list. Then, from the file list, you can continue to select subfolders until the file you want to open is located.

2

> **Change to the location where your student data files for this lab are located.**

Your screen should be similar to Figure 20

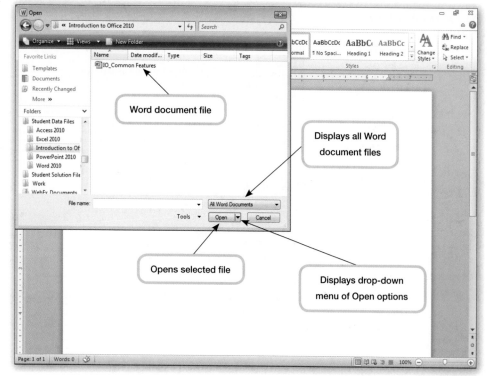

Figure 20

Now the file list displays the names of all Word files at that location. Next, you open the file by selecting it and clicking the Open button. In addition, in the Office applications you can specify how you want to open a file by choosing from the Open drop-down menu options described in the following table.

Open Options	Description
Open	Opens with all formatting and editing features enabled. This is the default setting.
Open Read-only	Opens file so it can be read or copied only, not modified in any way.
Open as Copy	Automatically creates a copy of the file and opens the copy with complete editing capabilities.
Open in Browser	Opens HTML type files in a Web browser.
Open with Transform	Opens certain types of documents and lets you change it into another type of document.
Open in Protected View	Opens files from potentially unsafe locations with editing functions disabled.
Open and Repair	Opens file and attempts to repair any damage.

You will open the file IO_Common Features. Clicking the Open button opens the file using the default Open option so you can read and edit the file.

3

- **Select** IO_Common Features.

- **Click** Open.

Your screen should be similar to Figure 21

File name of open Word document

Scroll bar

Open document file displayed in document window

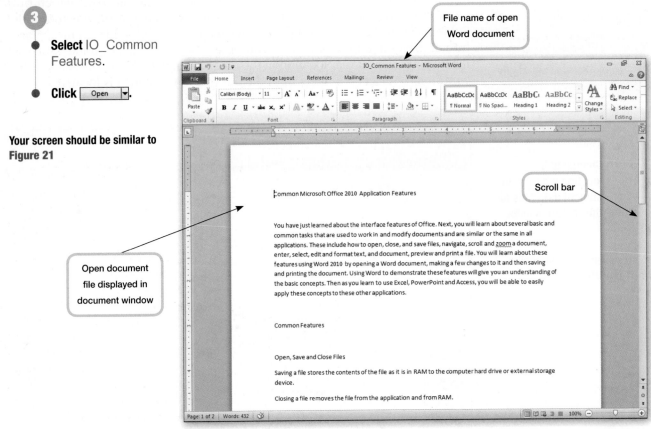

Figure 21

A Word document file describing the common Microsoft Office application features is displayed in the document window.

Scrolling the Document Window

As documents increase in size, they cannot be easily viewed in their entirety in the document window and much time can be spent moving to different locations in the document. All Office 2010 applications include features that make it easy to move around and view the information in a large document. The basic method is to scroll through a document using the scroll bar or keyboard. Both methods are useful, depending on what you are doing. For example, if you are entering text using the keyboard, using the keyboard method may be more efficient than using the mouse.

The table below explains the basic mouse and keyboard techniques that can be used to vertically scroll a document in the Office 2010 applications. There are many other methods for navigating through documents that are unique to an application. They will be discussed in the specific application text.

Mouse or Key Action	Effect in:			
	Word	**Excel**	**PowerPoint**	**Access**
Click ▼ Or ↓	Moves down line by line.	Moves down row by row	Moves down slide by slide	Moves down record by record
Click ▲ Or ↑	Moves up line by line.	Moves up row by row	Moves up slide by slide	Moves up record by record
Click above/below scroll box Or Page Up / Page Down	Moves up/down window by window	Moves up/down window by window	Displays previous/next slide	Moves up/down window by window
Drag ▤ Scroll Box	Moves up/down line by line	Moves up/down row by row	Moves up/down slide by slide	Moves up/down record by record
Ctrl + Home	Moves to beginning of document	Moves to first cell in worksheet or beginning of cell entry	Moves to first slide in presentation or beginning of entry in placeholder	Moves to first record in table or beginning of field entry
Ctrl + End	Moves to end of document	Moves to last-used cell in worksheet or end of cell entry	Moves to last slide in presentation or to end of placeholder entry	Moves to last record in table or end of field entry

You will use the vertical scroll bar to view the text at the bottom of the Word document. When you use the scroll bar to scroll, the actual location in the document where you can work does not change, only the area you are viewing changes. For example, in Word, the cursor does not move and in Excel the cell you can work in does not change. To move the cursor or make another cell active, you must click in a location in the window. However, when you scroll using the keyboard, the actual location as identified by the position of the cursor in the document also changes. For example, in Word the cursor attempts to maintain its position in a line as you scroll up and down through the document. In Excel the cell you can work in changes as you move through a worksheet using the keyboard.

1

- Click ▼ in the vertical scroll bar 10 times.

- Click at the beginning of the word Scroll in the Common Features section to move the cursor.

- Press ↓ 10 times to scroll the window and move the cursor down 10 lines.

Your screen should be similar to Figure 22

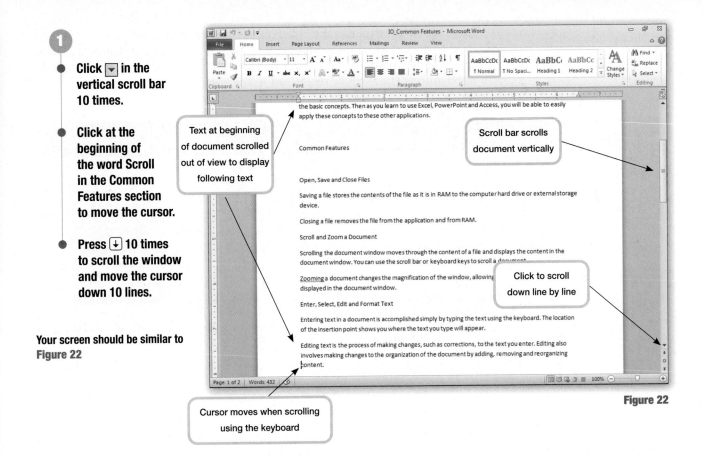

Text at beginning of document scrolled out of view to display following text

Scroll bar scrolls document vertically

Click to scroll down line by line

Cursor moves when scrolling using the keyboard

Figure 22

Having Trouble?

If your screen scrolls differently, this is a function of the type of monitor you are using.

The text at the beginning of the document has scrolled line by line off the top of the document window, and the following text is now displayed. In a large document, scrolling line by line can take a while. You will now try out several additional mouse and keyboard scrolling features that move by larger increments through the document.

2

- Click below the scroll box in the scroll bar.

- Press Ctrl + End to move to the end of the last line of the document.

- Drag the scroll box to the top of the scroll bar.

Your screen should be similar to Figure 23

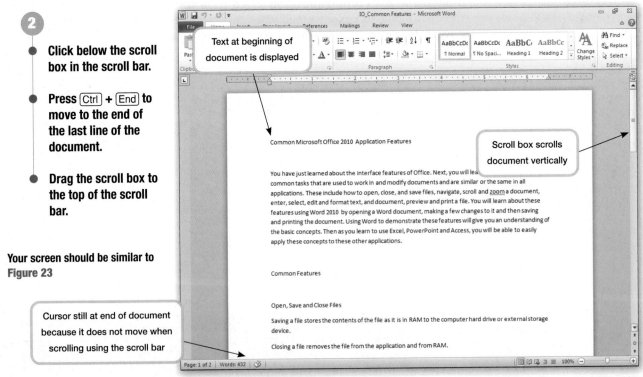

Text at beginning of document is displayed

Scroll box scrolls document vertically

Cursor still at end of document because it does not move when scrolling using the scroll bar

Figure 23

WWW.MHHE.COM/OLEARY

The document window displays the beginning of the document; however, the cursor is still at the end of the document. Using these features makes scrolling a large document much more efficient.

Using the Zoom Feature

Another way to see more or less of a document is to use the zoom feature. Although this feature is available in all Office 2010 applications, Excel and PowerPoint have fewer options than Word. In Access, the zoom feature is available only when specific features are used, such as viewing reports.

The Zoom Slider in the status bar is used to change the magnification. To use the Zoom Slider, click and drag the slider control. Dragging to the right zooms in on the document and increases the magnification whereas dragging to the left zooms out on the document and decreases the magnification. You also can change the zoom percentage by increments of 10 by clicking the ⊕ or ⊖ on each end of the slider control. In Word, the default display, 100 percent, shows the characters the same size they will be when printed. You can increase the onscreen character size up to five times the normal display (500 percent) or reduce the character size to 10 percent.

You will first "zoom out" on the document to get an overview of the file, and then you will "zoom in" to get a close-up look. When a document is zoomed, you can work in it as usual.

Additional Information

The degree of magnification varies with the different applications.

1

● **Click ⊖ in the Zoom Slider five times to decrease the zoom percentage to 50%.**

● **Press** Ctrl **+** Home **to move the cursor to the beginning of the document.**

● **Drag the Zoom Slider all the way to the right to increase the zoom to 500%.**

Your screen should be similar to Figure 24

Another Method

You can also hold down Ctrl while using the scroll wheel on your mouse to zoom a document.

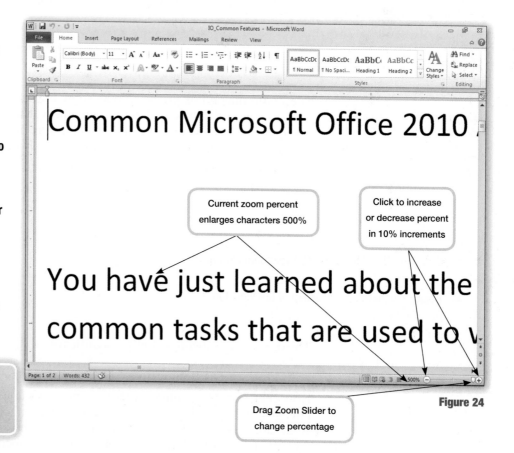

Current zoom percent enlarges characters 500%

Click to increase or decrease percent in 10% increments

Drag Zoom Slider to change percentage

Figure 24

Another Method

You can also click on the zoom percentage in the status bar to open the Zoom dialog box.

Another way to change the magnification is to use the [Zoom] button in the View tab. This method opens the Zoom dialog box containing several preset zoom options, or an option that lets you set a precise percentage using the Percent scroll box. You will use this feature next to zoom the document. This method is available in Word only.

2

- Open the View tab.

- Click in the Zoom group.

- Click **Whole Page** and note that the percent value in the Percent text box and the preview area reflect the new percentage setting.

- Click the ▲ up scroll button in the Percent scroll box to increase the zoom percentage to 57.

Another Method

You could also type a value in the Percent text box to specify an exact percentage.

Figure 25

Your screen should be similar to Figure 25

The Zoom dialog box preview areas show how the document will appear on your screen at the specified zoom percent. Not until you complete the command by clicking [OK] will the zoom percent in the document actually change. You will complete the command to apply the 57% zoom setting. Then, you will use the 🔲100% button in the Zoom group to quickly return to the default zoom setting.

3

- Click [OK] to apply the 57% zoom setting.

- Click 🔲100% in the Zoom group of the View tab.

The document is again at 100% magnification.

Entering and Editing Text

Now that you are familiar with the entire document, you will make a few changes to it. The keyboard is used to enter information into a document. In all applications, the location of the cursor shows you where the text will appear as you type. After text is entered into a document, you need to know how to move around within the text to edit or make changes to the text. Again, the process is similar for all Office applications.

Currently, in this Word document, the cursor is positioned at the top of the document. You will type your name at this location. As you type, the cursor moves to the right and the characters will appear to the left of the cursor. Then you will press Enter to end the line following your name and press Enter again at the beginning of a line to insert a blank line.

Additional Information

The effect of pressing Enter varies in the different Office applications. For example, in Excel, it completes the entry and moves to another cell. You will learn about these differences in the individual application labs.

Type your first and last name.

Press Enter **two times.**

Your screen should be similar to Figure 26

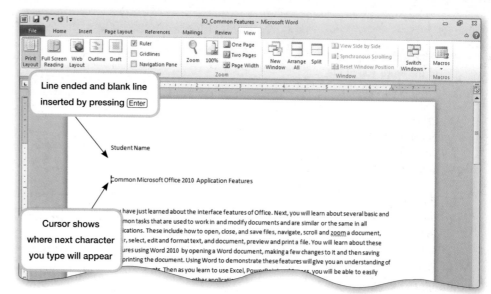

Line ended and blank line inserted by pressing Enter

Cursor shows where next character you type will appear

Student Name

Common Microsoft Office 2010 Application Features

...have just learned about the interface features of Office. Next, you will learn about several basic and ...mon tasks that are used to work in and modify documents and are similar or the same in all ...ications. These include how to open, close, and save files, navigate, scroll and <u>zoom</u> a document, ...r, select, edit and format text, and document, preview and print a file. You will learn about these ...ures using Word 2010 by opening a Word document, making a few changes to it and then saving ...printing the document. Using Word to demonstrate these features will give you an understanding of ...s. Then as you learn to use Excel, PowerP... ...s, you will be able to easily ...other applicati...

Figure 26

Additional Information

You can use the directional keys on the numeric keypad or the dedicated directional keypad area. If using the numeric keypad, make sure the Num Lock feature is off; otherwise, numbers will be entered in the document. The Num Lock indicator light above the keypad is lit when on. Press Num Lock to turn it off.

Additional Information

The mouse pointer also has other shapes whose meaning varies with the different applications. These specific features will be described in the individual application labs.

As you typed your name, to make space for the text on the line, the existing text moved to the right. Then, when you pressed Enter the first time, all the text following your name moved down one line. A blank line was inserted after pressing Enter the second time.

Next, you want to add a word to the first line of the first paragraph. To do this, you first need to move the cursor to the location where you want to make the change. The keyboard or mouse can be used to move through the text in the document window. Depending on what you are doing, one method may be more efficient than another. For example, if your hands are already on the keyboard as you are entering text, it may be quicker to use the keyboard rather than take your hands off to use the mouse.

You use the mouse to move the cursor to a specific location in a document simply by clicking on the location. When you can use the mouse to move the cursor, the mouse pointer is shaped as an ‖ I-beam. You use the arrow keys located on the numeric keypad or the directional keypad to move the cursor in a document. The keyboard directional keys are described in the following table.

Key	Word/PowerPoint	Excel	Access
→	Right one character	Right one cell	Right one field
←	Left one character	Left one cell	Left one field
↑	Up one line	Up one cell	Up one record
↓	Down one line	Down one cell	Down one record
Ctrl + →	Right one word	Last cell in row	One word to right in a field entry
Ctrl + ←	Left one word	First cell in row	One word to left in a field entry
Home	Beginning of line	First cell in row	First field of record
End	End of line		Last field of record

Additional Information

Many of the keyboard keys and key combinations have other effects depending on the mode of operation at the time they are used. You will learn about these differences in the specific application labs as they are used.

In the first line of the first paragraph, you want to add the word "common" before the word "interface" and the year "2010" after the word "Office." You will move to the correct locations using both the keyboard and the mouse and then enter the new text.

2

- **Click** at the beginning of the word You in the first paragraph.

- **Press** → **four times** to move to the beginning of the second word.

- **Press** Ctrl + → **five times to move to the beginning of the seventh word.**

Additional Information

Holding down a directional key or key combination moves quickly in the direction indicated, saving multiple presses of the key.

- **Type** basic **and press** Spacebar.

Having Trouble?

Do not be concerned if you make a typing error; you will learn how to correct them next.

- **Position the I-beam between the e in Office and the period at the end of the first sentence and click.**

- **Press** Spacebar **and type** 2010

Your screen should be similar to Figure 27

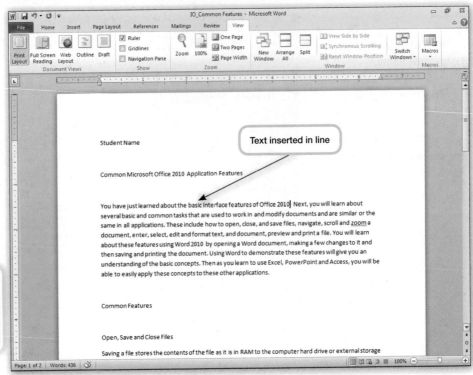

Figure 27

Next, you want to edit the text you just entered by changing the word "basic" to "common." Removing typing entries to change or correct them is one of the basic editing tasks. Corrections may be made in many ways. Two of the most basic editing keys that are common to the Office applications are the Backspace and Delete keys. The Backspace key removes a character or space to the left of the cursor. It is particularly useful when you are moving from right to left (backward) along a line of text. The Delete key removes the character or space to the right of the cursor and is most useful when moving from left to right along a line.

You will use these features as you make the correction.

3

- **Move the cursor between the s and i in "basic" (in the first sentence).**

- **Press** Del **to remove the two characters to the right of the insertion point.**

- **Press** Backspace **three times to remove the three characters to the left of the cursor.**

- **Type** common

- **Correct any other typing errors you may have made using** Backspace **or** Delete.

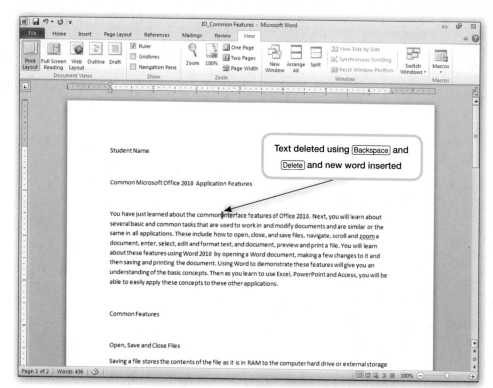

Figure 28

Your screen should be similar to Figure 28

The word "basic" was deleted from the sentence and the word "common" was entered in its place.

Selecting Text

While editing and formatting a document, you will need to select text. Selecting highlights text and identifies the text that will be affected by your next action. To select text using the mouse, first move the cursor to the beginning or end of the text to be selected, and then drag to highlight the text you want selected. You can select as little as a single letter or as much as the entire document. You also can select text using keyboard features. The following table summarizes common mouse and keyboard techniques used to select text in Word.

Additional Information

The capability to select text is common to all Office 2010 applications. However, many of the features that are designed for use in Word are not available in the other applications. Some are available only when certain modes of operation are in effect or when certain features are being used.

To Select	Mouse	Keyboard
Next/previous space or character	Drag across space or character.	Shift + → /Shift + ←
Next/previous word	Double-click in the word.	Ctrl + Shift + → /Ctrl + Shift + ←
Sentence	Press Ctrl and click within the sentence.	
Line	Click to the left of a line when the mouse pointer is ⇗.	
Multiple lines	Drag up or down to the left of a line when the mouse pointer is ⇗.	
Text going backward to beginning of paragraph	Drag left and up to the beginning of the paragraph when the mouse pointer is ⇗.	Ctrl + Shift + ↑
Text going forward to end of paragraph	Drag right and down to the end of the paragraph when the mouse pointer is ⇗.	Ctrl + Shift + ↓
Paragraph	Triple-click on the paragraph or double-click to the left of the paragraph when the mouse pointer is ⇗.	
Multiple paragraphs	Drag to the left of the paragraphs when the mouse pointer is ⇗.	
Document	Triple-click or press Ctrl and click to the left of the text when the mouse pointer is ⇗.	Ctrl + A

Having Trouble?

If you accidentally select the incorrect text, simply click anywhere in the document or press any directional key to clear the selection and try again.

You want to change the word "tasks" in the next sentence to "application features". Although you could use Delete and Backspace to remove the unneeded text character by character, it will be faster to select and delete the word. First you will try out several of the keyboard techniques to select text. Then you will use several mouse features to select text and finally you will edit the sentence.

- **Move the cursor to the beginning of the word "basic" in the second sentence.**

- **Press Shift + → five times to select the word basic.**

- **Press Shift + Ctrl + → to extend the selection word by word until the entire line is selected.**

- **Press Shift + Ctrl + ↓ to extend the selection to the end of the paragraph.**

Your screen should be similar to Figure 29

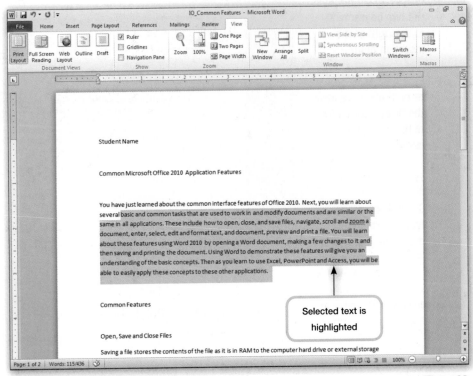

Figure 29

The text from the cursor to the end of the paragraph is selected. Next, you will clear this selection and then use the mouse to select text.

2

- Click anywhere in the paragraph to clear the selection.

- Click at the beginning of the word "basic" and drag to the right to select the text to the end of the line.

- Click in the left margin to the left of the fourth line of the paragraph when the mouse pointer is ⫞ to select the entire line.

- Double-click in the margin to the left of the paragraph when the mouse pointer is ⫞ to select the paragraph.

Your screen should be similar to Figure 30

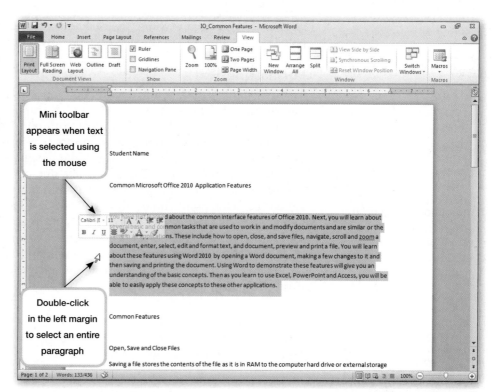

Figure 30

When you select text using the mouse, the **Mini toolbar** appears automatically in Word, Excel, and PowerPoint. You will learn about using this feature in the next section.

Text that is selected can be modified using many different features. In this case, you want to replace the word "tasks" in the second sentence with "application features".

3

- Double-click on the word "tasks" in the second sentence.

- Type **application features**

Your screen should be similar to Figure 31

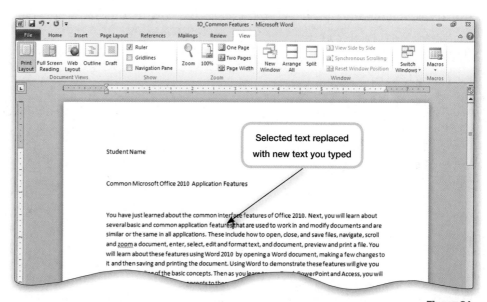

Figure 31

As soon as you began typing, the selected text was automatically deleted. The new text was inserted in the line just like any other text.

Formatting Text

An important aspect of all documents you create using Office 2010 is the appearance of the document. To improve the appearance you can apply many different formatting effects. The most common formatting features are font and character effects. A **font**, also commonly referred to as a **typeface**, is a set of characters with a specific design. The designs have names such as Times New Roman and Courier. Each font has one or more sizes. **Font size** is the height and width of the character and is commonly measured in points, abbreviated "pt." One point equals about 1/72 inch. **Character effects** are enhancements such as bold, italic, and color that are applied to selected text. Using font and character effects as design elements can add interest to your document and give readers visual cues to help them find information quickly.

First you want to change the font and increase the font size of the title of this document.

1

- Click in the left margin next to the title line when the mouse pointer is 𝄇 to select it.

- Open the Home tab.

- Open the [Calibri (Body) ▾] Font drop-down menu in the Font group.

- Point to the Arial Black font option in the menu.

Your screen should be similar to Figure 32

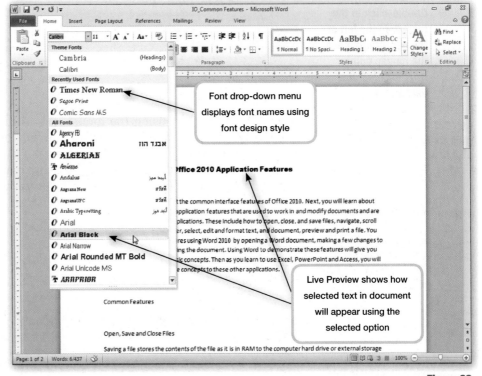

Figure 32

As you point to the font options, the **Live Preview** feature shows you how the selected text in the document will appear if this option is chosen.

- **Point to several different fonts in the menu to see the Live Preview.**

- **Scroll the menu and click Segoe Print to choose it.**

Your screen should be similar to Figure 33

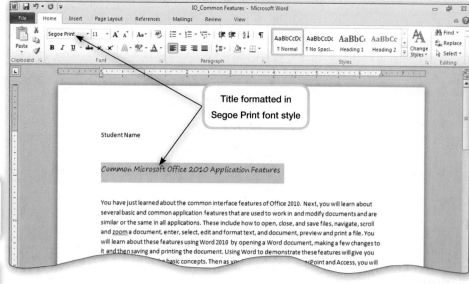

Figure 33

The title appears in the selected font and the name of the font used in the selection is displayed in the `Segoe Print` Font button. Next you want to increase the font size. The current (default) font size of 11 is displayed in the `11` Font Size button. You will increase the font size to 16 points.

- **Open the `11` Font Size drop-down menu in the Font group of the Home tab.**

- **Point to several different font sizes to see the Live Preview.**

- **Click 16 to choose it.**

Your screen should be similar to Figure 34

Figure 34

Now the title stands out much more from the other text in the document. Next you will use the Mini toolbar to add formatting to other areas of the document. As you saw earlier, the Mini toolbar appears automatically when you select text. Initially the Mini toolbar appears dimmed (semi-transparent) so that it does not interfere with what you are doing, but it changes to solid when you point at it. It displays command buttons for often-used commands from the Font and Paragraph groups that are used to format a document.

4 ● Select the line "Common Features" and point to the Mini toolbar.

● Click [11 ▾] **Font Size** and choose 14.

● Click **B** Bold.

● Click *I* Italic.

● Click <u>U</u> Underline.

Your screen should be similar to Figure 35

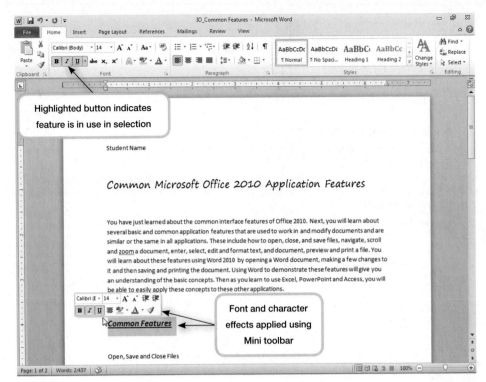

Highlighted button indicates feature is in use in selection

Student Name

Common Microsoft Office 2010 Application Features

You have just learned about the common interface features of Office 2010. Next, you will learn about several basic and common application features that are used to work in and modify documents and are similar or the same in all applications. These include how to open, close, and save files, navigate, scroll and zoom a document, enter, select, edit and format text, and document, preview and print a file. You will learn about these features using Word 2010 by opening a Word document, making a few changes to it and then saving and printing the document. Using Word to demonstrate these features will give you an understanding of the basic concepts. Then as you learn to use Excel, PowerPoint and Access, you will be able to easily apply these concepts to these other applications.

Font and character effects applied using Mini toolbar

Common Features

Open, Save and Close Files

Page: 1 of 2 | Words: 2/437 |

Figure 35

The increase in font size as well as the text effects makes this topic head much more prominent. Notice the command button for each selected effect is highlighted, indicating the feature is in use in the selection.

Using the Mini toolbar is particularly useful when the Home tab is closed because you do not need to reopen the Home tab to access the commands. It remains available until you clear the selection or press (Esc). If you do nothing with a selection for a while, the Mini toolbar will disappear. To redisplay it simply right-click on the selection again. This will also open the context menu.

You will remove the underline effect from the selection next.

5

● **Right-click on the selection to redisplay the Mini toolbar.**

● **Click U Underline on the Mini toolbar.**

Your screen should be similar to Figure 36

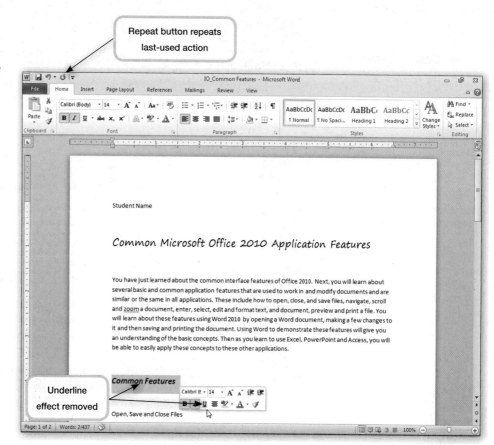

Figure 36

The context menu and Mini toolbar appeared when you right-clicked the selection. The context menu displayed a variety of commands that are quicker to access than locating the command on the Ribbon. The commands that appear on this menu change depending on what you are doing at the time. The context menu disappeared after you made a selection from the Mini toolbar. Both the Mini toolbar and context menus are designed to make it more efficient to execute commands.

Also notice that the 🔁 Redo button in the Quick Access Toolbar has changed to a 🔄 Repeat button. This feature allows you to quickly repeat the last-used command at another location in the document.

Undoing and Redoing Editing Changes

Instead of reselecting the U Underline command to remove the underline effect, you could have used 🔙 ▾ Undo to reverse your last action or command. You will use this feature to restore the underline (your last action).

1

Click Undo in the Quick Access Toolbar.

Another Method

The keyboard shortcut is Ctrl + Z.

Your screen should be similar to Figure 37

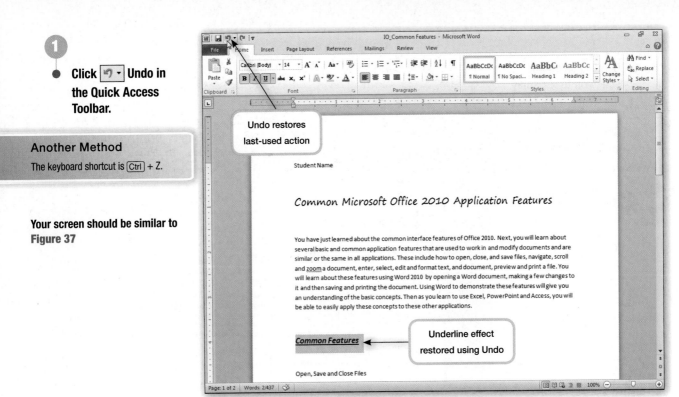

Undo restores last-used action

Underline effect restored using Undo

Figure 37

Undo reversed the last action and the underline formatting effect was restored. Notice that the Undo button includes a drop-down menu button. Clicking this button displays a menu of the most recent actions that can be reversed, with the most-recent action at the top of the menu. When you select an action from the drop-down menu, you also undo all actions above it in the menu.

2

Open the Undo drop-down menu.

Choose **Bold**.

Your screen should be similar to Figure 38

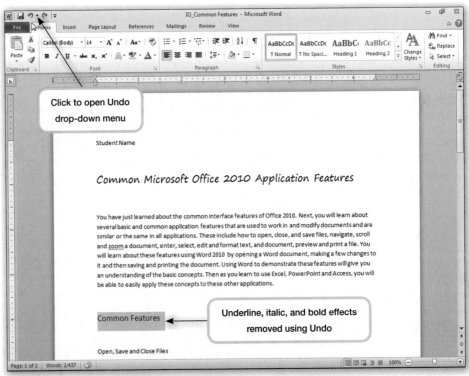

Click to open Undo drop-down menu

Underline, italic, and bold effects removed using Undo

Figure 38

The underline, italic, and bold effects were all removed. Immediately after you undo an action, the Repeat button changes to the Redo button and is available so you can restore the action you just undid. You will restore the last-removed format, bold.

Copying and Moving Selections

Common to all Office applications is the capability to copy and move selections to new locations in a document or between documents, saving you time by not having to recreate the same information. A selection that is moved is cut from its original location, called the **source**, and inserted at a new location, called the **destination**. A selection that is copied leaves the original in the source and inserts a duplicate at the destination.

When a selection is cut or copied, the selection is stored in the system **Clipboard**, a temporary Windows storage area in memory. It is also stored in the **Office Clipboard**. The system Clipboard holds only the last cut or copied item, whereas the Office Clipboard can store up to 24 items that have been cut or copied. This feature allows you to insert multiple items from various Office documents and paste all or part of the collection of items into another document.

First, you will copy the text "Office 2010" to two other locations in the first paragraph.

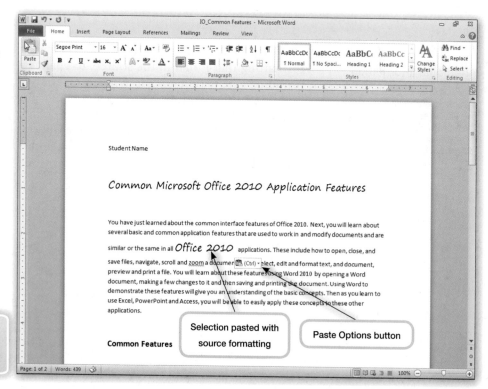

Figure 39

The copied selection is inserted at the location you specified with the same formatting as it has in the title. The Paste Options button appears automatically whenever a selection is pasted. It is used to control the format of the pasted item.

2

● **Click the** **Paste Options button.**

Your screen should be similar to Figure 40

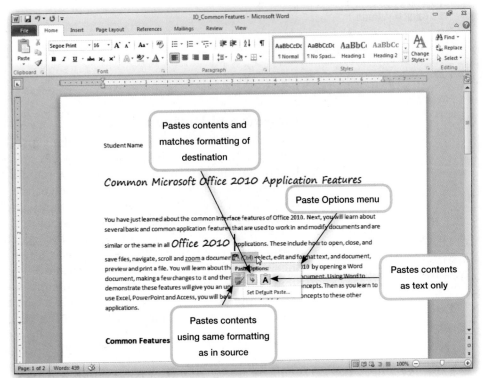

Figure 40

Additional Information

The Paste Options vary with the different applications. For example, Excel has 14 different Paste Options. The Paste Options feature is not available in Access and Paste Preview is not available in Excel.

The Paste Options are used to specify whether to insert the item with the same formatting that it had in the source, to change it to the formatting of the surrounding destination text, or to insert text only (from a selection that is a combination of text and graphics). The default as you have seen is to keep the formatting from the source. You want to change it to the formatting of the surrounding text. As you point to a Paste Options button, a **Paste Preview** will show how that option will affect the selection. Then you will copy it again to a second location.

3

- Click 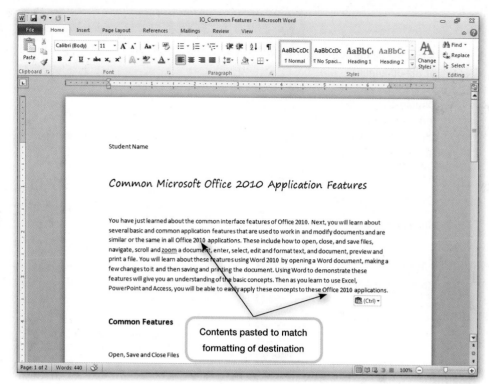 Merge Formatting.

- Select "other" in the last line of the first paragraph.

- Right-click on the selection and point to each of the Paste Options in the context menu to see the Paste Preview.

- Click Merge Formatting.

Your screen should be similar to Figure 41

Figure 41

The selected text was deleted and replaced with the contents of the system Clipboard. The system Clipboard contents remain in the Clipboard until another item is copied or cut, allowing you to paste the same item multiple times.

Now you will learn how to move a selection by rearranging several lines of text in the description of common features. You want to move the last sentence in the document, beginning with "Opening a file", to the top of the list. The Cut and Paste commands in the Clipboard group of the Home tab are used to move selections.

4 ● Scroll to see the end of the document.

● Double-click in the left margin next to the last sentence in the document to select it.

● Click ✂ Cut in the Clipboard group.

Your screen should be similar to Figure 42

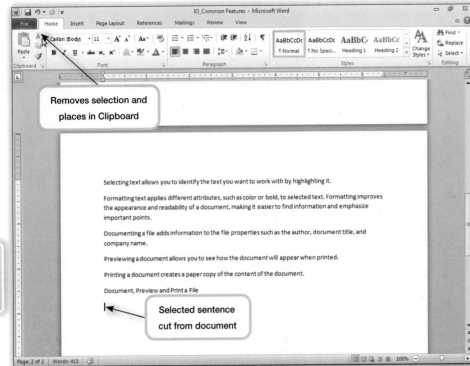

Figure 42

The selected paragraph is removed from the source and copied to the Clipboard. Next, you need to move the cursor to the location where the text will be inserted and paste the text into the document from the Clipboard.

5 ● Move to the beginning of the word "Saving" at the top of the Common Features list.

● Press Ctrl + V.

Your screen should be similar to Figure 43

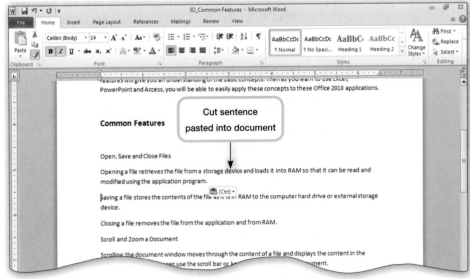

Figure 43

The cut sentence is reentered into the document at the cursor location. That was much quicker than retyping the whole sentence! Because the source has the same formatting as the text at the destination, the default setting to keep the source formatting is appropriate.

Using Drag and Drop

Another way to move or copy selections is to use the drag-and-drop editing feature. This feature is most useful for copying or moving short distances in a document. To use drag and drop to move a selection, point to the selection and drag it to the location where you want the selection inserted. The mouse pointer appears as as you drag, and a temporary insertion point shows you where the text will be placed when you release the mouse button.

1

● Select the last line of text in the document.

● Drag the selection to the beginning of the word "Documenting" (four lines up).

Your screen should be similar to Figure 44

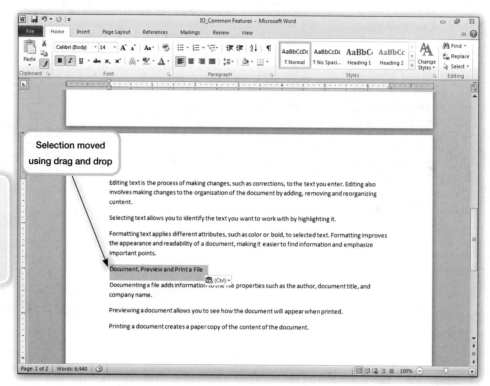

Figure 44

The selection moved to the new location. However, the selection is not copied and stored in the Clipboard and cannot be pasted to multiple locations in the document.

Copying Formats

Many times, you will find you want to copy the formats associated with a selection, but not the text. It is easy to do this using the Format Painter tool.

1

- Apply bold and italic effects and increase the font size to 14 of the currently selected text.

- Click Format Painter in the Clipboard group.

- Scroll the document up and select the topic line of text "Enter, Select, Edit and Format text".

Your screen should be similar to Figure 45

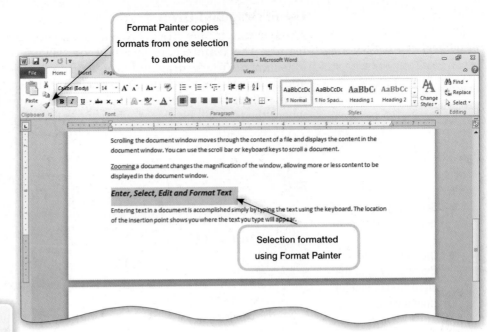

Format Painter copies formats from one selection to another

Selection formatted using Format Painter

Figure 45

The text you selected is formatted using the same formats. This feature is especially helpful when you want to copy multiple formats at one time. Next, you want to format the other topic heads in the Common Features list using the same formats. To do this, you can make the Format Painter "sticky" so that it can be used to copy the format multiple times in succession.

2

- Double-click Format Painter in the Clipboard group.

- Select the remaining two topic heads in the Common Features list:

- Scroll and Zoom a Document

- Open, Save and Close Files

- Click Format Painter to turn off this feature.

- Clear the selection.

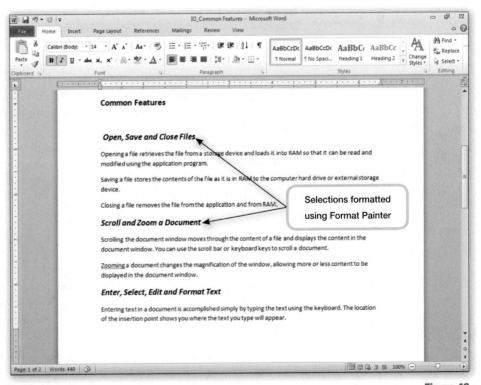

Selections formatted using Format Painter

Figure 46

Your screen should be similar to Figure 46

Specifying Document Properties

In addition to the content of the document that you create, all Office 2010 applications automatically include details about the document that describe or identify it called **metadata** or document **properties**. Document properties include details such as title, author name, subject, and keywords that identify the document's topic or contents (described below). Some of these properties are automatically generated. These include statistics such as the number of words in the file and general information such as the date the document was created and last modified. Others such as author name and tags or keywords are properties that you can specify. A **tag** or **keyword** is a descriptive word that is associated with the file and can be used to locate a file using a search.

By specifying relevant information as document properties, you can easily organize, identify, and search for your documents later.

Property	Action
Title	Enter the document title. This title can be longer and more descriptive than the file name.
Tags	Enter words that you associate with the presentation to make it easier to find using search tools.
Comments	Enter comments that you want others to see about the content of the document.
Categories	Enter the name of a higher-level category under which you can group similar types of presentations.
Author	Enter the name of the presentation's author. By default this is the name entered when the application was installed.

You will look at the document properties that are automatically included and add documentation to identify you as the author, and specify a document title and keywords to describe the document.

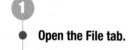

- Open the File tab.

- Click the "Show all properties" link at the bottom of the Properties panel in the Info window to display all properties.

Your screen should be similar to Figure 47

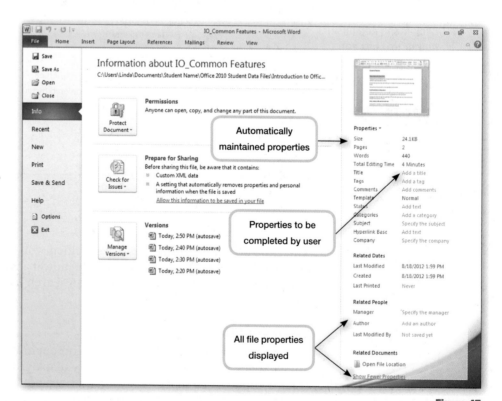

Figure 47

The Properties panel in the right section of the Info tab is divided into four groups and displays the properties associated with the document. Properties such as the document size, number of words, and number of pages are automatically maintained. Others such as the title and tag properties are blank waiting for you to specify your own information.

You will add a title, a tag, and your name as the author name.

2

● Click in the Title text box and type **Common Office Features**

● In the same manner, enter **common, features, interface** as the tags.

● Click in the Add an Author text box and enter your name.

Your screen should be similar to Figure 48

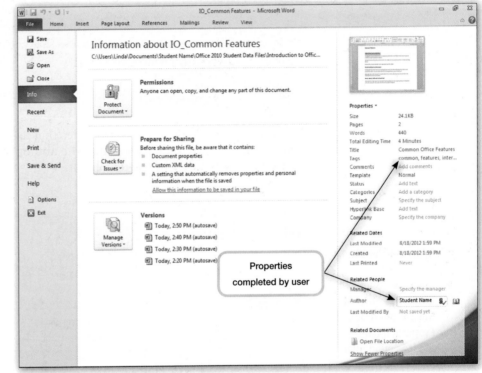

Figure 48

Once the document properties are specified, you can use them to identify and locate documents. You also can use the automatically updated properties for the same purpose. For example, you can search for all files created by a specified user or on a certain date.

Saving a File

As you enter and edit text to create a document in Word, Excel, and PowerPoint, the changes you make are immediately displayed onscreen and are stored in your computer's memory. However, they are not permanently stored until you save your work to a file on a disk. After a document has been saved as a file, it can be closed and opened again at a later time to be edited further. Unlike Word, Excel, and PowerPoint, where you start work on a new document and then save your changes, Access requires that you name the new database file first and create a table for your data. Then, it saves your changes to the data automatically as you work. This allows multiple users to have access to the most up-to-date data at all times.

As a backup against the accidental loss of work from power failure or other mishap, Word, Excel, and PowerPoint include an AutoRecover feature. When this feature is on, as you work you may see a pulsing disk icon briefly appear in the status bar. This icon indicates that the program is saving your work to a temporary recovery file. The time interval between automatic saving can be set to any period you specify; the default is every 10 minutes. After a problem has occurred, when you restart the program, the recovery file is automatically opened containing all changes you made up to the last time it was saved by AutoRecover. You then need to save the recovery file. If you do not save it, it is deleted when closed. AutoRecover is a great feature for recovering lost work but should not be used in place of regularly saving your work.

You will save the work you have done so far on the document. You use the Save or Save As commands to save files. The ⊟ **Save** command on the File tab or the ⊟ Save button on the Quick Access Toolbar will save the active file using the same file name by replacing the contents of the existing disk file with the document as it appears on your screen. The ⊠ **Save As** command on the File tab is used to save a file using a new file name, to a new location, or as a different file type. This leaves the original file unchanged. When you create a new document, you can use either of the Save commands to save your work to a file on the disk. It is especially important to save a new document very soon after you create it because the AutoRecover feature does not work until a file name has been specified.

You will save this file using a new file name to your solution file location.

Additional Information

You can specify different AutoRecover settings by choosing Options/Save in Backstage view and specifying the AutoRecover settings of your choice.

Another Method

The keyboard shortcut for the Save command is [Ctrl] + S.

Additional Information

Saving a file is the same in all Office 2010 applications, except Access.

1

• **Click** **in the left section of Backstage view.**

Your screen should be similar to Figure 49

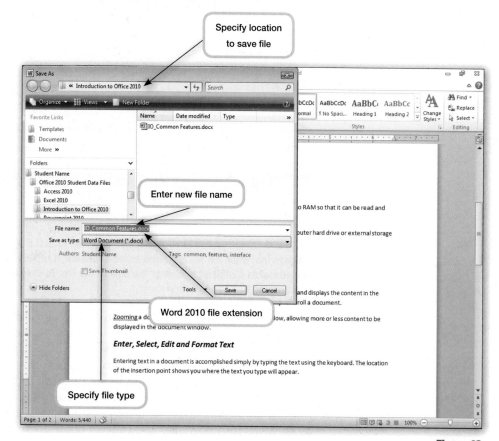

Specify location to save file

Enter new file name

Word 2010 file extension

Specify file type

Figure 49

The Save As dialog box is used to specify the location where you will save the file and the file name. The Address bar displays the folder location from which the file was opened and the File name text box displays the name of the open file. The file name is highlighted, ready for you to enter a new file name. The Save as type box displays "Word Document.docx" as the default format in which the file will be saved. Word 2010 documents are identified by the file extension .docx. The file type you select determines the file extension that will be automatically added to the file name when the file is saved. The file types and extensions for the four Office 2010 applications are described in the following table.

Extensions	File Type
Word 2010	
.docx	Word 2007-2010 document without macros or code
.dotx	Word 2007-2010 template without macros or code
.docm	Word 2007-2010 document that could contain macros or code
.xps	Word 2007-2010 shared document (see Note)
.doc	Word 95–2003 document
Excel 2010	
.xlsx	Excel 2007-2010 default workbook without macros or code
.xlsm	Excel 2007-2010 default workbook that could contain macros
.xltx	Excel 2007-2010 template without macros
.xltm	Excel 2007-2010 template that could contain macros
.xps	Excel 2007-2010 shared workbook (see Note)
.xls	Excel 97–2003 workbook
PowerPoint	
.pptx	PowerPoint 2007-2010 default presentation format
.pptm	PowerPoint 2007-2010 presentation with macros
.potx	PowerPoint 2007-2010 template without macros
.potm	PowerPoint 2007-2010 template that may contain macros
.ppam	PowerPoint 2007-2010 add-in that contains macros
.ppsx	PowerPoint 2007-2010 slide show without macros
.ppsm	PowerPoint 2007-2010 slide show that may contain macros
.thmx	PowerPoint 2007-2010 theme
.ppt	PowerPoint 2003 or earlier presentation
Access	
.accdb	Access 2007-2010 database
.mdb	Access 2003 or earlier database

NOTE XPS file format is a fixed-layout electronic file format that preserves document formatting and ensures that when the file is viewed online or printed, it retains exactly the format that you intended. It also makes it difficult to change the data in the file. To save as an XPS file format, you must have installed the free add-in.

Office 2007 and 2010 save Word, Excel, and PowerPoint files using the XML format (Extensible Markup Language) and a four-letter file extension. This format makes your documents safer by separating files that contain macros (small programs in a document that automate tasks) to make it easier for a virus checker to identify and block unwanted code or macros that could be dangerous to your computer. It also makes file sizes smaller by compressing the content upon saving and makes files less susceptible to damage. In addition, XML format makes it easier to open documents created with an Office application using another application.

Previous versions of Word, Excel, and PowerPoint did not use XML and had a three-letter file extension. If you plan to share a file with someone using an Office 2003 or earlier version, you can save the document using the three-letter file type; however, some features may be lost. Otherwise, if you save it as a four-letter file type, the recipient may not be able to view all features. There also may be loss of features for users of Office 2007 (even though it has an XML file type) because the older version does not support several of the new features in Office 2010. Office 2010 includes a feature that checks for compatibility with previous versions and advises you what features in the document may be lost if opened by an Office 2007 user or if the document is saved in the 2003 format.

If you have an Office Access 2007 (.accdb) database that you want to save in an earlier Access file format (.mdb), you can do so as long as your .accdb database does not contain any multivalued lookup fields, offline data, or attachments. This is because older versions of Access do not support these new features. If you try to convert an .accdb database containing any of these elements to an .mdb file format, Access displays an error message.

First you may need to change the location to the location where the file will be saved. The same procedures you used to specify a location to open a file are used to specify the location to save a file. Then, you will change the file name to Common Features using the default Word document type (.docx).

2

● If necessary, select the location where you save your solution files.

● If necessary, triple-click or drag in the File Name text box to highlight the existing file name.

● Type **Common Features**

● Click [Save].

Your screen should be similar to Figure 50

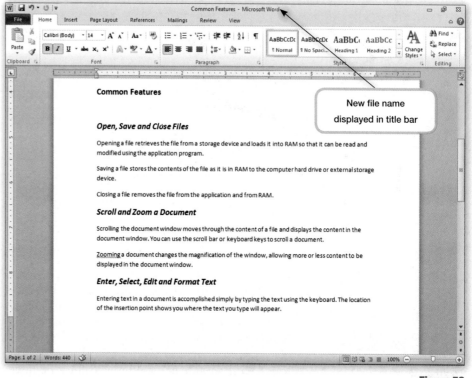

Figure 50

The document is saved as Common Features.docx at the location you selected, and the new file name is displayed in the Word application window title bar.

Printing a Document

Once a document appears how you want, you may want to print a hard copy for your own reference or to give to others. All Office 2010 applications include the capability to print and have similar options. You will print this document next.

1

- **Open the File tab and choose Print.**

Another Method

The keyboard shortcut for the Print command is [Ctrl] + P.

Your screen should be similar to Figure 51

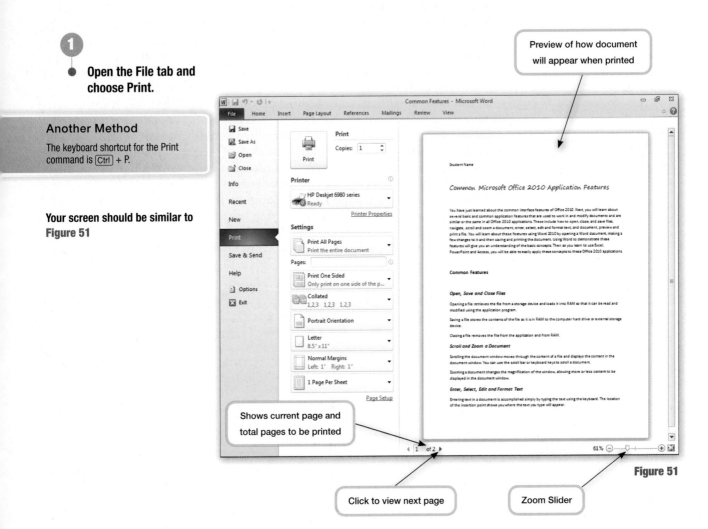

Preview of how document will appear when printed

Shows current page and total pages to be printed

Click to view next page

Zoom Slider

Figure 51

The right section of the Print window displays a preview of the current page of your document. To save time and unnecessary printing and paper waste, it is always a good idea to preview each page of your document before printing. Notice below the preview, the page scroll box shows the page number of the page you are currently viewing and the total number of pages. The scroll buttons on either side are used to scroll to the next and previous pages. Additionally, a Zoom Slider is available to adjust the size of the preview.

Having Trouble?

If necessary, use the Zoom Slider to change the preview zoom to 60%.

2

● Click ► to view the second page of the document.

● Increase the zoom to 70%.

Your screen should be similar to Figure 52

Specify area of document to print

Changes page orientation

Click to print using specified settings

Currently selected printer

Preview of second page

Current page is page two

Click to view previous page

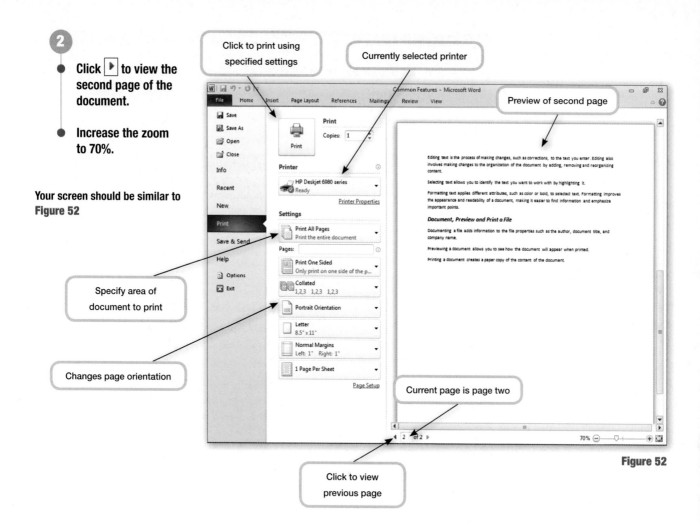

Figure 52

If you see any changes you want to make to the document, you would need to close the File tab and make the changes. If the document looks good, you are ready to print.

The second section of the Print window is divided into three areas: Print, Printer, and Settings. In the Print section you specify the number of copies you want printed. The default is to print one copy. The Printer section is used to specify the printer you will use and the printer properties such as paper size and print quality. The name of the default printer on your computer appears in the list box. The Settings area is used to specify what part of the document you want to print, whether to print on one or both sides of the paper or to collate (sort) the printed output, the page orientation, paper size, margins, and sheet settings. The Word print setting options are explained in the following table. The Print settings will vary slightly with the different Office applications. For example, in Excel, the options to specify what to print are to print the entire worksheet, entire workbook, or a selection. The differences will be demonstrated in the individual labs.

Option	Setting	Action
Print what	All	Prints entire document (default)
	Current page	Prints selected page or page where the cursor is located.
	Pages	Prints pages you specify by typing page numbers in Pages text box
	Selection	Prints selected text only (default)
Sides	One	Prints on one side of the paper.
	Both (short)	Prints on both sides by flipping the page vertically using a duplex printer
	Both (long)	Prints on both sides by flipping the page horizontally using a duplex printer
	Manually both	Reload the paper when prompted to print on the other side
Collate	Collated	Prints all of specified document before printing second or multiple copies; for example, pages 1,2 then 1,2 again (default)
	Uncollated	Prints multiple copies of each specified page sequentially (for example, pages 1,1 then 2,2)
Orientation	Portrait	Prints across the width of the paper (default)
	Landscape	Prints across the length of the paper
Paper	Size	Select the paper size (8.5 × 11 is default)
	Envelope	Select an envelope size
Margins	Normal	One-inch margins all around (default)
	Narrow, Wide	Select alternative margin settings
Sheet	One Page Per Sheet	Prints each page of the document on a separate sheet (default)
	Multiple pages per sheet	Specify number of pages to print on a sheet

NOTE Please consult your instructor for printing procedures that may differ from the following directions.

You will specify several different print settings to see the effect on the preview, then you will print using the default print settings.

3

- If you need to change the selected printer to another printer, open the Printer drop-down menu and choose the appropriate printer (your instructor will tell you which printer to select).

- Click

  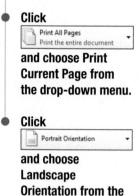

  Print All Pages
  Print the entire document

  and choose Print Current Page from the drop-down menu.

- Click

  Portrait Orientation

  and choose Landscape Orientation from the drop-down menu.

Your screen should be similar to Figure 53

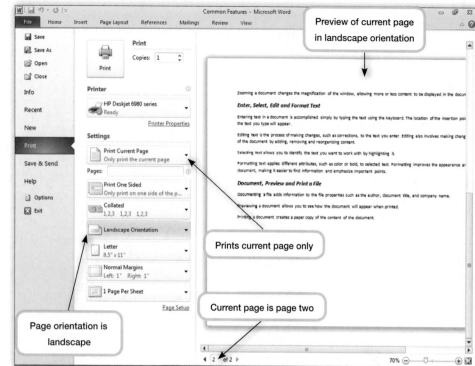

Preview of current page in landscape orientation

Prints current page only

Current page is page two

Page orientation is landscape

Figure 53

The preview window displays the current page in landscape orientation and the page indicator shows that page two of two will print. You will return these settings to their defaults and then print the document.

4

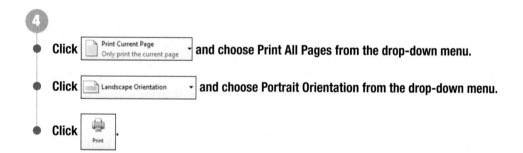

- Click **Print Current Page** / Only print the current page and choose Print All Pages from the drop-down menu.

- Click **Landscape Orientation** and choose Portrait Orientation from the drop-down menu.

- Click **Print** .

Your printer should be printing the document.

Closing a File

Finally, you want to close the document.

1

● **Open the File tab and click** [📄 Close].

Another Method

The keyboard shortcut is Ctrl + F4.

Your screen should be similar to Figure 54

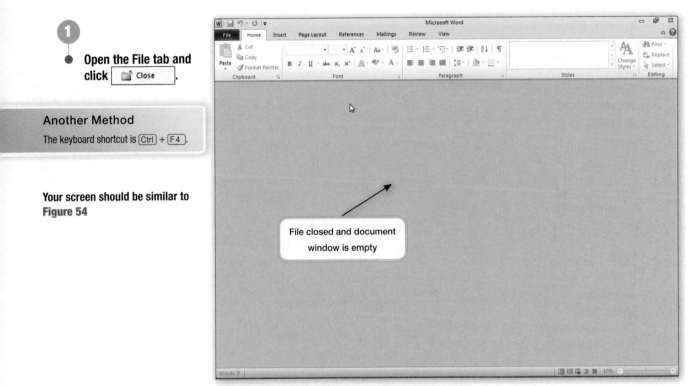

File closed and document window is empty

Figure 54

Additional Information

Do not click 🗙 Close in the window title bar as this closes the application.

Now the Word window displays an empty document window. Because you did not make any changes to the document since saving it, the document window closed immediately. If you had made additional changes, the program would ask whether you wanted to save the file before closing it. This prevents the accidental closing of a file that has not been saved first.

USING OFFICE HELP

Another Method

You also can press F1 to access Help.

Notice the 🔵 in the upper-right corner of the Ribbon. This button is used to access the Microsoft Help system. The Help button is always visible even when the Ribbon is hidden. Because you are using the Microsoft Word 2010 application, Word Help will be accessed.

1

● Click ❓ Microsoft Word Help.

● If a Table of Contents pane is not displayed along the left side of the Help window, click 🖼 Show Table of Contents in the Help window toolbar to open it.

Your screen should be similar to Figure 55

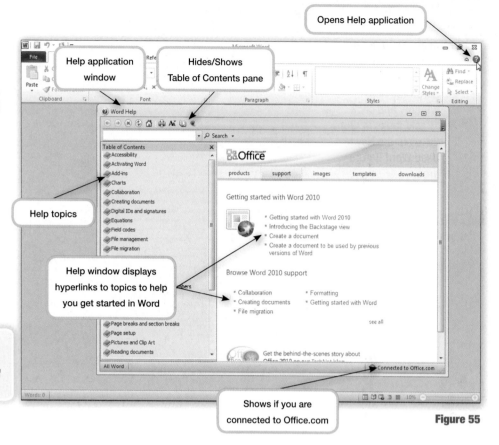

Opens Help application

Help application window

Hides/Shows Table of Contents pane

Help topics

Help window displays hyperlinks to topics to help you get started in Word

Shows if you are connected to Office.com

Connected to Office.com

Figure 55

Additional Information

Click 🖼 Hide Table of Contents in the Help window toolbar to hide the Table of Contents pane when it is open.

Additional Information

Because Help is an online feature, the information is frequently updated. Your screens may display slightly different information than those shown in the figures in this lab.

Additional Information

Depending on the size of your Help window, you may need to scroll the window to see all the Help information provided.

Having Trouble?

In addition to being connected to the Internet, the Help feature to show content from the Internet must be selected. If necessary, click

 at the bottom of the Help window and choose Show content from Office.com.

The Word Help feature is a separate application and is opened and displayed in a separate window. The Help window on your screen will probably be a different size and arrangement than in Figure 56. A list of help topics is displayed in the Table of Contents pane along the left side of the window and the Help window on the right side displays several topics to help you get started using Word. If you are connected to the Internet, the Microsoft Office Online Web site, Office.com, is accessed and help information from this site is displayed in the window. If you are not connected, the offline help information that is provided with the application and stored on your computer is located and displayed. Generally, the listing of topics is similar but fewer in number.

Selecting Help Topics

There are several ways you can get help. The first is to select a topic from the listing displayed in the Help window. Each topic is a **hyperlink** or connection to the information located on the Office.com Web site or in Help on your computer. When you point to a hyperlink, it appears underlined and the mouse pointer appears as 🖑. Clicking the hyperlink accesses and displays the information associated with the hyperlink.

1

- Click "Getting started with Word 2010."

- Scroll the Help window and click "Basic tasks in Word 2010" in the Never Used Word Before area.

Your screen should be similar to Figure 56

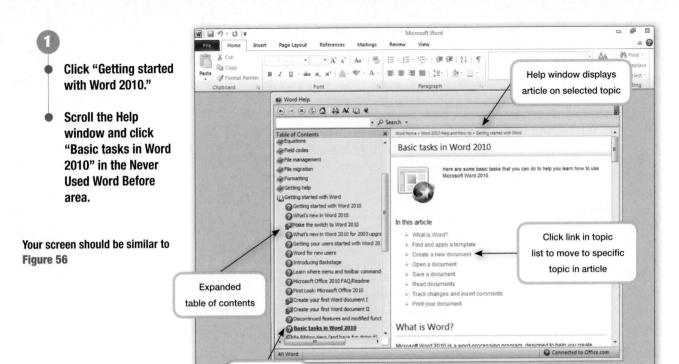

Help window displays article on selected topic

Click link in topic list to move to specific topic in article

Expanded table of contents

Selected topic

Figure 56

An article containing information about basic features of Word 2010 is displayed and the table of contents has expanded and current topic is underlined to show your location in Help. A topic list appears at the top of the article. You can either scroll the article to read it, or you can jump to a specific location in the article by clicking on a topic link.

2

- Click "Create a new document."

Your screen should be similar to Figure 57

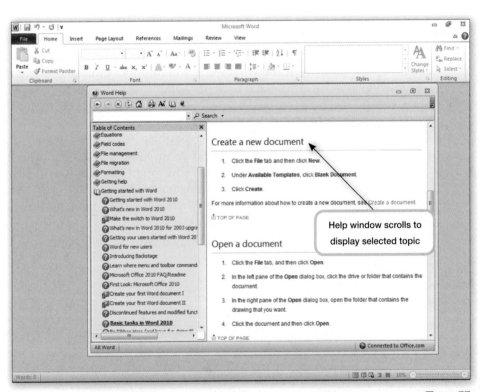

Help window scrolls to display selected topic

Figure 57

The information on the selected topic is displayed in the window. Notice, as you made selections in the Help window, that the Table of Contents pane shows your current location in Help.

Using the Help Table of Contents

Choosing a topic from the Table of Contents is another method of locating Help information. Using this method allows you to browse the entire list of Help topics to locate topics of interest to you. In this case, the Getting Started with Word topic has expanded to show the subtopics and the topic you are currently viewing is underlined, indicating it is selected. Notice the 📖 Open Book and 📗 Closed Book icons in the Table of Contents. The 📖 Open Book icon identifies those chapters that are open. Clicking on an item preceded with a 📗 Closed Book icon opens a chapter, which expands to display additional chapters or topics. Clicking on an item preceded with 📄 displays the specific Help information.

Additional Information

Pointing to a topic that is not fully displayed in the Table of Contents displays a ScreenTip of the entire topic heading.

● Click "Word for new users" in the Table of Contents list.

● Click "A tour of the Word user interface" in the Help window.

Your screen should be similar to Figure 58

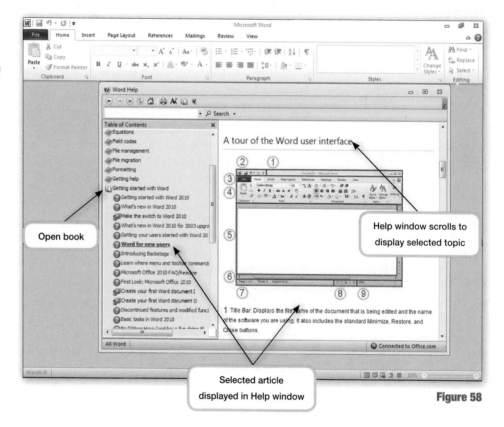

Open book

Help window scrolls to display selected topic

Selected article displayed in Help window

Figure 58

Now information about the user interface features of Word 2010 is displayed in the Help window. To move through previously viewed Help topics, you can use the ⬅ Back and ➡ Forward buttons in the Help toolbar. You can quickly redisplay the opening Help window using 🏠 Home on the Help toolbar.

2

- Click ◄ Back to display the previous topic.

- Click ⌂ Home in the Help window toolbar.

- Click "Getting started with Word" in the Table of Contents pane to close this topic.

Your screen should be similar to Figure 59

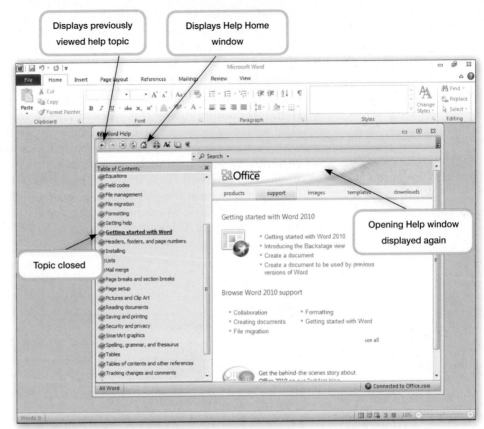

Displays previously viewed help topic

Displays Help Home window

Topic closed

Opening Help window displayed again

Figure 59

The opening Help window is displayed, the Table of Contents topic is closed, and the ➡ Forward button in the Help window toolbar is now available for use.

Searching Help Topics

Another method to find Help information is to conduct a search by entering a word or phrase you want help on in the Search text box. When searching, you can specify the scope of the search by selecting from the 🔍 Search ▾ drop-down menu. The broadest scope for a search, All Word under Content from Office .com, is preselected. You will use this feature to search for Help information about the Office user interface.

- **Click in the Search text box to display the cursor and type user interface**

Additional Information

The search is not case sensitive.

- **Click 🔍 Search ▾.**

- **Scroll the Help window to see the search results.**

Additional Information

You also could press [Enter] to start the search.

Your screen should be similar to Figure 60

Figure 60

The Help window displays links to articles that contain both the words "user" and "interface." The results are shown in order of relevance, with the most likely matches at the top of the list.

EXITING AN OFFICE 2010 APPLICATION

Now you are ready to close the Help window and exit the Word program. The ⊠ Close button located on the right end of the window title bar can be used to exit most application windows. Alternatively, you can use the ⊠ Exit command on the File tab. If you attempt to close an application without first saving your document, a warning appears asking if you want to save your work. If you do not save your work and you exit the application, any changes you made since last saving it are lost.

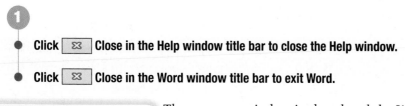

- **Click ⊠ Close in the Help window title bar to close the Help window.**

- **Click ⊠ Close in the Word window title bar to exit Word.**

Another Method

The keyboard shortcut for the Exit command is [Alt] + [F4].

The program window is closed and the Windows desktop is visible again.

KEY TERMS

Backstage view IO.24
buttons IO.15
character effects IO.40
Clipboard IO.45
commands IO.18
context menu IO.17
contextual tabs IO.20
cursor IO.15
database IO.7
default IO.27
destination IO.45
dialog box launcher IO.23
document window IO.15
edit IO.3
Enhanced ScreenTip IO.20
fields IO.7
font IO.40
font size IO.40
format IO.3
groups IO.18
hyperlink IO.61
insertion point IO.15
keyboard shortcut IO.16
keyword IO.51
Live Preview IO.40
metadata IO.51

Mini toolbar IO.39
Office Clipboard IO.45
on-demand tabs IO.20
Paste Preview IO.46
properties IO.27, 51
Quick Access Toolbar IO.15
records IO.7
Ribbon IO.15
ScreenTip IO.16
scroll bar IO.15
shortcut menu IO.17
slide IO.10
slide shows IO.10
source IO.45
status bar IO.15
tables IO.7
tabs IO.18
tag IO.51
task pane IO.23
template IO.26
tooltip IO.16
typeface IO.40
user interface IO.14
View buttons IO.15
worksheet IO.5
Zoom Slider IO.15

COMMAND SUMMARY

Command/Button	Shortcut	Action
Quick Access Toolbar		
↩ ▾ Undo	Ctrl + Y	Restores last change
↪ Redo	Ctrl + Y	Restores last Undo action
↪ Repeat	Ctrl + Y	Repeats last action
❓ Microsoft Word Help	F1	Opens Microsoft Help

COMMAND SUMMARY (CONTINUED)

Command/Button	Shortcut	Action
File tab		
🖫 Save	Ctrl + S or 🖫	Saves document using same file name
🖫 Save As	F12	Saves document using a new file name, type, and/or location
📂 Open	Ctrl + O	Opens existing file
📁 Close	Ctrl + F4 or ⊠	Closes document
Info		Displays document properties
Print/ 🖶 Print	Ctrl + P	Prints document using specified settings
⊠ Exit	Alt + F4 or ⊠	Exits Office program
View tab		
Zoom group		
🔍 Zoom		Changes magnification of document
Home tab		
Clipboard group		
📋 Paste	Ctrl + V	Inserts copy of Clipboard at location of cursor
✂ Cut	Ctrl + X	Removes selection and copies to Clipboard
📋 Copy	Ctrl + C	Copies selection to Clipboard
✿ Format Painter		Duplicates formats of selection to other locations
Font group		
Calibri (Body) ▾ Font	Ctrl + Shift + F	Changes typeface
11 ▾ Font Size	Ctrl + Shift + P	Changes font size
B Bold	Ctrl + B	Adds/removes bold effect
I Italic	Ctrl + I	Adds/removes italic effect
U Underline	Ctrl + U	Adds/removes underline effect

STEP-BY-STEP

EXPLORING EXCEL 2010

1. In this exercise you will explore the Excel 2010 application and use many of the same features you learned about while using Word 2010 in this lab.

   a. Use the Start menu or a shortcut icon on your desktop to start Office Excel 2010.

   b. What shape is the mouse pointer when positioned in the document window area? _____

   c. Excel has _____ tabs. Which tabs are not the same as in Word? _____

   d. Open the Formulas tab. How many groups are in the Formulas tab? _____

   e. Which tab contains the group to work with charts? _____

   f. From the Home tab, click the Number group dialog box launcher. What is the name of the dialog box that opens? _____ How many number categories are there? _____ Close the dialog box.

   g. Display ScreenTips for the following buttons located in the Alignment group of the Home tab and identify what action they perform.

       ▤ _____

       ▤ _____

       ▤ _____

   h. Open the Excel Help window. From the Help window choose "Getting started with Excel 2010" and then choose "Basic tasks in Excel 2010." Read this article and answer the following question: What is Excel used for? _____

   i. In the Table of Contents, open the "Worksheets" topic and then "Entering Data." Read the topic "Enter data manually in worksheet cells" and answer the following:

   - What is the definition of worksheet? Hint: Click on the grayed term "worksheet" to view a definition.

     _____

   - What four types of data can be entered in a worksheet? _____, _____, _____, _____

   j. Read the topic "Quick Start: Edit and enter data in a worksheet." If you have an Internet connection, click the Watch the video link and view the video. Close your browser window.

   k. Enter the term "formula" in the Search text box. Look at several articles and answer the following question: All formula entries begin with what symbol? _____

   l. Close the Help window. Exit Excel.

EXPLORING POWERPOINT 2010

2. In this exercise you will explore the PowerPoint 2010 application and use many of the same features you learned about while using Word 2010 in this lab.

   a. Use the Start menu or a shortcut icon on your desktop to start Office PowerPoint 2010.

   b. PowerPoint has _____ tabs. Which tabs are not the same as in Word?

   _____

   c. Open the Animations tab. How many groups are in this tab? _____

   d. Which tab contains the group to work with themes? _____

   e. Click on the text "Click to add title." Type your name. Select this text and change the font size to 60; add italic and bold. Cut this text. Click in the box containing "Click to add subtitle" and paste the cut selection. Use the Paste Options to keep the source formatting.

   f. Click on the text "Click to add title" and type the name of your school. Select the text and apply a font of your choice.

   g. Open the PowerPoint Help window. From the Help window, choose "Getting Started with PowerPoint 2010" and then choose "Basic tasks in PowerPoint 2010." Read the information in this article and answer the following questions:

      • In the "What is PowerPoint?" topic, what is the primary use of PowerPoint?_____.

      • In the "Save a presentation" topic, what is the default file format for a presentation?

        _____

      • What is the first tip in the "Tips for creating an effective presentation" topic?

        _____

   h. Enter the term "placeholder" in the Search text box. Look at several articles and write the definition of this term. Hint: Click on a word in an article that appears in light gray to view a definition.

      _____

   i. In the Table of Contents, open the "Delivering your presentation" topic. Choose "Create and print notes pages" and answer the following questions:

      • What are notes pages?

        _____

      • What is the Green Idea?

        _____

   j. Close the Help window. Exit PowerPoint and do not save the changes you made to the presentation.

LAB EXERCISES

EXPLORING ACCESS 2010

3. As noted in this Introduction to Microsoft Office 2010, when you start Access 2010 you need to either open an existing database file or create and name a new database. Therefore, in this exercise, you simply explore the Access 2010 Help information without opening or creating a database file.

    a. Use the Start menu or a shortcut icon on your desktop to start Office Access 2010.

    b. Open the Help tab in Backstage view and choose Microsoft Office Help.

    c. From the Help window, choose "Basic tasks in Access 2010." Read the information in this article and answer the following questions:

    - In the "What is Access?" topic, what are the two locations where you can keep your data? _____ and _____.

    - In the "Create a Database from Scratch" topic, what are the two choices? _____ or _____.

    d. In the Table of Contents pane, open the "Access basics" topic. Choose "Database basics" and answer the following questions:

    - In the "What is a database?" topic, define "database."

      _____

    - In "The parts of an Access database" topic, what are the six main parts? _____, _____, _____, _____, _____, _____.

    - In "The parts of an Access database" topic, how is data in a table stored? _____ and _____.

    - In "The parts of an Access database" topic, each row in a table is referred to as a _____.

    e. Enter the term "field" in the Search text box. Look at several articles and write the definition of this term. Hint: Click on a word in an article that appears in light gray to view a definition.

      _____

    f. Close the Help window. Exit Access.

ON YOUR OWN

EXPLORING WORD HELP

1. In addition to the Help information you used in this lab, Office 2010 Help also includes many interactive tutorials. Selecting a Help topic that starts a tutorial will open the browser program on your computer. Both audio and written instructions are provided. You will use one of these tutorials to learn more about using Word 2010.

    Start Word 2010. Open Help and choose "Getting started with Word" from the Help window. Click on the training topic "Create your first Word document I." Follow the directions in your browser to run the tutorial. When you are done, close the browser window, close Help, and exit Word 2010.

Objectives

After completing this lab, you will know how to:

1 Use a template to create a presentation.

2 View and edit a presentation.

3 Copy and move selections.

4 Move, copy, and delete slides.

5 Move, demote, and promote items.

6 Use a numbered list.

7 Check spelling.

8 Size and move placeholders.

9 Change fonts and formatting.

10 Insert and modify clip art.

11 Run a slide show.

12 Document a file.

14 Preview and print a presentation.

Animal Rescue Foundation

You are the volunteer coordinator at the local Animal Rescue Foundation. This nonprofit organization rescues unwanted pets from local animal shelters and finds foster homes for them until a suitable adoptive family can be found. The agency has a large volunteer group called the Animal Angels that provides much-needed support for the foundation.

The agency director has decided to launch a campaign to increase community awareness about the foundation. As part of the promotion, you have been asked to create a powerful and persuasive presentation to entice more members of the community to join Animal Angels.

The agency director has asked you to preview the presentation at the weekly staff meeting tomorrow and has asked you to present a draft of the presentation by noon today.

To help you create the presentation, you will use Microsoft PowerPoint 2010, a graphics presentation application that is designed to create presentation materials such as slides, overheads, and handouts. Using PowerPoint 2010, you can create a high-quality and interesting onscreen presentation with pizzazz that will dazzle your audience.

Each main topic in your presentation should have a supporting slide with a title and bulleted points.

The presentation can be reorganized easily by adding, deleting, and moving slides.

Enhance the presentation with the addition of graphics and text colors.

The following concepts will be introduced in this lab:

1 Slide A slide is an individual "page" of your presentation.

2 Spelling Checker The spelling checker locates all misspelled words, duplicate words, and capitalization irregularities as you create and edit a presentation, and proposes possible corrections.

3 AutoCorrect The AutoCorrect feature makes some basic assumptions about the text you are typing and, based on those assumptions, automatically corrects the entry.

4 Layout A layout defines the position and format for objects and text on a slide. A layout contains placeholders for the different items such as bulleted text, titles, charts, and so on.

5 Graphic A graphic is a nontext element or object such as a drawing or picture that can be added to a slide.

Starting a New Presentation

The Animal Rescue Foundation has just installed the latest version of the Microsoft Office suite of applications, Office 2010, on its computers. You will use the graphics presentation program, Microsoft PowerPoint 2010, included in the Office suite, to create your presentation. Using this program, you should have no problem creating the presentation in time for tomorrow's staff meeting.

DEVELOPING A PRESENTATION

During your presentation, you will present information about the Animal Rescue Foundation and why someone should want to join the Animal Angels volunteer group. As you prepare to create a new presentation, you should follow several basic steps: plan, create, edit, enhance, and rehearse.

Step	Description
Plan	The first step in planning a presentation is to understand its purpose. You also need to find out the length of time you have to speak, who the audience is, what type of room you will be in, and what kind of audiovisual equipment is available. These factors help to determine the type of presentation you will create.
Create	To begin creating your presentation, develop the content by typing your thoughts or notes into an outline. Each main idea in your presentation should have a supporting slide with a title and bulleted points.
Edit	While typing, you will probably make typing and spelling errors that need to be corrected. This is one type of editing. Another type is to revise the content of what you have entered to make it clearer, or to add or delete information. To do this, you might insert a slide, add or delete bulleted items, or move text to another location.
Enhance	You want to develop a presentation that grabs and holds the audience's attention. Choose a design that gives your presentation some dazzle. Wherever possible, add graphics to replace or enhance text. Add effects that control how a slide appears and disappears and that reveal text in a bulleted list one bullet at a time.
Rehearse	Finally, you should rehearse the delivery of your presentation. For a professional presentation, your delivery should be as polished as your materials. Use the same equipment that you will use when you give the presentation. Practice advancing from slide to slide and then back in case someone asks a question. If you have a mouse available, practice pointing or drawing on the slide to call attention to key points.

After rehearsing your presentation, you may find that you want to go back to the editing phase. You may change text, move bullets, or insert a new slide. Periodically, as you make changes, rehearse the presentation again to see how the changes affect your presentation. By the day of the presentation, you will be confident about your message and at ease with the materials.

EXPLORING THE POWERPOINT DOCUMENT WINDOW

During the planning phase, you have spoken with the foundation director regarding the purpose of the presentation and the content in general. The purpose of your presentation is to educate members of the community about the organization and to persuade many to volunteer. In addition, you want to impress the director by creating a professional presentation.

1

- **Start the PowerPoint 2010 application.**

- **If necessary, maximize the window.**

Having Trouble?

See "Common Office 2010 Interface Features," page IO.14, for information on how to start the application and use features that are common to all 2010 Office applications.

Your screen should be similar to Figure 1.1

Figure 1.1

Additional Information

Because the Office 2010 applications remember settings that were on when the program was last exited, your screen may look slightly different.

When you first start PowerPoint, a new blank presentation file, named Presentation1, is opened and displayed in the document window. It is like a blank piece of paper that already has many predefined settings. These default settings are generally the most commonly used settings and are stored in the Blank Presentation template file.

Many other templates that are designed to help you create professional-looking presentations are also available within PowerPoint and from the Microsoft Office Online Web site. They include design templates, which provide a design concept, fonts, and color scheme; and content templates, which suggest content for your presentation based on the type of presentation you are making. You also can design and save your own presentation templates.

The Blank Presentation template consists of a single slide that is displayed in the document window.

Concept 1 Slide

A **slide** is an individual "page" of your presentation. The first slide of a presentation is the title slide, which is used to introduce your presentation. Additional slides are used to support each main point in your presentation. The slides give the audience a visual summary of the words you speak, which helps them understand the content and keeps them engaged. The slides also help you, the speaker, organize your thoughts and prompt you during the presentation.

When you first start PowerPoint, it opens in a view called Normal view. A **view** is a way of looking at a presentation and provides the means to interact with the presentation. PowerPoint provides several views you can use to look at and modify your presentation. Depending on what you are doing, one view may be preferable to another.

View	Button	Description
Normal		Provides four working areas of the window that allow you to work on all aspects of your presentation in one place.
Slide Sorter		Displays a miniature of each slide to make it easy to reorder slides, add special effects such as transitions, and set timing between slides.
Reading View		Displays each slide in final form within the PowerPoint window so you can see how it will look during a presentation but still have access to the Windows desktop.
Slide Show		Displays each slide in final form using the full screen space so you can practice or present the presentation.

Normal view is displayed by default because it is the main view you use while creating a presentation. Normal view has four working areas: Outline tab, Slides tab, Slide pane, and Notes pane. These areas allow you to work on all components of your presentation in one convenient location. The **Outline tab** displays the text content of each slide in outline format, and the **Slides tab** displays a miniature version or **thumbnail** of each slide. You can switch between the Slides and Outline tabs by clicking on the tab. The **Slide pane** displays the selected slide. The **Notes pane** includes space for you to enter notes that apply to the current slide.

Below the document window is the status bar, which displays the slide indicator, messages and information about various PowerPoint settings, buttons to change the document view, and a window zoom feature. The **slide indicator** identifies the number of the slide that is displayed in the Slide pane, along with the total number of slides in the presentation. You will learn about the other features of the status bar shortly.

You decide to try to create your first presentation using the Blank Presentation template. It is the simplest and most generic of the templates. Because it has minimal design elements, it is good to use when you first start working with PowerPoint, as it allows you to easily add your own content and design changes.

Notice the slide contains two boxes with dotted borders. These boxes, called **placeholders**, are containers for all the content that appears on a slide. Slide content consists of text and **objects** such as, graphics, tables and charts. In this case, the placeholders are text placeholders that are designed to contain text and display standard **placeholder text** messages that prompt the user to enter a title and subtitle.

ENTERING AND EDITING TEXT

As suggested, you will enter the title for the presentation. As soon as you click on the placeholder, the placeholder text will disappear and will be replaced by the text you want to appear in the slide.

1

Click the "Click to add title" placeholder.

Your screen should be similar to Figure 1.2

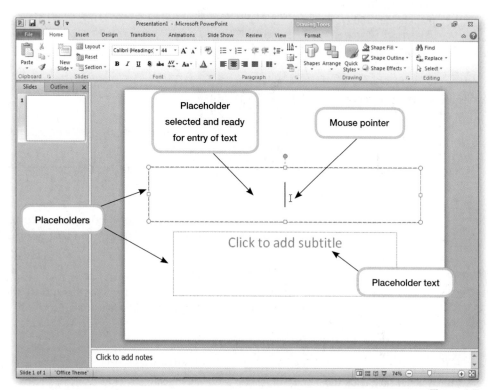

Figure 1.2

Additional Information

A solid border indicates that you can format the placeholder box itself. Clicking the dashed-line border changes it to a solid border.

Notice that the placeholder is surrounded with a dashed-line border. This indicates that you can enter, delete, select, and format the object inside the placeholder. Because this placeholder contains text, the cursor is displayed to show your location in the text and to allow you to select and edit the text. Additionally, the mouse pointer appears as a I to be used to position the cursor.

Next you will type the title text you want to appear on the slide. Then you will enter the subtitle.

Having Trouble?

See the section "Entering and Editing Text" in the Introduction to Microsoft Office 2010 to review this feature.

2

Type **Join Animal Angels**

Having Trouble?

If you make a typing error, press [Backspace] to delete the characters back to the error and retype the entry.

● Click in the "Click to add subtitle" placeholder and type **Animal Rescue Foundation**

Your screen should be similar to Figure 1.3

Figure 1.3

The content for the first slide is complete. Notice that the thumbnail of the slide in the Slides tab now displays the text you just entered.

INSERTING A SLIDE

Next you want to add the content for a second slide. To continue creating the presentation, you need to add another slide.

1

● If necessary, click the Home tab to open it.

● Click [New Slide] in the Slides group.

Another Method

You also can use the keyboard shortcut [Ctrl] + M to insert a new slide.

Your screen should be similar to Figure 1.4

Figure 1.4

A new slide with a slide title placeholder and a content placeholder was added to the presentation. It is displayed in the Slide pane and is the **current slide**, or the slide that will be affected by any changes you make. The Slides tab displays a second slide thumbnail. It is highlighted, further indicating it is the current slide. The status bar displays the number of the current slide and the total number of slides in the presentation.

Now you could add text to the new slide and continue adding slides to create the presentation.

OPENING A PRESENTATION TEMPLATE

Although the Blank presentation template is opened automatically when you start PowerPoint, it is not the only method that can be used to create a presentation. Another is to use one of the many supplied design templates. A third is to save the design elements of an existing presentation as a custom template, which you would then use as the basis for your new presentation. Finally, you can open an existing presentation and modify the design and content as needed for the new presentation.

Because you have not decided exactly what content should be presented next in the presentation, you decide that it might be easier to use one of the templates that will suggest the content to include. You will close this file without saving it and then open a presentation template file.

1

● Open the File tab and click ☐ Close.

● Click Do_n't Save.

● Open the File tab and choose New.

Your screen should be similar to Figure 1.5

Having Trouble?

To complete steps 2 and 3 you need an Internet connection. If you are not connected to the Internet, choose New from Existing, change to the location containing your data files, and double-click on the file pp01_Training. Then skip to the next section, Viewing the Presentation.

Figure 1.5

The Available Templates and Themes window of Backstage view is open. The upper section of this window displays six options from which you can choose to start a new presentation from files that are stored on your computer. The Blank presentation template is selected, as this is the default template that is opened when you first start PowerPoint. The five other choices provide the means of starting a presentation from recent templates you have opened, templates you have created, or other existing presentations.

The lower section of the window displays categories of templates that are available online from Microsoft. When you choose a category, folders of additional subcategories are displayed that contain the available presentation template files. For this presentation, you want to look at the online templates.

2

- **Choose Presentations from the Office.com Templates category.**

- **Choose the Training folder.**

- **Scroll the list of template files in the Training folder and select "Employee Training Presentation".**

Your screen should be similar to Figure 1.6

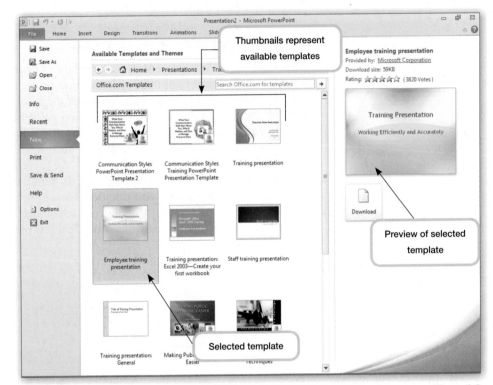

Figure 1.6

Thumbnail images representing the first slide in each template file are displayed in alphabetical order by name. The preview area displays a larger image of the selected thumbnail and information about the template.

You think the design of the selected template looks good and decide to begin your presentation for the volunteers using the content in this template as a guide.

3

● Click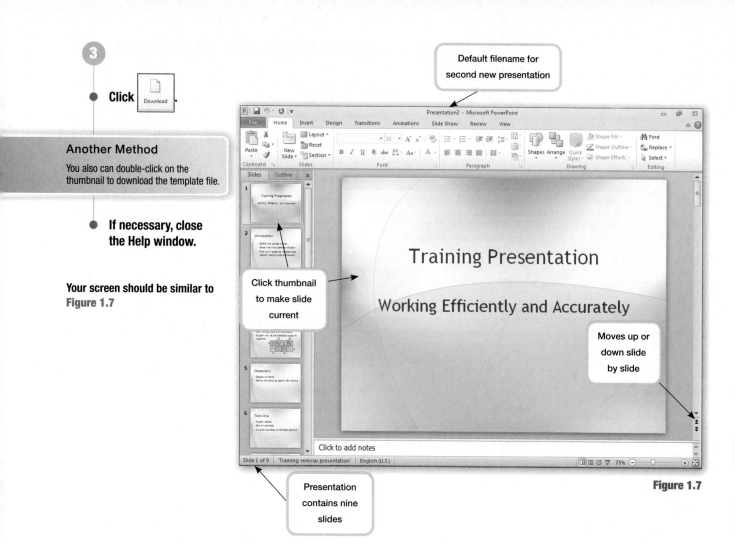

Another Method

You also can double-click on the thumbnail to download the template file.

● If necessary, close the Help window.

Your screen should be similar to Figure 1.7

Default filename for second new presentation

Click thumbnail to make slide current

Moves up or down slide by slide

Presentation contains nine slides

Figure 1.7

The template file is downloaded and opened in PowerPoint. It contains a total of nine slides. Because this is the second new presentation you have worked on since starting PowerPoint 2010, the default file name is Presentation2.

MOVING AMONG SLIDES

You want to look at the slides in the presentation to get a quick idea of their content. There are many ways to move from slide to slide in PowerPoint. Most often, the quickest method is to click on the slide thumbnail in the Slides tab. Clicking on a slide in the Slides tab displays it in the Slide pane and makes it the current slide. However, if your hands are already on the keyboard, you may want to use the keyboard directional keys. The following table shows both keyboard and mouse methods to move among slides in Normal view.

To Display	Action
Previous slide	Click ⬆️ Click above scroll box Press Page Up ⬆️ One slide up
Next slide	Click ⬇️ Click below scroll box Press Page Down ⬇️ One slide down
Any slide	Drag the Slide pane's scroll box until the ScreenTip displays the slide you want to view. ScreenTip — Slide: 2 of 9 / Introduction — Scroll box
Last slide in presentation	End
First slide in presentation	Home

You will try out several of these methods as you look at the slides in the presentation. First you will use the Slides tab. This tab makes it easy to move from one slide to another. You also will increase the width of the Slide tab pane to make the slide thumbnails larger and easier to see.

1

- Point to the splitter bar between the Slide pane and the Slides tab pane and when the mouse pointer is shaped as ↔ drag to the right to increase the width of the pane as in Figure 1.8.

- Press ⬇️ or Page Down to move to the next slide.

- Scroll the Slides tab to display slides 4 to 7.

- Click on slide 4.

Your screen should be similar to Figure 1.8

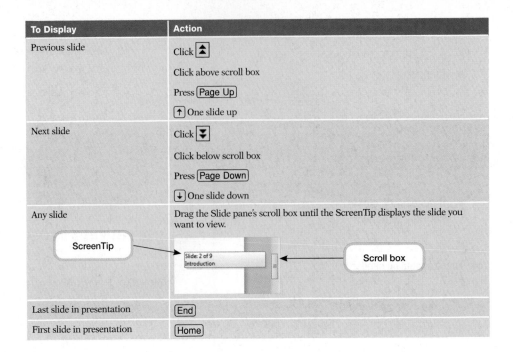

Figure 1.8

Slide 4 is the current slide and is displayed in the Slide pane. This slide contains two placeholders: title and content. The content placeholder consists of two bulleted items as well as a graphic. Next you will use the Slide pane scroll bar to display the next few slides.

● Click ▼ Next Slide to display slide 5.

Having Trouble?
The ▲ Previous Slide and ▼ Next Slide buttons are located at the bottom of the Slide pane's vertical scroll bar.

● Drag the scroll box and stop when the ScreenTip displays Slide 6 of 9.

● Click below the scroll box to display slide 7.

● Press End to display the last slide.

Your screen should be similar to Figure 1.9

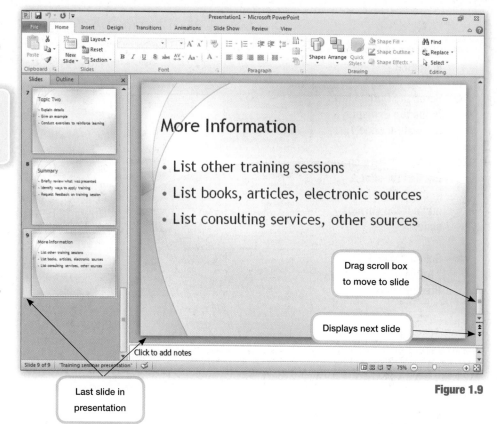

Figure 1.9

You can see this template will help you to create your presentation because the content provides some basic guidance as to how to organize a presentation.

Editing a Presentation

Now you need to edit the presentation to replace the sample content with the appropriate information for your presentation. Editing involves making text changes and additions to the content of your presentation. It also includes making changes to the organization of content. This can be accomplished quickly by rearranging the order of bulleted items on slides as well as the order of slides.

USING THE OUTLINE TAB

You have already entered text in a slide in the Slide pane. Another way to make text-editing changes is to use the Outline tab in Normal view. The Outline tab displays the content of the presentation in outline form, making it easy to see the organization of your presentation as you enter and edit content. The first change you want to make is to enter a title for the presentation on slide 1. First, you will open the Outline tab and select the sample title text on the slide and delete it.

1

- Click the Outline tab to open it.

- Scroll the Outline tab to the top to display the text for slide 1.

- Click anywhere on the text for slide 1 in the Outline tab to make it the current slide.

- Select the text "Training Presentation".

Having Trouble?

Refer to the topic "Selecting Text" in the Introduction to Microsoft Office 2010 to review these features.

- Press [Delete].

Your screen should be similar to Figure 1.10

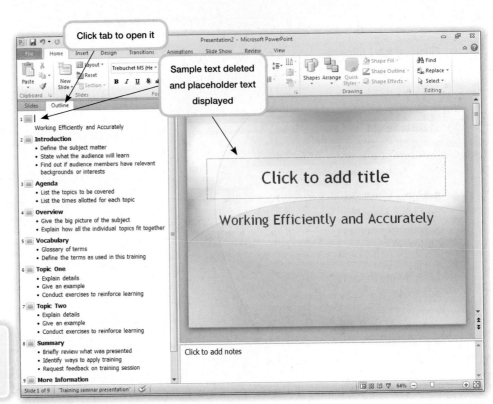

Figure 1.10

The sample text is deleted. As you change the text content in the Outline tab, it also appears in the slide displayed in the Slide pane. Notice that although you deleted the sample text, the slide still displays the title placeholder text.

You will enter the title and subtitle for the presentation next.

2
● **Type** Join
Animal Angels

Having Trouble?

If you make a typing error, use
[Backspace] or [Delete] to correct the
errors.

● **Select the text
"Working Efficiently
and Accurately"
on the second line
of slide 1 in the
Outline tab and type**
Animal Rescue
Foundation

**Your screen should be similar to
Figure 1.11**

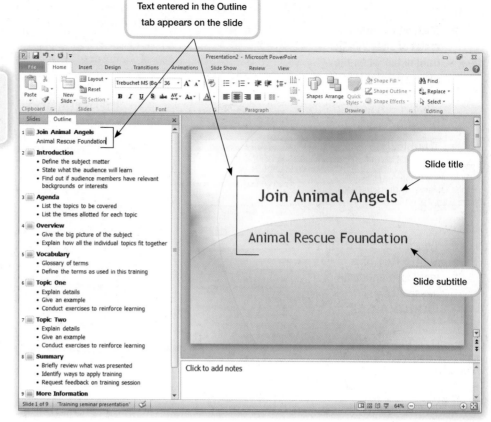

Figure 1.11

Additional Information

If you click the slide icon to the right of
the slide number in the Outline tab, all
text on the slide is selected.

As soon as you pressed a key, the selected text was deleted and replaced with
the text you typed. When entering the title for a slide, it is a common practice
to use title case, in which the first letter of most words is capitalized.

The next change you want to make is in the Introduction slide. The sample
text recommends that you define the subject of the presentation and what the
audience will learn. You will replace the sample text next to the first bullet
with the text for your slide. In the Outline tab, you can select an entire paragraph and all subparagraphs by pointing to the left of the line and clicking
when the mouse pointer is a ⊕.

3

● **Click on the first bullet of slide 2 in the Outline tab when the mouse pointer is a** **.**

Having Trouble?

If you accidentally drag selected text, it will move. To return it to its original location, immediately click ↺ ▾ Undo on the Quick Access Toolbar.

● **Type Your Name, Volunter (this word is intentionally misspelled) Coordinator**

Your screen should be similar to Figure 1.12

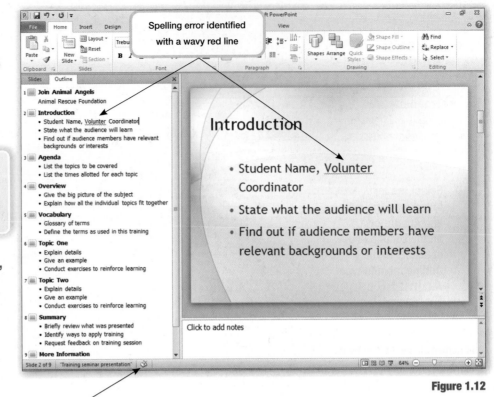

Figure 1.12

Spelling error identified with a wavy red line

Indicates document contains a spelling error

Having Trouble?

Do not be concerned if the spelling checker identifies your name as misspelled.

Having Trouble

If the Spelling indicator is not displayed, right click on the status bar and choose Spell Check from the context menu.

The sample text has been replaced with the text you typed. Depending on the length of your name, the text in this bullet may not have wrapped to a second line.

CORRECTING ERRORS

As you enter text, the program checks each word for accuracy. In this case, a spelling error was located. PowerPoint identified the word as misspelled by underlining it with a wavy red line. The Spelling indicator 📝 in the status bar also shows a spelling error has been detected in the document.

Concept ② Spelling Checker

The **spelling checker** locates all misspelled words, duplicate words, and capitalization irregularities as you create and edit a presentation, and proposes possible corrections. This feature works by comparing each word to a dictionary of words. If the word does not appear in the main dictionary or in a custom dictionary, it is identified as misspelled. The **main dictionary** is supplied with the program; a **custom dictionary** is one you can create to hold words you commonly use, such as proper names and technical terms, that are not included in the main dictionary.

If the word does not appear in either dictionary, the program identifies it as misspelled by displaying a red wavy line below the word. You can then correct the misspelled word by editing it. Alternatively, you can display a list of suggested spelling corrections for that word and select the correct spelling from the list to replace the misspelled word in the presentation.

To quickly correct the misspelled word, you can select the correct spelling from a list of suggested spelling corrections displayed on the shortcut menu.

1

● **Right-click on the misspelled word in the Outline tab to display the shortcut menu.**

Your screen should be similar to Figure 1.13

Figure 1.13

The shortcut menu displays two suggested correct spellings. The menu also includes several related menu options described below.

Option	Effect
Ignore All	Instructs PowerPoint to ignore the misspelling of this word throughout the rest of this session.
Add to Dictionary	Adds the word to the custom dictionary list. When a word is added to the custom dictionary, PowerPoint will always accept that spelling as correct.
Spelling	Opens the Spelling dialog box to check the entire presentation.

You will replace the word with the correct spelling and then enter the information for the second bullet.

2

- Choose "Volunteer" from the shortcut menu.

- In the Outline tab, select the text in the second bullet on slide 2 by clicking the bullet.

- Press Delete.

- In the Outline tab, select the text in the second bullet on slide 2.

- Type **volunteer oppotunities** (this word is intentionally misspelled) and press Spacebar.

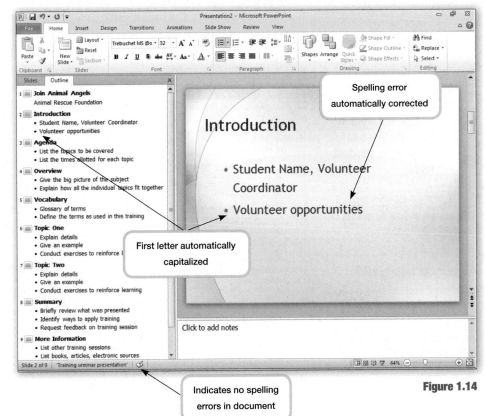

Figure 1.14

Your screen should be similar to Figure 1.14

Additional Information

Bulleted items in a presentation are capitalized in sentence case format. Ending periods, however, are not included.

Notice that the first letter of "volunteer" was automatically capitalized. Also notice that the incorrect spelling of the word "oppotunities" was corrected. These corrections are part of the AutoCorrect feature of PowerPoint.

Concept ③ AutoCorrect

The **AutoCorrect** feature makes some basic assumptions about the text you are typing and, based on those assumptions, automatically corrects the entry. The AutoCorrect feature automatically inserts proper capitalization at the beginning of sentences and in the names of days of the week. It also will change to lowercase letters any words that were incorrectly capitalized due to the accidental use of the Caps Lock key. In addition, it also corrects many common typing and spelling errors automatically.

One way the program makes corrections automatically is by looking for certain types of errors. For example, if two capital letters appear at the beginning of a word, the second capital letter is changed to a lowercase letter. If a lowercase letter appears at the beginning of a sentence, the first letter of the first word is capitalized. If the name of a day begins with a lowercase letter, the first letter is capitalized.

Another way the program makes corrections is by automatically replacing a misspelled word with the correct spelling in situations where the spelling checker offers only one suggested spelling correction. AutoCorrect also checks all words against the AutoCorrect list, a built-in list of words that are commonly spelled or typed incorrectly. If it finds the entry on the list, the program automatically replaces the error with the correction. For example, the typing error "aboutthe" is automatically changed to "about the" because the error is on the AutoCorrect list. You also can add words to the AutoCorrect list that you want to be corrected automatically. Any such words are added to the list on the computer you are using and will be available to anyone who uses the machine after you.

COPYING AND MOVING SELECTIONS

You are now ready to enter the text for the next slide in your presentation by entering the three main topics of discussion. You want to enter a new slide title, Topics of Discussion, with three bulleted items describing the topics to be discussed. Two placeholder bullets with sample text are displayed. You will edit these and then add a third bulleted item.

1

- Move to slide 3.

- In the Outline tab, replace the sample title, Agenda, with **Topics of Discussion**

- Select and replace the text in the first bullet with **Why are pets abandoned?**

- Select and replace the text in the second bullet with **How can you help?**

- Press Enter.

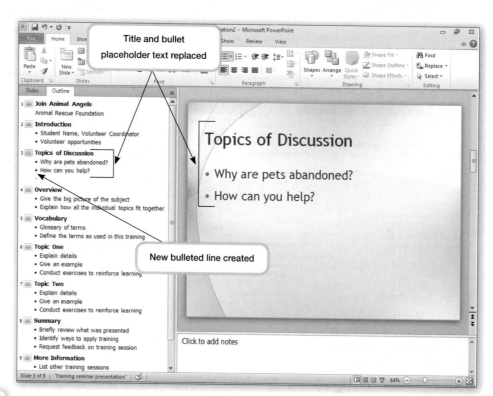

Figure 1.15

Having Trouble?

If you accidentally insert an extra bullet and blank line, press Backspace twice to remove them.

Your screen should be similar to Figure 1.15

Having Trouble?

Refer to "Copying and Moving Selections" in the Introduction to Microsoft Office 2010 to review this feature.

A new bulleted line is automatically created whenever you press Enter at the end of a bulleted item. Because the text you want to enter for this bullet is similar to the text in the second bullet, you decide to save time by copying and pasting the bullet text. Then you will modify the text in the third bullet.

2

- Select the second bulleted item.

- Click [Copy] Copy in the Clipboard group of the Home tab.

- Click on the third bullet line and click [Paste].

Another Method

You also can press [Ctrl] + C to copy a selection and [Ctrl] + V to paste a selection.

- Select "can you" in the third bullet item.

- Type **does the Foundation**

- If necessary, delete the fourth blank bullet line.

Your screen should be similar to Figure 1.16

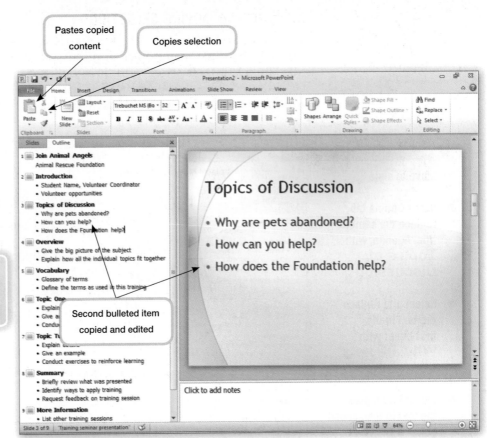

Figure 1.16

The text you copied to the third bullet has been quickly modified. Copying is especially helpful when the entries are long and complicated.

As you review what you have entered so far in your presentation, you decide that it would be better to introduce yourself on the first slide. Rather than retyping this information, you will move your introduction from slide 2 to slide 1. You will do this using drag and drop.

3

- In the Outline tab, press Enter at the end of the subtitle in slide 1 to create a blank line.

- Select the first bulleted item on aslide 2.

- Drag the selection to the blank line on slide 1.

Another Method

You can also use 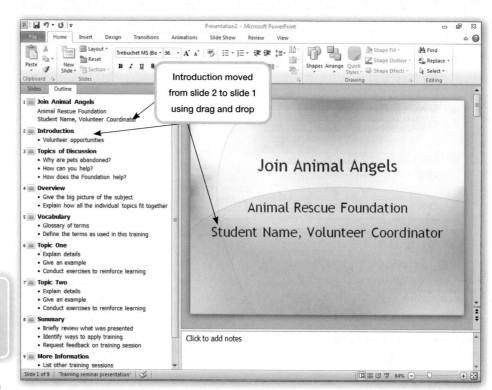 Cut or Ctrl + X to cut a selection and then paste it to the new location.

- Move to the blank line at the end of slide 1 and press Backspace to delete it.

Your screen should be similar to Figure 1.17

Additional Information

You can also delete and move slides in the Outline tab by clicking on the slide icon next to the slide number to select the entire slide and then use the appropriate command.

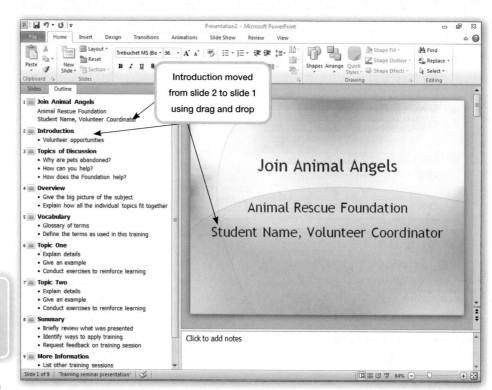

Figure 1.17

Because the Outline tab lets you see the content in multiple slides at once, it makes it easy to see the organization of the presentation and to quickly make text changes within and between slides.

MOVING, COPYING, AND DELETING SLIDES

As you continue to plan the presentation content and organization, you decide you will not use the Vocabulary slide and want to delete it. You also think a more appropriate location for the Overview slide may be above the agenda. Finally, you plan to have three slides to present the three main topics you plan to cover in the presentation. For this purpose, you want to add a third topic slide. Because you are not working with slide content, you will use the Slides tab to make these changes.

First you will delete slide 5, Vocabulary.

① • **Click on the Slides tab to open it.**

• **Scroll the Slides tab to see slide 5.**

• **Click on slide 5 to select the slide.**

• **Press ⌜Delete⌝.**

Another Method
You can also choose Delete Slide from the selected slide's context menu.

Your screen should be similar to Figure 1.18

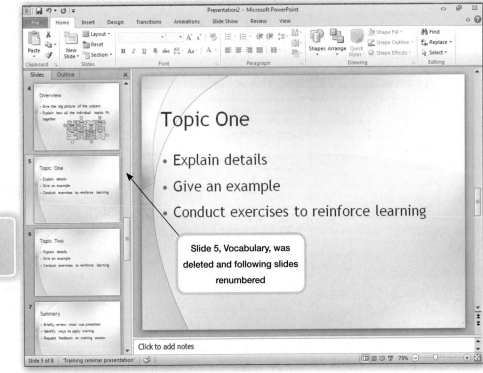

Figure 1.18

The slide has been deleted and all subsequent slides renumbered. Next, you will move the Overview slide (4) above slide 3 using drag and drop

② • **Select slide 4 in the Slides tab.**

• **If necessary, scroll the Slides tab to show slide 3.**

• **Drag slide 4 above slide 3 in the Slides tab.**

Additional Information
A solid horizontal line identifies the location where the slide will be placed when you stop dragging.

Your screen should be similar to Figure 1.19

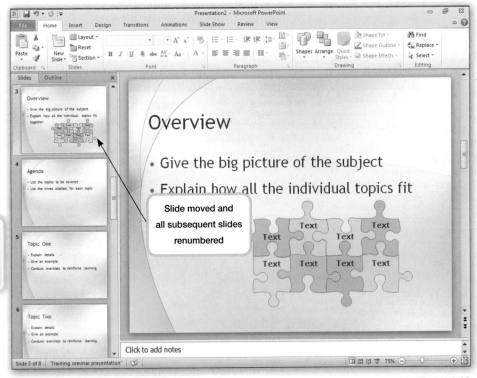

Figure 1.19

The Overview slide is now slide 3 and, again, all following slides are appropriately renumbered. Finally, you will make a copy of slide 6.

3

- Select slide 6 in the Slides tab.

- Open the 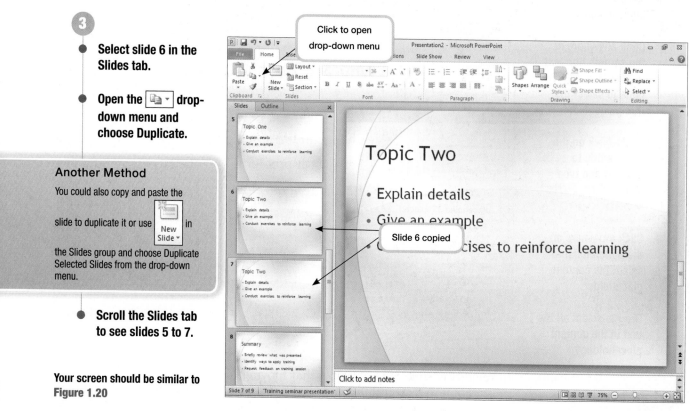 drop-down menu and choose Duplicate.

Another Method

You could also copy and paste the slide to duplicate it or use New Slide in the Slides group and choose Duplicate Selected Slides from the drop-down menu.

- Scroll the Slides tab to see slides 5 to 7.

Your screen should be similar to Figure 1.20

Figure 1.20

There are now three topic slides. The duplicate slide was inserted directly below the slide that was copied and is the selected slide.

MOVING, DEMOTING, AND PROMOTING BULLETED ITEMS

Now you are ready to enter the text for the three topic slides. You decide to enter the text for these slides using the Slide pane rather than the Outline tab. Simply clicking in an area of the slide in the Slide pane will make it the active area.

1

- Make slide 5 the current slide.

- Click anywhere in the sample title text of slide 5 in the Slide pane to select the title placeholder.

- Triple-click on the sample title to select it and type **Why Are Pets Abandoned?**

- Click anywhere on the bulleted list to select the content placeholder.

- Drag to select all the text in the content placeholder.

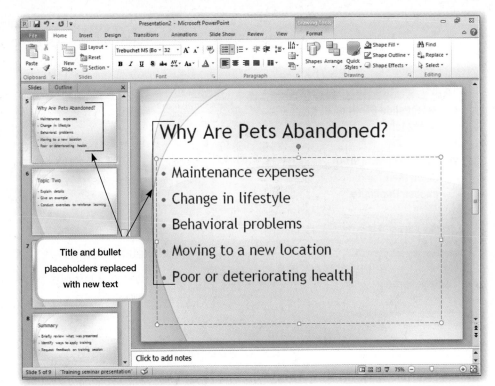

Figure 1.21

In reviewing slide 5, you realize that moving to a new location is one of the most common reasons for pets to be abandoned, so you decide to move that to the top of the list. You can rearrange bulleted items in the Slide pane by selecting the item and dragging it to a new location in the same way you moved selections in the Outline tab.

- Enter the following bulleted items (Press [Enter] after each line, except the last, to create a new bullet):

Maintenance expenses

Change in lifestyle

Behavioral problems

Moving to a new location

Poor or deteriorating health

Your screen should be similar to **Figure 1.21**

2

- Select all the text in the fourth bulleted item in the Slide pane.

- Drag the selection to the beginning of the first bulleted item.

Your screen should be similar to Figure 1.22

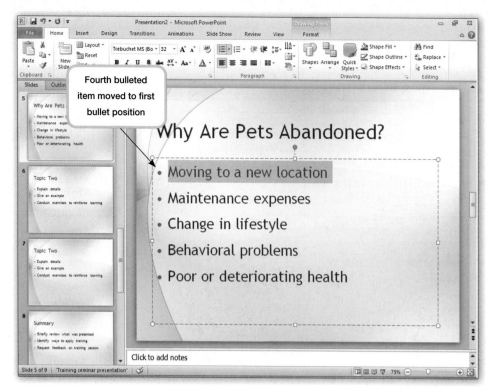

Figure 1.22

The fourth bullet is now the first bulleted item in the list.

In the next slide, you will enter information about how people can help the Animal Rescue Foundation.

3

- Make slide 6 the current slide.

- Replace the sample title text with **How Can You Help?**

- Select all the text in the bulleted text placeholder.

- Type **Donate your time and talent**

- Press (Enter).

Your screen should be similar to Figure 1.23

Figure 1.23

You want the next bulleted item to be indented below the first bulleted item. Indenting a bulleted point to the right **demotes** it, or makes it a lower or subordinate topic in the outline hierarchy.

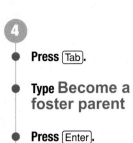
4

- Press Tab.

- Type **Become a foster parent**

- Press Enter.

- Type **Work at adoption fairs**

- Press Enter.

Your screen should be similar to Figure 1.24

Figure 1.24

When you demote a bulleted point, PowerPoint continues to indent to the same level until you cancel the indent. Before entering the next item, you want to remove the indentation, or **promote** the line. Promoting a line moves it to the left, or up a level in the outline hierarchy.

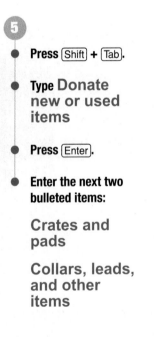
5

- Press Shift + Tab.

- Type **Donate new or used items**

- Press Enter.

- Enter the next two bulleted items:

Crates and pads

Collars, leads, and other items

Your screen should be similar to Figure 1.25

Figure 1.25

You also can promote or demote bulleted items after the text has been entered. The insertion point must be at the beginning of the line to be promoted or demoted, or all the text must be selected. You will demote the last two bulleted items.

6

- Select the two bulleted items "Crates and pads" and "Collars, leads, and other items".

- Press Tab.

- Move to the end of "Collars, leads, and other items".

- Press Enter.

Your screen should be similar to Figure 1.26

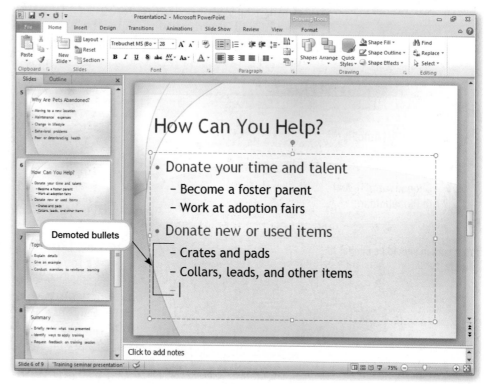

Figure 1.26

The last two items have been demoted. Next you will add more items to the bulleted list.

7

- Type **Provide financial support**

- Press Enter.

- Enter the following three bulleted items:

  Send a donation

  Sponsor a foster pet

  Sponsor an adoption

- Promote the "Provide financial support" bullet.

Your screen should be similar to Figure 1.27

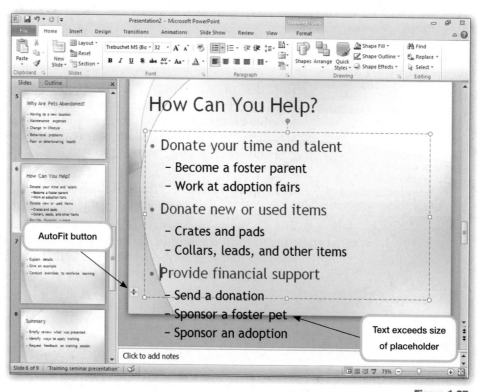

Figure 1.27

As you entered more bulleted items, the slide's text exceeds the size of the placeholder. When this happens a AutoFit Options button appears at the bottom left corner of the placeholder. It provides options that allow you to control the AutoFit feature and to handle any overspilling text. The AutoFit feature will automatically adjust the line spacing and text size as needed to display the content inside the placeholder appropriately. Currently, this feature is off in this template.

8

● Click AutoFit Options.

● Choose AutoFit Text to Placeholder.

Your screen should be similar to Figure 1.28

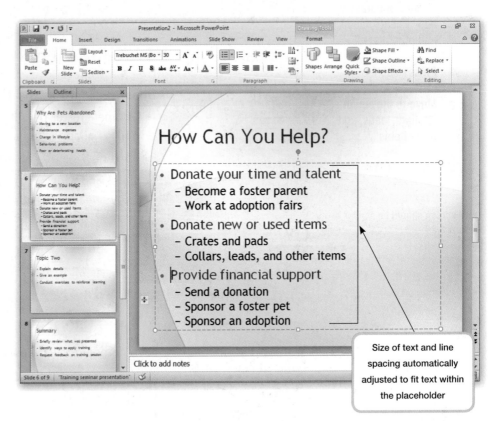

Figure 1.28

Now that the AutoFit Text to Placeholder option is on, the text size and line spacing of the bulleted items have been reduced to display the text more comfortably on the slide. If you were to add more text or increase or decrease the size of the placeholder, the AutoFit feature would continue to adjust the text size and spacing.

SPLITTING TEXT BETWEEN SLIDES

Although using AutoFit solved the problem, you decide that 10 bulleted items are too many for a single slide. Generally, when creating slides, it is a good idea to limit the number of bulleted items on a slide to six. It also is recommended that the number of words on a line should not exceed five. You decide to split the slide content between two slides.

1

- With the bullet placeholder in slide 6 still selected, click **AutoFit Options** and choose Split Text Between Two Slides.

- If necessary, scroll the Slides tab so that slides 6 and 7 are visible.

Your screen should be similar to Figure 1.29

Having Trouble?

You may have noticed that slide 6 in the Slides tab still displays all the bulleted items. Do not be concerned. The five bullets have been removed; however, the Slides tab has not updated to reflect the change.

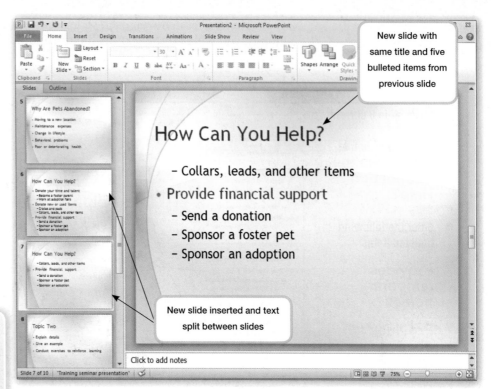

Figure 1.29

A new slide containing the same title as the previous slide and five of the bulleted items from the previous slide is inserted into the presentation. Often when splitting text between slides, the content may not split appropriately and you may still need to make adjustments to the slides. You will move the first bulleted item on slide 7 to the last item on slide 6 using the keyboard shortcuts for the Cut and Paste commands. You also will edit the slide title of slide 7.

2

- On slide 7, replace the title text with **More Ways to Help!**

- Select the first bulleted item on slide 7 and press Ctrl + X to cut the selection.

- Move to the end of the last item on slide 6 and press Enter.

- Press Ctrl + V to paste the item.

- If necessary, delete the new blank bullet line.

Your screen should be similar to Figure 1.30

Figure 1.30

Now the number of items on each slide seems much more reasonable. Finally, you will add the text for the third topic slide.

3

- **Make slide 8 current.**

- **Enter the slide title** **How Does the Foundation Help?**

- **Enter the following bulleted items:**

  Provides temporary homes

  Provides obedience training

  Provides veterinary care

  Finds loving permanent homes

- **Open the Outline tab and scroll the tab to see slides 4 through 8.**

Your screen should be similar to Figure 1.31

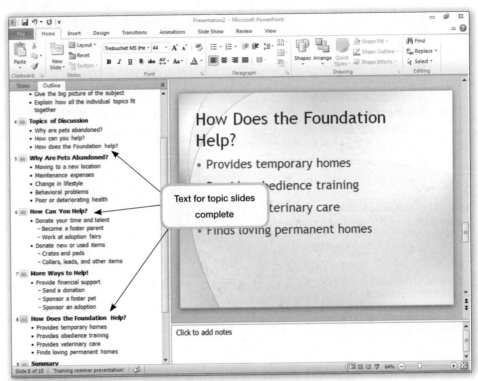

Figure 1.31

The text for the three topic slides reflects the order of the topics in the Topics of Discussion slide.

CREATING A NUMBERED LIST

After looking at slide 4, you decide that it would be better if the topics of discussion were a numbered list. You can easily change the format of the bulleted items to a numbered list using the [numbering icon] Numbering command in the Paragraph group on the Home tab.

1

- Open the Slides tab and make slide 4 current.

- Click anywhere in the bulleted items placeholder on slide 4.

- Click on the dashed-line border of the placeholder box to change it to a solid line.

- Click ▤ ▾ Numbering in the Paragraph group on the Home tab.

Your screen should be similar to Figure 1.32

Figure 1.32

Notice the cursor does not appear in the placeholder box. This is because a solid line around the placeholder indicates your action will affect the entire placeholder rather than individual parts, such as the text, of the placeholder. The bullets have been replaced with an itemized numbered list.

MOVING, DEMOTING, AND PROMOTING NUMBERED ITEMS

Now it is obvious to you that you entered the topics in the wrong order. You want to present the information about the Foundation before information about how individuals can help. Just like a bulleted item, an item in a numbered list can be moved easily by selecting it and dragging it to a new location.

1

- Select the third item in the placeholder on slide 4.

- Drag the selection up to the beginning of the second line.

Your screen should be similar to Figure 1.33

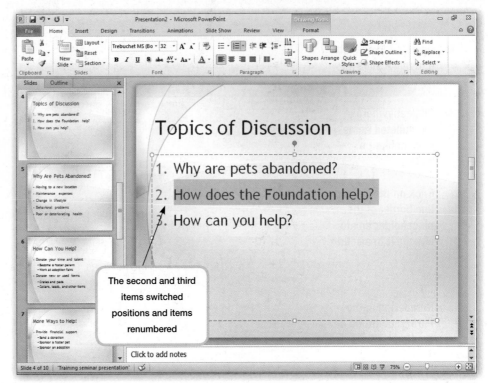

Figure 1.33

As soon as you clicked inside the placeholder, the cursor appeared and the solid-line border changed to a dashed-line border, indicating you can edit the contents of the placeholder. The third item in the numbered list is now the second item, and PowerPoint automatically renumbered the list for you.

Because you don't want to miss anything, you decide to go back and review the information you've entered so far. As you go back through the slides, you realize that you forgot to include the Animal Angels volunteer group as a topic to be discussed. You will add it to the Topics of Discussion slide as a subtopic below the "How can you help?" topic.

2

- Open the Outline tab to review the slide content.

- Click at the end of the third numbered list item on slide 4 and press [Enter].

- Press [Tab] and type **Who are Animal Angels?**

Your screen should be similar to Figure 1.34

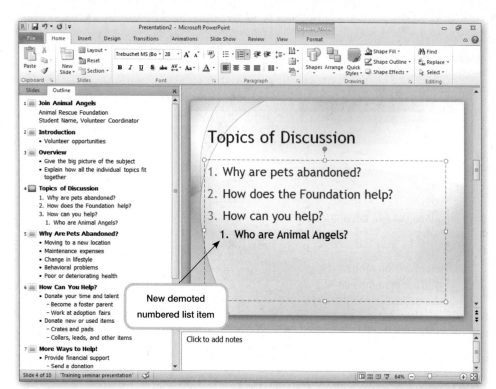

Figure 1.34

The numbering for the subtopic begins with one again. The new item is too important to be demoted on the list, so you decide to promote it and move it higher on the list.

3

- Select the entire fourth line.

- Press [Shift] + [Tab] to promote the fourth line.

- Drag the selected item to the beginning of the third line.

Your screen should be similar to Figure 1.35

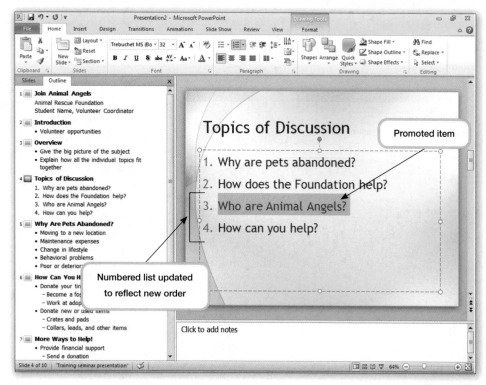

Figure 1.35

The numbered list has again been appropriately adjusted.

SAVING A PRESENTATION

Having Trouble?

See "Saving a File," in the Introduction to Microsoft Office 2010 to review this feature.

You have just been notified about an important meeting that is to begin in a few minutes. Before leaving for the meeting, you want to save the presentation so that you don't lose your work.

The Save or Save As commands on the File tab are used to save files. When a presentation is saved for the first time, either command can be used to display the Save As dialog box, in which you specify the location to save the file and the file name.

- Open the File tab and click ![Save As]

- Replace the proposed file name in the File Name text box with **Volunteer**

Having Trouble?

If you used the student data file pp01_ Training for this lab, choose Save As from the File tab. The file name in the Save As dialog box will be the name of the file you opened.

- Select the location where you will save your solution files.

Your screen should be similar to Figure 1.36

Figure 1.36

Additional Information

The file extensions may or may not be displayed, depending upon your Windows folder settings.

The file list displays folder names as well as the names of PowerPoint files (if any) stored in the current location. Only PowerPoint presentation files are listed, because the selected file type in the Save As Type list box is PowerPoint Presentation. Depending on what file type you choose, a different file extension will be added to the file name. Presentation files have a default file extension of .pptx.

You can also save PowerPoint presentations as an image file using the .gif, .tif, or .jpg file extension. When you save a presentation as an image file, you are given the choice to save the Current Slide Only or Every Slide as an image, in which case each slide will be saved as a separate image file.

In this case, you will use the default presentation file type (.pptx).

● Click [Save].

Your screen should be similar to Figure 1.37

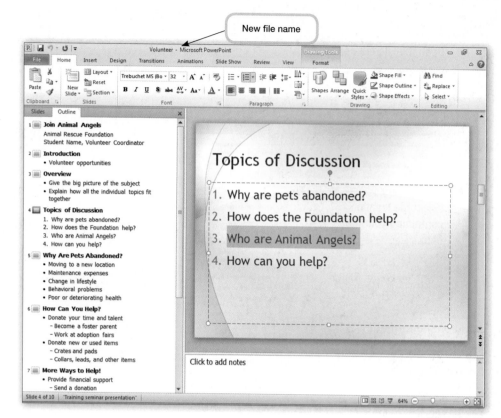

New file name

Figure 1.37

The presentation is now saved to the location you specified in a new file named Volunteer and the new file name is displayed in the application window title bar. The view in use at the time the file is saved also is saved with the file.

You are now ready to close the file.

● Open the File tab and click [Close].

The presentation is closed, and an empty workspace is displayed. Always save your slide presentation before closing a file or leaving the PowerPoint program. As a safeguard against losing your work if you forget to save the presentation, PowerPoint will remind you to save any unsaved presentation before closing the file or exiting the program.

Opening an Existing Presentation

Additional Information

If you are ending your lab session now, open the File tab and click [Exit] to exit the program.

After returning from your meeting, you continued to work on the presentation. You revised the content of several of the slides and added information for several new slides. Then you saved the presentation using a new file name. You will open this file to see the changes and will continue working on the presentation.

1

● **Open the File tab and click** **Open .**

Another Method

The keyboard shortcut to open a file is [Ctrl] + O.

● **If necessary, select the location containing your data files.**

● **Select pp01_Volunteer1.**

Additional Information

You also can quickly open a recently used file by selecting it from the Recent Documents list in the File tab.

● **Click** Open ▼.

Another Method

You also could double-click the file name to both select it and choose Open ▼.

● **Open the Outline tab.**

● **Replace "Your Name" in slide 1 with your name.**

● **Scroll the Outline tab to see the additional content that has been added to the presentation.**

Your screen should be similar to Figure 1.38

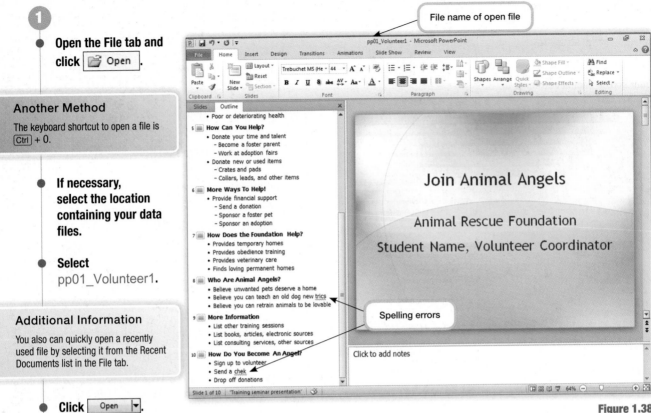

File name of open file

Spelling errors

Figure 1.38

The presentation now contains 10 slides, and all the sample text has been replaced with text for the volunteer recruitment presentation, except for slide 9.

Using Spelling Checker

As you entered the information on the additional slides, you left some typing errors uncorrected. To correct the misspelled words, you can use the shortcut menu to correct each individual word or error, as you learned earlier. However, in many cases, you may find it more efficient to wait until you are finished writing before you correct any spelling or grammatical errors. Rather than continually break your train of thought to correct errors as you type, you can check the spelling on all slides of the presentation at once by running the spelling checker.

Additional Information

Unlike Word 2010, Powerpoint does not check for grammar errors.

1

● **Open the Review tab.**

● **Click** **in the Proofing group.**

Another Method

The keyboard shortcut to check spelling is `F7`.

Your screen should be similar to Figure 1.39

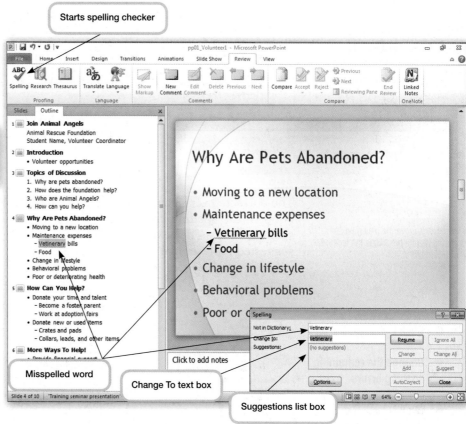

Figure 1.39

Additional Information

The spelling checker identifies many proper names and technical terms as misspelled. To stop this from occurring, use the Add Words To option to add those names to the custom dictionary.

The program jumps to slide 4; highlights the first located misspelled word, "Vetinerary," in the Outline pane; and opens the Spelling dialog box. The Spelling dialog box displays the misspelled word in the Not in Dictionary text box. The Suggestions list box typically displays the words the spelling checker has located in the dictionary that most closely match the misspelled word.

In this case, the spelling checker does not display any suggested replacements because it cannot locate any words in the dictionaries that are similar in spelling. If there are no suggestions, the Not in Dictionary text box simply displays the word that is highlighted in the text. When none of the suggestions is correct, you must edit the word yourself by typing the correction in the Change To text box.

● **Type** Veterinary **in the Change To text box.**

Additional Information

The replacement text must be entered exactly as you want it to appear, including capitalization.

● **Click** Change .

Additional Information

You also can edit words directly in the presentation and then click Resume to continue checking spelling.

Your screen should be similar to Figure 1.40

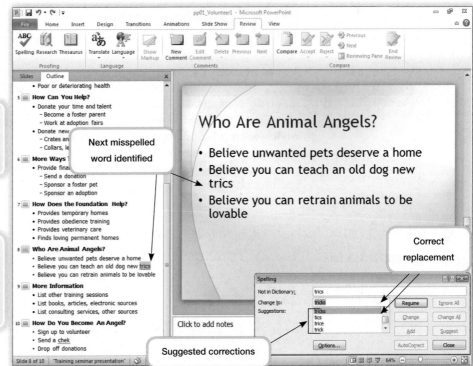

Figure 1.40

Having Trouble?

If necessary, move the dialog box by dragging its title bar to see the located misspelled word.

The corrected replacement is made in the slide. After the Spelling dialog box is open, the spelling checker continues to check the entire presentation for spelling errors. The next misspelled word, "trics," is identified. In this case, the suggested replacement is correct.

● **Click** Change .

● **Change the remaining spelling errors.**

● **Click** OK **in response to the message telling you that the spelling check is complete.**

● **Open the File tab, click** Save As **and save the revised presentation as** Volunteer1 **to your solution file location.**

Your screen should be similar to Figure 1.41

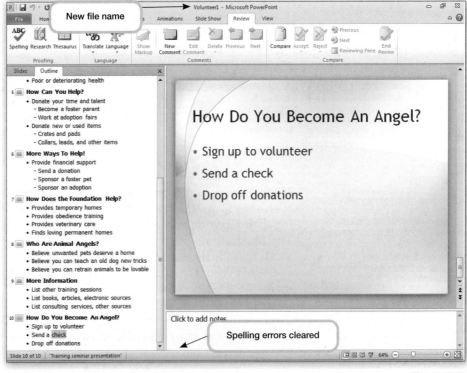

Figure 1.41

The Spelling indicator in the Status bar shows that all spelling errors have been resolved.

Using Slide Sorter View

To get a better overall picture of the presentation, you will switch to Slide Sorter view. This view displays thumbnail images of each slide in the work area and is particularly useful for rearranging slides to improve the flow and organization of the presentation. Clicking on a thumbnail selects the slide and makes it the current slide.

1

Click ⊞ **Slide Sorter** in the status bar.

Having Trouble?

Pointing to a view button displays its name in a ScreenTip.

Another Method

You also could switch to Slide Sorter view by clicking ⊞ Slide Sorter in the Presentation Views group of the View tab.

• Set the zoom to 90%.

• Click on slide 1.

Your screen should be similar to Figure 1.42

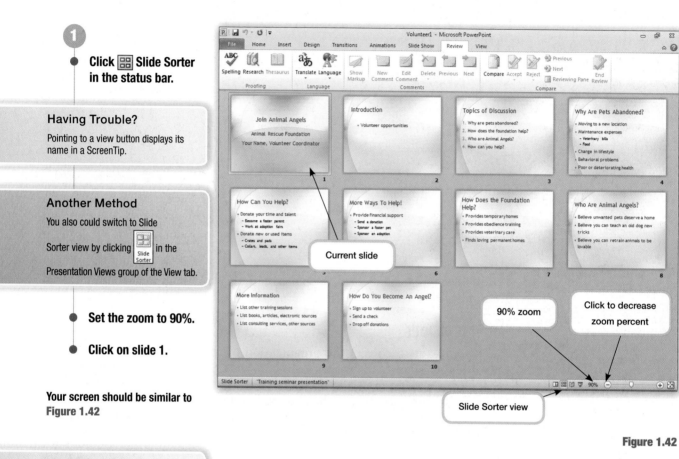

Figure 1.42

Having Trouble?

Do not be concerned if your screen displays a different number of slides per row. This is a function of the size of your monitor and your monitor settings.

The currently selected slide, slide 1, appears with a yellow border around it. Viewing all the slides side by side helps you see how your presentation flows. You realize that the second slide is no longer necessary because you added your name to the opening slide. You also decide to delete slide 9 because you plan to add any necessary information to other slides. As you continue to look at the slides, you can now see that slides 7 and 8 are out of order and do not follow the sequence of topics in the Topics of Discussion slide.

SELECTING AND DELETING SLIDES

You will delete slides 2 and 9. In this view, it is easy to select and work with multiple slides at the same time. To select multiple slides, hold down Ctrl while clicking on each slide to select it.

- Select slide 2, hold down Ctrl, and click on slide 9.

- Press Delete.

- Increase the zoom to 100%.

Additional Information

You can use Delete to delete a slide in Slide Sorter view and in the Slides tab. However, in the Slide pane, using Delete deletes text or placeholder content.

Additional Information

The zoom setting for each view is set independently and remains in effect until changed to another zoom setting.

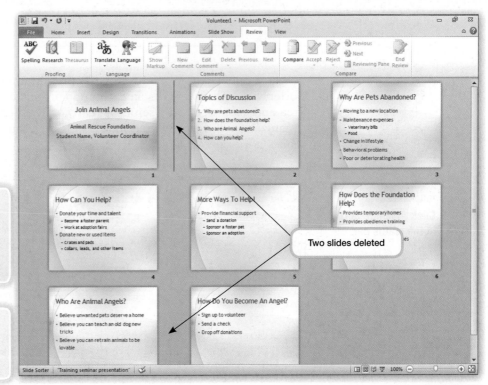

Figure 1.43

Your screen should be similar to Figure 1.43

The slides have been deleted, and all remaining slides have been appropriately renumbered.

MOVING SLIDES

Now you want to correct the organization of the slides by moving slides 6 and 7 before slide 4. To reorder a slide in Slide Sorter view, you drag it to its new location using drag and drop. As you drag the mouse, an indicator line appears to show you where the slide will appear in the presentation. When the indicator line is located where you want the slide to be placed, release the mouse button. You will select both slides and move them at the same time.

- **Select slides 6 and 7.**

- **Point to either selected slide and drag the mouse until the indicator line is displayed before slide 4.**

Additional Information

The mouse pointer appears as when you drag to move a slide.

- **Release the mouse button.**

Another Method

You also can use the ✂ Cut and 📋 Paste commands in the Clipboard group on the Home tab to move slides in Slide Sorter view.

Your screen should be similar to Figure 1.44

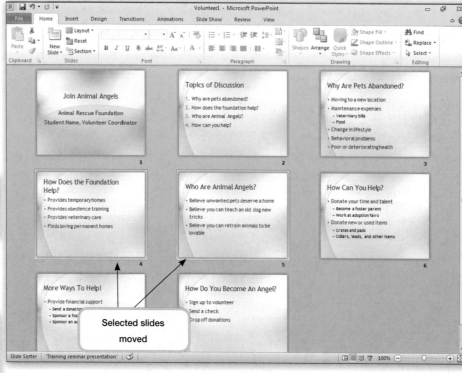

Figure 1.44

The slides now appear in the order in which you want them.

SELECTING A SLIDE LAYOUT

During your discussion with the foundation director, it was suggested that you add a slide showing the history of the organization. To include this information in the presentation, you will insert a new slide after slide 4.

- **Click in the space before slide 5.**

Additional Information

The indicator line shows you where the new slide will be inserted.

- **Open the Home tab.**

- **Open the New Slide drop-down menu in the Slides group.**

Your screen should be similar to Figure 1.45

Figure 1.45

Using Slide Sorter View   **PP1.41**

The drop-down menu displays 9 built-in slide layouts. The number of available layouts varies with the template you are using.

Concept ④ Layout

A layout defines the position and format for objects and text on a slide. Layouts provide placeholders for slide titles and slide content such as text, tables, diagrams, charts, or clip art. Many of these placeholders are shown in the following diagram.

Background object — / Title placeholder

Background fill — / Subtitle placeholder

Body placeholder

Headers and footers
(date, footer, slide#)

Placeholder formatting

You can change the layout of an existing slide by selecting a new layout. If the new layout does not include placeholders for objects that are already on your slide (for example, if you created a chart and the new layout does not include a chart placeholder), you do not lose the information. All objects remain on the slide, and the selected layout is automatically adjusted by adding the appropriate type of placeholder for the object. Alternatively, as you add new objects to a slide, the layout automatically adjusts by adding the appropriate type of placeholder. You also can rearrange, size, and format placeholders on a slide any way you like to customize the slide's appearance.

To make creating slides easy, use the predefined layouts. The layouts help you keep your presentation format consistent and, therefore, more professional.

You need to choose the layout that best accommodates the changes you discussed with the director. Because this slide will contain two columns of text about the history of the organization, you will use the Two Content layout.

● **Choose Two Content.**

● **Double-click on the slide to switch back to Normal view.**

Additional Information
The current slide does not change when you switch views.

● **Open the Slides tab.**

Your screen should be similar to Figure 1.46

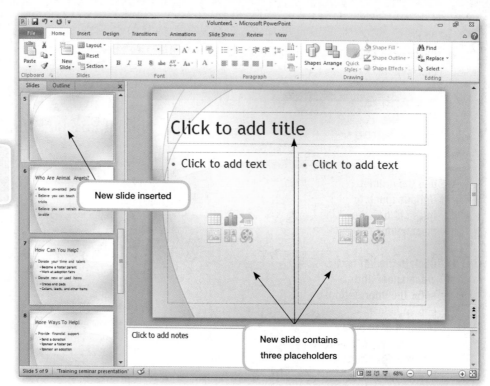

Figure 1.46

A new Two Content slide is inserted with the same design elements as the other slides in the presentation. The Two Content layout contains three placeholders, but unlike the template slides, the placeholders on the inserted slide do not contain sample text. When you select the placeholder, you can simply type in the text without having to select or delete any sample text.

CHANGING A PLACEHOLDER

You will add text to the slide presenting a brief history of the Animal Rescue Foundation. First, you will enter the slide title and then the list of dates and events.

1

- Click in the title placeholder.

- Type **Animal Rescue Foundation History**

- Use the AutoFit Options menu to fit the title to the placeholder.

- Click in the left text placeholder and enter the information shown below. Remember to press Enter to create a new line (except after the last entry).

  1995

  1996

  1997

  2005

- In the same manner, enter the following text in the right text placeholder:

  Founded by Steve Dow

  Built first shelter

  Began volunteer program

  Rescued 3000 animals!

Your screen should be similar to Figure 1.47

Figure 1.47

The left placeholder is too big for its contents and the right is too small, forcing some items to wrap to a second line. To correct the size, you can adjust the size of the placeholders.

SIZING A PLACEHOLDER

The four circles and squares that appear at the corners and sides of a selected placeholder's border are **sizing handles** that can be used to adjust the size of the placeholder. Dragging the corner sizing handles will adjust both the height and width at the same time, whereas the center handles adjust the associated side borders. When you point to the sizing handle, the mouse pointer appears as ⤡, indicating the direction in which you can drag the border to adjust the size.

1

- On the right placeholder, drag the left-center sizing handle to the left until each item appears on one line.

- Select the left text placeholder and drag the right-center sizing handle to the left (see Figure 1.48).

- With the left placeholder still selected, hold down (Shift) while clicking on the right placeholder border to select both.

- Use the bottom-middle sizing handle to decrease the height of the placeholders to fit the text.

Your screen should be similar to Figure 1.48

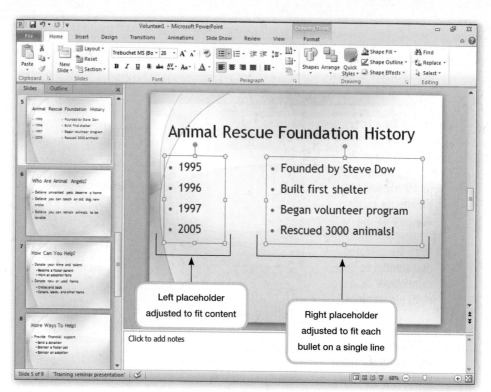

Figure 1.48

MOVING A PLACEHOLDER

Next, you want to decrease the blank space between the two columns. Then you want to move both placeholders so they appear more centered in the space. An object can be moved anywhere on a slide by dragging the place-holder's border. The mouse pointer appears as ⁺⟨ when you can move a place-holder. As you drag the placeholder, an opaque white copy of the placeholder is displayed to show your new location.

- Click outside the placeholders to clear the selection.

- Select the left placeholder and point to the edge of the placeholder (not a handle) until the mouse pointer appears as .

- Drag the selected placeholder to the right closer to the right placeholder.

- Select both placeholders and drag to center them horizontally in the slide as shown in Figure 1.49.

- Save your changes to the presentation.

Your screen should be similar to Figure 1.49

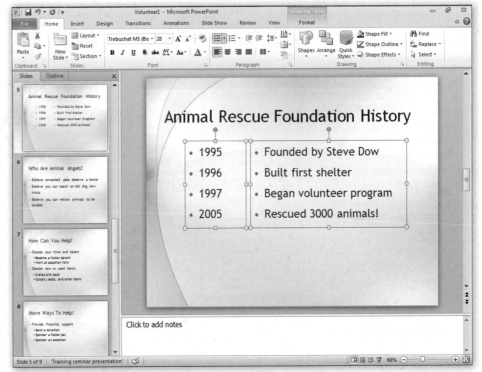

Figure 1.49

ADDING AND REMOVING BULLETS

Next, you want to remove the bullets from the items on the history slide. You can quickly apply and remove bullets using ▤ ▾ Bullets in the Paragraph group on the Home tab. This button applies the bullet style associated with the design template you are using. Because the placeholder items already include bullets, using this button will remove them.

- With both text placeholders still selected, click ▤ ▾ Bullets from the Paragraph group in the Home tab to remove all bullets.

Your screen should be similar to Figure 1.50

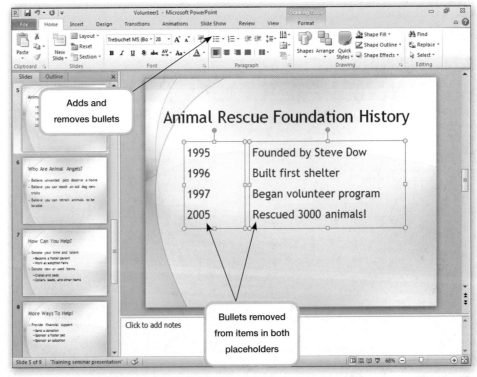

Adds and removes bullets

Bullets removed from items in both placeholders

Figure 1.50

The bullets are removed from all the items in both placeholders. Now, however, you think it would look better to add bullets back to the years in the first column.

2

- Select the four years in the left column.

- Click ⬚ Bullets from the Paragraph group in the Home tab.

- Click outside the selected placeholder to deselect it.

- Save the presentation again.

Your screen should be similar to Figure 1.51

Figure 1.51

Bullets appear before the selected text items only.

Formatting Slide Text

The next change you want to make to the presentation is to improve the appearance of the title slide. Although the design template you are using already includes many formatting features, you want this slide to have more impact.

Applying different formatting to characters and paragraphs can greatly enhance the appearance of the slide. **Character formatting** features affect the selected characters only. They include changing the character style and size, applying effects such as bold and italics, changing the character spacing, and adding animated text effects. **Paragraph formatting** features affect an entire paragraph. A paragraph is text that has an (Enter) at the end of it. Each item in a bulleted list, title, and subtitle is a paragraph. Paragraph formatting features include the position of the paragraph or its alignment between the margins, paragraph indentation, spacing above and below a paragraph, and line spacing within a paragraph.

CHANGING FONTS

First, you will improve the appearance of the presentation title by changing the font of the title text. There are two basic types of fonts: serif and sans serif. **Serif fonts** have a flair at the base of each letter that visually leads the reader to the next letter. Two common serif fonts are Roman and Times New Roman.

Having Trouble?

Refer to the section "Formatting Text" in the Introduction to Microsoft Office 2010 to review this feature.

Serif fonts generally are used for text in paragraphs. **Sans serif fonts** do not have a flair at the base of each letter. Arial and Helvetica are two common sans serif fonts. Because sans serif fonts have a clean look, they are often used for headings in documents.

Each font can appear using a different font size. Several common fonts in different sizes are shown in the following table.

Font Name	Font Type	Font Size
Calibri	Sans serif	This is 10 pt. This is 16 pt.
Courier New	Serif	This is 10 pt. This is 16 pt.
Garamond	Serif	This is 10 pt. This is 16 pt.

Using fonts as a design element can add interest to your presentation and give your audience visual cues to help them find information quickly. It is good practice to use only two or three different fonts in a presentation, because too many can distract from your presentation content and can look unprofessional.

To change the font before typing the text, use the command and then type. All text will appear in the specified setting until another font setting is selected. To change a font setting for existing text, select the text you want to change and then use the command. If you want to apply font formatting to a word, simply move the insertion point to the word and the formatting is automatically applied to the entire word.

Additional Information

The font used in the title is Trebuchet MS (Headings), as displayed in the Trebuchet MS (He ▼) Font button. It is automatically used in all headings in this template.

The Trebuchet MS (He ▼) Font button in the Font tab or on the Mini toolbar that appears when you select text is used to change the font style. As you select a font from the drop-down menu, a live preview of how the selected font will appear is displayed in the document.

1

- Select the text "Join Animal Angels" in the Slide pane on slide 1.

- Open the [Trebuchet ▾] Font drop-down list in the Mini toolbar.

- Point to several fonts to see the live preview.

Having Trouble?

Refer to the section "Using the Mini Toolbar" in the Introduction to Microsoft Office 2010 to review this feature.

Your screen should be similar to Figure 1.52

Additional Information

The Live Preview feature is also available with many other formatting features.

Figure 1.52

The selected text in the document appears in the font style you have selected in the menu. With Live Preview, you can see how the text will look with the selected font before you click the one that you want. You want to change the font to a design that has a less serious appearance.

2

- Scroll the menu and choose Comic Sans MS.

Another Method

You also could use Font in the Font group of the Home tab to change the font.

Your screen should be similar to Figure 1.53

Figure 1.53

The text has changed to the new font style, and the Font button displays the font name used in the current selection.

CHANGING FONT SIZE

The title text is also a little smaller than you want it to be.

Open the 44 ▾ **Font Size drop-down list on the Mini toolbar.**

Having Trouble?

If the Mini toolbar is no longer displayed, right click on the selection to display it again.

Point to several different sizes to see how the font size changes using Live Preview.

Scroll the list and choose 60.

Another Method

You also could use 44 ▾ Font Size in the Font group.

Another Method

Using **A˄** Increase Font Size in the Font group or the Mini toolbar will incrementally increase the font size. The keyboard shortcut is Ctrl + Shift + >.

Your screen should be similar to Figure 1.54

Additional Information

Use **A˅** Decrease Font Size or Ctrl + Shift + < to incrementally decrease the point size of selected text.

Additional Information

If a selection includes text in several different sizes, the smallest size appears in the Font Size button followed by a plus sign.

Figure 1.54

The font size increased from 44 points to 60 points. The Font Size button displays the point size of the current selection.

APPLYING TEXT EFFECTS

Next, you want to further enhance the title slide by adding **text effects** such as color and shadow to the title and subtitle. The table below describes some of the effects and their uses. The Home tab and the Mini toolbar contain buttons for many of the formatting effects.

Format	Example	Use
Bold, italic	**Bold Italic**	Adds emphasis
Underline	<u>Underline</u>	Adds emphasis
Superscript	"To be or not to be."[1]	Used in footnotes and formulas
Subscript	H_2O	Used in formulas
Shadow	Shadow	Adds distinction to titles and headings
Color	Color Color **Color**	Adds interest

You decide to add color and a shadow effect to the main title first.

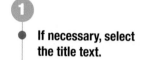

- If necessary, select the title text.

- Click **S** Text Shadow in the Font group.

Additional Information

Many formatting commands are toggle commands. This means the feature can be turned on and off simply by clicking on the command button.

- Open the **A** ▾ Font Color menu to display a gallery of colors.

- Choose Green, Accent 1, Darker 25% in the Theme Colors section.

Additional Information

A ScreenTip displays the name of the color when selected.

Additional Information

You will learn about themes in Lab 2.

- Click the subtitle placeholder to select it.

Your screen should be similar to Figure 1.55

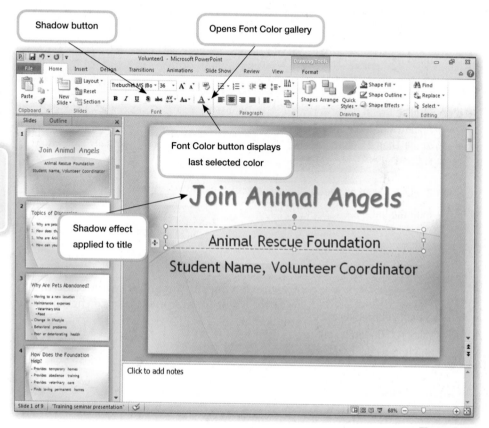

Figure 1.55

The selected color and slight shadow effect make the title much more interesting. Also notice the color in the Font Color button is the green color you just selected. This color can be quickly reapplied to other selections now simply by clicking the button.

Next you will enhance the two subtitle lines. Notice that the subtitle placeholder box does not include the second subtitle line. Although the second line was included in the placeholder when it was moved to this slide, the placeholder did not automatically increase in size to accommodate the new text. You will increase the size of the placeholder to visually include this text.

2

- Drag the bottom-middle sizing handle down to increase the size of the placeholder to include both subtitle lines.

- Select the text "Animal Rescue Foundation".

- Open the A ▾ Font Color gallery.

- Choose Green, Accent 1, Darker 50% in the Theme Colors section.

- Click **B** Bold on the Mini toolbar.

Another Method

The keyboard shortcut is Ctrl + B.

- Select your name and click **U** Underline on the Home tab.

Another Method

The keyboard shortcut is Ctrl + U.

Your screen should be similar to Figure 1.56

Figure 1.56

After reviewing your changes, you decide that underlining your name doesn't have the right look. You'll italicize the entire line instead and make the font smaller.

3

- Click [U] Underline.
- Select the entire second line of the subtitle.
- Click [I] Italic.
- Click [A˅] Decrease Font Size three times.
- Click somewhere outside the placeholder.

Your screen should be similar to Figure 1.57

Figure 1.57

Now the title slide has much more impact.

Working with Graphics

Finally, you want to add a picture to the presentation. A picture is one of several different graphic objects that can be added to a slide.

Concept 5 Graphics

A **graphic** is a nontext element or object, such as a drawing or picture, that can be added to a slide. A graphic can be a simple drawing object consisting of shapes such as lines and boxes. A **drawing object** is part of your presentation document. A **picture** is an image such as a graphic illustration or a scanned photograph. Pictures are graphics that were created from another program and are inserted in a slide as **embedded objects**. An embedded object becomes part of the presentation file and can be opened and edited using the **source program**, the program in which it was created. Any changes made to the embedded object are not made to the original picture file because they are independent. Several examples of drawing objects and pictures are shown below.

Photograph

Graphic illustration

Drawing object

Add graphics to your presentation to help the audience understand concepts, to add interest, and to make your presentation stand out from others.

Graphic files can be obtained from a variety of sources. Many simple drawings called **clip art** are available in the Clip Organizer, a Microsoft Office tool that arranges and catalogs clip art and other media files stored on the computer's hard disk. The Clip Organizer's files, or clips, include art, sound, animation, and movies you can add to a presentation. Additionally, if you are connected to the Internet, Microsoft's Office.com Web site is automatically accessed for even more graphics.

Digital images created using a digital camera are one of the most common types of graphic files. You also can create graphic files using a scanner to convert any printed document, including photographs, to an electronic format. Most images that are scanned and inserted into documents are stored as Windows bitmap files (.bmp). All types of graphics, including clip art, photographs, and other types of images, can be found on the Internet. These files are commonly stored as .jpg or .pcx files. Keep in mind that any images you locate on the Internet may be protected by copyright and should only be used with permission. You also can purchase CDs containing graphics for your use.

Additional Information

When your computer is connected to a scanner, you also can scan a picture and insert it directly into a slide without saving it as a file first.

INSERTING A GRAPHIC FROM THE CLIP ORGANIZER

You want to add a graphic to the second slide. First you decide to check the Clip Art gallery to see if you can find an image that will work as an attention getter. The Insert tab includes commands that are designed to enhance a presentation by adding features such as shapes and illustrations to movies and sounds.

1

● Select slide 2.

● Open the Insert tab.

● Click **Clip Art**.

Having Trouble?

Your Clip Art task pane may already display graphics if this feature was previously used while the application was still running.

Your screen should be similar to Figure 1.58

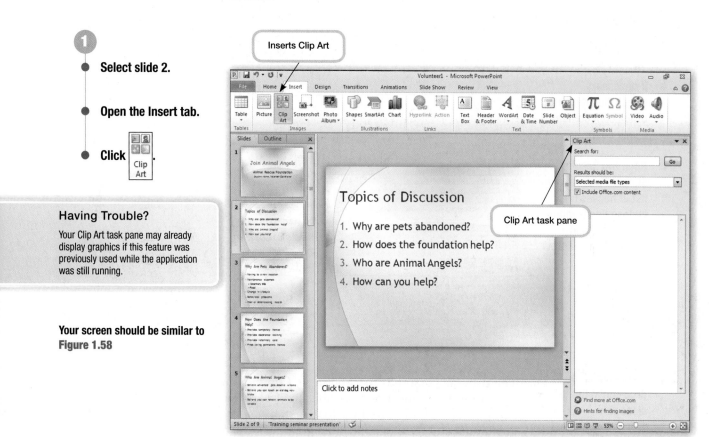

Figure 1.58

In the Clip Art task pane, you enter a word or phrase that is representative of the type of picture you want to locate. You also can specify the location to search and the type of media files, such as clip art, movies, photographs, or sound, to display in the search results. Since each of the items on this slide is a question, you decide to look for graphics of question marks.

2

- If necessary, select any existing text in the Search For text box.

- In the Search For text box, type **question**

- If necessary, select the Include Office.com content check box.

- Open the Results Should Be drop-down list, if necessary, choose Illustrations to select it, and deselect the all other options.

Having Trouble?

Click the box next to an option to select or deselect (clear the checkmark).

Figure 1.59

- Click outside the drop-down list to close it.

- Click [Go] .

Having Trouble?

If your thumbnails appear in a single column, increase the width of your task pane by dragging the left edge of the pane until two columns are displayed.

Having Trouble?

Do not worry if the thumbnails displayed on your screen do not match those shown in Figure 1.59, because the online clip art is continuously changing.

Your screen should be similar to Figure 1.59

The program searches the Microsoft Clip Organizer on your computer and, if an Internet connection is established, searches Microsoft's Office.com Web site for clip art and graphics that match your search term. The Results list displays thumbnails of all located graphics. The pictures stored on your computer in the Microsoft Clip Art gallery appear first in the results list, followed by the Office Online clip art.

Pointing to a thumbnail displays a ScreenTip containing the **keywords**, descriptive words or phrases, associated with the graphic and other information about the picture properties. It also displays a drop-down list bar that accesses the item's shortcut menu. The shortcut menu commands are used to work with and manage the items in the Clip Organizer. Because it is sometimes difficult to see the graphic in the thumbnail, you can preview it in a larger size.

3

● Scroll the Results list to view additional images.

● Point to any graphic and click · to open the thumbnail menu.

● Choose Preview/ Properties.

Your screen should be similar to Figure 1.60

Having Trouble?

Do not worry if your preview image does not match Figure 1.60. It will only match if you selected the same graphic in the results area.

Figure 1.60

The Preview/Properties dialog box displays the selected graphic in a larger size so it is easier to see. It also displays more information about the properties associated with the graphic. Notice the search word you entered appears as one of the keywords. Now you will scroll the results list of graphics to find one you like.

4

● Click [Close] to close the dialog box.

● Scroll the Results list to locate the graphic shown in Figure 1.61.

● Click on the graphic to insert it in the slide.

Another Method

You also could choose Insert from the thumbnail's shortcut menu to insert the graphic.

Your screen should be similar to Figure 1.61

Having Trouble?

If this graphic is not available in the Clip Organizer, just choose a question mark graphic that you like from the results list.

Figure 1.61

The clip art image is inserted in the center of the slide on top of the text. It is a selected object and can be sized and moved like any other selected object. The Picture Tools Format tab is automatically displayed in the Ribbon, in anticipation that you may want to modify the graphic.

SIZING AND MOVING A GRAPHIC

First you need to size and position the picture on the slide. A graphic object is sized and moved just like a placeholder. You want to decrease the graphic size slightly and move it to the bottom right of the slide.

1

- **If necessary, click on the graphic to select it.**

- **Drag the graphic to position it as shown in Figure 1.62.**

- **Drag the top left corner sizing handle inward to decrease its size to that shown in Figure 1.62.**

Additional Information

To maintain an object's proportions while resizing it, hold down (Shift) while dragging the sizing handle.

- **Close the Clip Art task pane.**

Your screen should be similar to Figure 1.62

Additional Information

Be careful when increasing the size of a picture (bitmap) image, as it can lose sharpness and appear blurry if enlarged too much.

Figure 1.62

The clip art image is now smaller and placed in the correct position on the slide.

ADDING GRAPHIC EFFECTS

You can use the picture effects on the Picture Tools Format tab to customize the look of the graphic to suit your presentation. There are many effects that you can use to improve the appearance of graphics in your presentation. The first enhancement you would like to make is to change the color of the question mark so it coordinates with the slide design.

1

- With the clip art selected, click **Color** in the Adjust group of the Picture Tools Format tab.

- Point to the choices in the Recolor gallery to see live previews.

- Choose Light Green, Accent Color 5 Dark from the gallery (second row, fifth column).

Your screen should be similar to Figure 1.63

Figure 1.63

Next, you want to enhance the graphic by applying a picture style to it. A **style** is a combination of formatting options that can be applied in one easy step. In the case of **picture styles**, the combinations consist of border, shadow, and shape effects. You also can create your own picture style effects by selecting specific style elements, such as borders and shadows, individually using the ☑ Picture Border ▾ , ⬤ Picture Effects ▾ , and 🔲 Picture Layout ▾ commands.

2

- Click ▾ More in the Picture Styles group to open the Picture Styles gallery.

Your screen should be similar to Figure 1.64

Figure 1.64

When you point to a style, the style name appears in a ScreenTip, and the Live Preview feature shows how the selected graphic will look with the selected picture style.

3

● **Point to several picture styles to see the live previews.**

● **Choose the** 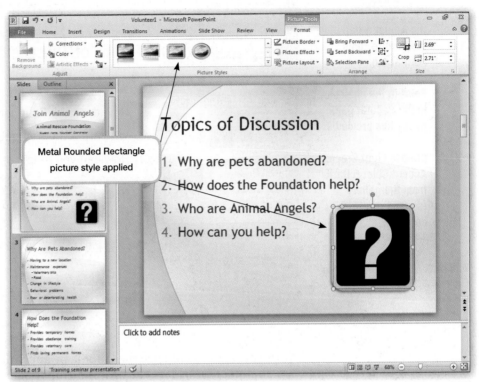 **Metal Rounded Rectangle style (bottom row, third column).**

Your screen should be similar to Figure 1.65

Figure 1.65

As you look at the picture, you decide to remove the rectangle and use the oval shape with the thin black border instead. You will then modify the picture style by changing the border color and removing the reflection.

4

- Choose the Beveled Oval, Black style in the Picture Styles gallery.

- Click ✐ Picture Border ▾ in the Picture Styles group.

- Choose Blue, Accent 2 from the Theme Colors group.

- Click ✐ Picture Effects ▾ in the Picture Styles group.

- From the Shadow group, choose No Shadow.

- Click outside the graphic to deselect the object.

Your screen should be similar to Figure 1.66

Figure 1.66

The addition of a customized graphic image gives your presentation a more polished look. Now that the slides are in the order you want and formatted, you would like to see how the presentation will look when viewed by an audience.

Rehearsing a Presentation

Rather than projecting the presentation on a large screen as you would to present it for an audience, a simple way to rehearse a presentation is to view it on your computer screen as a **slide show**. A slide show displays each slide full screen and in order. While the slide show is running during this rehearsal, you can plan what you will say while each slide is displayed.

USING SLIDE SHOW VIEW

When you view a slide show, each slide fills the screen, hiding the PowerPoint application window, so you can view the slides as your audience would. You will begin the slide show starting with the first slide.

1
- **Select slide 1 in the Slides tab.**
- **Click** **Slide Show (in the status bar).**

Another Method

You also can use [From Beginning] or [From Current Slide] on the Slide Show tab or the shortcut keys [F5] and [Shift] + [F5], respectively, to start the slide show.

Your screen should be similar to Figure 1.67

First slide of the presentation displayed full screen

Join Animal Angels

Animal Rescue Foundation

Student Name, Volunteer Coordinator

Figure 1.67

The presentation title slide is displayed full screen, as it will appear when projected on a screen using computer projection equipment. The easiest way to see the next slide is to click the mouse button. You also can use the keys shown below to move to the next or previous slide.

Next Slide	Previous Slide
[Spacebar]	[Backspace]
[Enter]	
[→]	[←]
[↓]	[↑]
[Page Down]	[Page Up]
[N] (for Next)	[P] (for Previous)

You also can select Next, Previous, or Last Viewed from the shortcut menu. Additionally, moving the mouse pointer to the lower-left corner of the window in Slide Show displays the Slide Show toolbar. Clicking ◁ or ▷ moves to the previous or next slide, and ▤ opens the shortcut menu.

2

● **Click to display the next slide.**

● **Using each of the methods described, slowly display the entire presentation.**

● **When the last slide displays a black window, click again to end the slide show.**

Additional Information

You can press [Esc] or use End Show on the shortcut menu at any time to end the slide show.

Your screen should be similar to Figure 1.68

Figure 1.68

After the last slide is displayed, the program returns to the view you were last using, in this case, Normal view.

Documenting a File

Having Trouble?

Refer to the section "Specifying Document Properties" in the Introduction to Microsoft Office 2010 to review this feature.

Finally, you want to update the presentation file properties by adding your name as the author, and a tag. The default title does not need to be changed.

1

- **Return to Normal view and display slide 1, if necessary.**

- **Open the File tab and, if necessary, choose Info.**

- **In the Tags text box, enter Volunteer, Recruit**

- **In the Author text box, enter your name**

- **Click anywhere outside the text box.**

Your screen should be similar to Figure 1.69

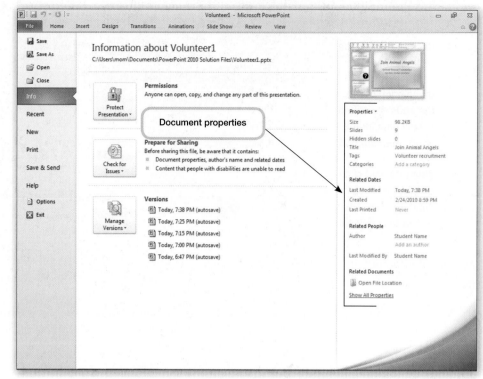

Figure 1.69

Previewing and Printing the Presentation

Although you still plan to make many changes to the presentation, you want to provide a printed copy of the presentation to the foundation director to get feedback regarding the content and layout.

PRINTING A SLIDE

Having Trouble?

Refer to the section "Printing a Document" in the Introduction to Microsoft Office 2010 to review basic printing features.

Although your presentation looks good on your screen, it may not look good when printed. Shading, patterns, and backgrounds that look good on the screen can make your printed output unreadable. Fortunately, PowerPoint displays a preview of how your printed output will appear as you specify the print settings. This allows you to make changes to the print settings before printing and reduces unnecessary paper waste.

From the File tab choose Print.

Your screen should be similar to Figure 1.70

Print options

Preview shows how the slide will appear when printed

Previous Page button

Next Page button

Page scroll box

Join Animal Angels

Animal Rescue Foundation
Student Name, Volunteer Coordinator

Figure 1.70

The Print window displays the print options in the left pane that are used to modify the default print settings. The preview area displays the first slide in the presentation as it will appear when printed using the current settings. It appears in color if your selected printer is a color printer; otherwise, it appears in grayscale (shades of gray). Even if you have a color printer, you can print the slides in grayscale or pure black and white. You want to print using the black and white option. The page scroll box shows the page number of the page you are currently viewing and the number of total pages. The scroll buttons on either side are used to scroll to the next and previous page.

The other change you want to make to the print settings is to only print the first slide in the presentation. To do this, you will change the settings to print the current slide only.

Additional Information

Use grayscale when your slides include patterns whose colors you want to appear in shades of gray.

2

- If you need to select a different printer, open the Printer drop-down list and select the appropriate printer.

- Click in the Settings group.

- Choose Pure Black and White.

- Click
in the Settings area.

- Choose Print Current Slide from the submenu.

Another Method
You could also type 1 in the Slides text box to select only the title slide.

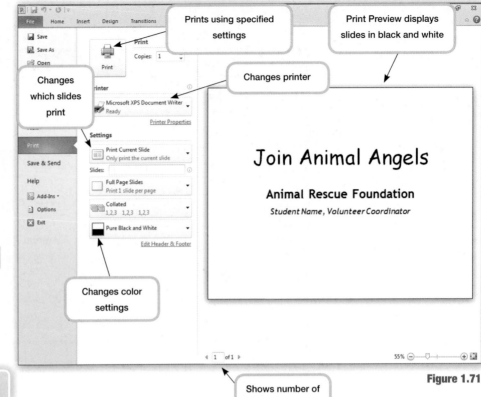

> Prints using specified settings

> Print Preview displays slides in black and white

> Changes which slides print

> Changes printer

> Changes color settings

> Shows number of slides that will print

Figure 1.71

Join Animal Angels

Animal Rescue Foundation

Student Name, Volunteer Coordinator

Your screen should be similar to Figure 1.71

The preview area displays how the slide will look when printed in black and white. Notice the page scroll box in the preview area now show 1 of 1, indicating that only the first slide will be printed.

Additional Information
Please consult your instructor for printing procedures that may differ from the following directions.

3

- If necessary, make sure your printer is on and ready to print.

- Click Print.

A printing progress bar appears in the status bar, indicating that the program is sending data to the printer and the title slide should be printing.

PRINTING HANDOUTS

You also can change the type of printed output from full page slides to any one of the output settings described in the table below. Only one type of output can be printed at a time.

Additional Information
You will learn about notes in Lab 2.

Output Type	Description
Full Page Slides	Prints one slide on a page.
Notes Pages	Prints the slide and the associated notes on a page.
Outline	Prints the slide content as it appears in Outline view.
Handouts	Prints multiple slides on a page.

To help the foundation's director get a better feel for the flow of the presentation, you decide to also print out the presentation as a handout. The handout format will allow him to see each slide as it appears onscreen.

1

- **Open the File menu and choose Print.**

- **Click** **Print Current Slide / Only print the current slide ▾** **in the Settings area and choose Print All Slides.**

- **Click** **Full Page Slides / Print 1 slide per page ▾** **in the Settings area and choose** **6 Slides Vertical**.

Your screen should be similar to Figure 1.72

Figure 1.72

Additional Information

The Orientation setting will override the Slide Layout setting. So, even if you leave the Slide Layout setting as 6 Slides Vertical, the presentation will print horizontal to match the Orientation setting.

The preview area shows the handouts as they will print. The vertical arrangement of the slides displays the slides down a row and then across. You decide to change the orientation from the default of portrait to landscape so that the slides print across the length of the paper, to change the arrangement to horizontal, and also to increase the number of slides per page so that the entire presentation fits on one page.

2

- Change the Color setting to Pure Black and White, if necessary.

- Click and choose 9 Slides Horizontal.

- Click

  Portrait Orientation ▼

  and choose Landscape Orientation.

Your screen should be similar to Figure 1.73

Figure 1.73

The preview area reflects your changes to the print settings. The horizontal layout displays the slides in order across a row and then down, making the presentation easier to follow.

3

- Click Print.

Your printed output should be similar to that shown in the Case Study at the beginning of the lab.

PRINTING AN OUTLINE

The final item you want to print is an outline of the presentation. An outline will make it easier for the director to provide feedback on the overall organization of the presentation.

- Open the File tab and choose Print.

- Change the Color setting to Pure Black and White again, if necessary.

- Change the orientation to Portrait Orientation.

- Click 9 Slides Horizontal Handouts (9 slides per page) ▼ and choose | Outline |.

- Ensure that the correct printer is selected and ready and click | Print |.

The printed outline will be a two-page document that looks similar to the preview.

Exiting PowerPoint

Another Method

You also can exit PowerPoint using ⊠ Exit in the File tab.

You have finished working on the presentation for now and will exit the PowerPoint program.

1

- Click ⊠ Close in the title bar.

- If asked to save the file again, click | Save |.

FOCUS ON CAREERS

EXPLORE YOUR CAREER OPTIONS

Account Executive

Sales is an excellent entry point for a solid career in any company. Account executive is just one of many titles that a sales professional may have; field sales and sales representative are two other titles. Account executives take care of customers by educating them on the company's latest products, designing solutions using the company's product line, and closing the deal to make the sale and earn their commission. These tasks require the use of effective PowerPoint presentations that educate and motivate potential customers. The salary range of an account executive is limited only by his or her ambition; salaries range from $30,000 to more than $120,540. To learn more about this career, visit the Web site for the Bureau of Labor Statistics of the U.S. Department of Labor.

Slide (PP1.6)

A slide is an individual "page" of your presentation.

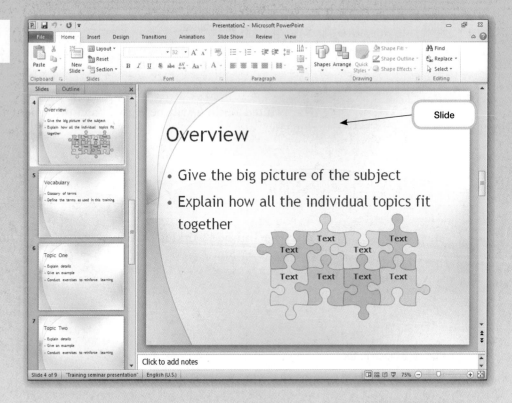

Spelling Checker (PP1.16)

The spelling checker locates most misspelled words, duplicate words, and capitalization irregularities as you create and edit a presentation, and proposes possible corrections.

AutoCorrect (PP1.18)

The AutoCorrect feature makes some basic assumptions about the text you are typing and, based on those assumptions, automatically corrects the entry.

Layout (PP1.42)

A layout defines the position and format for objects and text on a slide. A layout contains placeholders for the different items such as bulleted text, titles, charts, and so on.

Graphic (PP1.54)

A graphic is a nontext element or object, such as a drawing or picture, that can be added to a slide.

KEY TERMS

AutoCorrect PP1.18
character formatting PP1.47
clip art PP1.54
current slide PP1.9
custom dictionary PP1.16
default settings PP1.5
demote PP1.25
drawing object PP1.54
embedded object PP1.54
graphic PP1.54
keyword PP1.56
layout PP1.42
main dictionary PP1.16
Notes pane PP1.6
object PP1.6
Outline tab PP1.6
paragraph formatting PP1.47
picture PP1.54

picture style PP1.59
placeholder PP1.6
placeholder text PP1.6
promote PP1.26
sans serif font PP1.48
serif font PP1.47
sizing handles PP1.44
slide PP1.6
Slide indicator PP1.6
Slide pane PP1.6
slide show PP1.61
Slides tab PP1.6
source program PP1.54
spelling checker PP1.16
style PP1.59
text effects PP1.50
thumbnail PP1.6
view PP1.6

COMMAND SUMMARY

Command	Shortcut	Action
File tab		
Save	Ctrl + S	Saves presentation
🖫 Save As	F12	Saves presentation using new file name and/or location
📂 Open	Ctrl + O	Opens existing presentation
📑 Close		Closes presentation
Info		Document properties
New	Ctrl + N	Opens New Presentation dialog box
Print	Ctrl + P	Opens print settings and a preview pane
✕ Exit		Closes PowerPoint
Quick Access Toolbar		
🖫 Save	Ctrl + S	Saves presentation
↺ ▾ Undo	Ctrl + Z	Reverses last action
Home tab		
Clipboard group		
Paste ▾	Ctrl + V	Pastes item from Clipboard
✂ Cut	Ctrl + X	Cuts selection to Clipboard
📋 ▾ Copy	Ctrl + C	Copies selection to Clipboard
Slides group		
New Slide ▾	Ctrl + M	Inserts new slide with selected layout
📄 Layout ▾		Changes layout of a slide
Font group		
Trebuchet MS (He ▾) Font		Changes font type
44 ▾ Size		Changes font size

COMMAND SUMMARY (CONTINUED)

Command	Shortcut	Action
A˄		Increases font size
A˅		Decreases font size
I		Italicizes text
U		Underlines text
S		Applies a shadow effect
A ˅		Changes font color
Paragraph group		
Bullets/Bullets		Formats bulleted list
Numbering/Bulleted		Formats numbered lists
Editing group		
Select / Select All	Ctrl + A	Selects everything in the placeholder box
Insert tab		
Illustrations group		
Clip Art		Inserts clip art
Slide Show tab		
Start Slide Show group		
From Beginning	F5	Displays presentation starting with the first slide
From Current Slide	Shift + F5	Displays presentation starting with the current slide
Review tab		
Proofing group		
ABC Spelling	F7	Spell-checks presentation

COMMAND SUMMARY (CONTINUED)

Command	Shortcut	Action
View tab		
Presentation Views group		
Normal		Switches to Normal view
Slide Sorter		Switches to Slide Sorter view
Picture Tools Format tab		
Adjust group		
9 Slides Horizontal Handouts (9 slides per page)		Modifies the color of the picture
Picture Styles group		
More		Opens Picture styles gallery to choose an overall visual style for a picture
Picture Layout		Changes layout of a drawing
Picture Border		Applies a border style to picture
Picture Effects		Applies a visual effect to picture

LAB EXERCISES

SCREEN IDENTIFICATION

1. In the following PowerPoint screen, letters identify important elements. Enter the correct term for each screen element in the space provided.

Possible answers for the screen identification are:

Clip art   Presentation template

Object   Outline tab

Picture Styles   Sizing handle

Slide Show view   Slides tab

Slide pane   Note pane

Slide title   Thumbnail

Current slide

A. _____   H. _____

B. _____   I. _____

C. _____   J. _____

E. _____   K. _____

F. _____   L. _____

G. _____   M. _____

MATCHING

Match the item on the left with the correct description on the right.

1. AutoFit   ____ a. small image
2. demote   ____ b. sample text that suggests the content for the slide
3. embedded object   ____ c. moves the slide back to the previous slide in a presentation
4. Previous Slide button   ____ d. individual page of a presentation
5. layout   ____ e. displays each slide as a thumbnail
6. Notes pane   ____ f. indents a bulleted point to the right
7. placeholder text   ____ g. defines the position and format for objects and text that will be added to a slide
8. slide   ____ h. includes space to enter notes that apply to the current slide
9. Slides tab   ____ i. becomes part of the presentation file and can be opened and edited using the source program
10. thumbnail   ____ j. tool that automatically resizes text to fit within the placeholder

TRUE/FALSE

Circle the correct answer to the following questions.

1. A layout contains placeholders for different items such as bulleted text, titles, and charts.   **True**   **False**
2. PowerPoint will continue to indent to the same level when you demote a bulleted point until you cancel the indent.   **True**   **False**
3. A slide is a set of characters with a specific design.   **True**   **False**
4. PowerPoint identifies a word as misspelled by underlining it with a wavy blue line.   **True**   **False**
5. PowerPoint can print multiple types of output at a time.   **True**   **False**
6. The Previous Slide and Next Slide buttons are located at the bottom of the horizontal scroll bar.   **True**   **False**
7. Content templates focus on the design of a presentation.   **True**   **False**
8. Graphics are objects, such as charts, drawings, pictures, and scanned photographs, that provide visual interest or clarify data.   **True**   **False**
9. You can rely on AutoCorrect to ensure your document is error free.   **True**   **False**
10. After the final slide is displayed in Slide Sorter view, the program will return to the view you were last using.   **True**   **False**

LAB EXERCISES

FILL-IN

Complete the following statements by filling in the blanks with the correct terms.

1. _____ is a set of picture files or simple drawings that comes with Office 2010.
2. The size of a _____ can be changed by dragging its sizing handles.
3. A _____ is an individual "page" of your presentation.
4. _____ define the position and format for objects and text that will be added to a slide.
5. A _____ is text or graphics that appears at the bottom of each slide.
6. When selected, a placeholder is surrounded with eight _____.
7. A _____ is a miniature of a slide.
8. _____ is a PowerPoint feature that advises you of misspelled words as you add text to a slide and proposes possible corrections.
9. A _____ is a file containing predefined settings that can be used as a pattern to create many common types of presentations.
10. An embedded object is edited using the _____ program.

MULTIPLE CHOICE

Circle the correct response to the questions below.

1. The step in the development of a presentation that focuses on determining the length of your speech, the audience, the layout of the room, and the type of audiovisual equipment available is _____.
   a. editing
   b. creating
   c. planning
   d. enhancing

2. A _____ is a file containing predefined settings that can be used as a pattern to create many common types of presentations.
   a. presentation
   b. slide
   c. template
   d. graphic

3. The _____ feature makes some basic assumptions about the text you are typing and, based on those assumptions, automatically corrects the entry.
   a. grammar checker
   b. AutoCorrect
   c. spelling checker
   d. template

4. If you want to work on all aspects of your presentation, switch to _____ view, which displays the Slide pane, Outline pane, and Notes pane.
   a. Normal
   b. Outline
   c. Slide
   d. Slide Sorter

5. _____ displays a miniature of each slide to make it easy to reorder slides, add special effects such as transitions, and set timing between slides.
   a. Slide Show view
   b. Normal view
   c. Reading view
   d. Slide Sorter view

6. If you want to provide copies of your presentation to the audience showing multiple slides on a page, you would print _____.
   a. note pages
   b. slides
   c. handouts
   d. outline area

7. A(n) _____ is an onscreen display of your presentation.
   a. slide
   b. handout
   c. outline
   d. slide show

8. A _____ is a nontext element or object, such as a drawing or picture, that can be added to a slide.
   a. slide
   b. template
   c. text box
   d. graphic

9. When the spelling checker is used, you can create a(n) _____ dictionary to hold words that you commonly use but are not included in the main dictionary.
   a. official
   b. common
   c. personal
   d. custom

10. The keyboard shortcut to view a slide show is _____.
    a. F5
    b. Alt + V
    c. F3
    d. Ctrl + V

STEP-BY-STEP

RATING SYSTEM

★ Easy

★★ Moderate

★★★ Difficult

TRIPLE CROWN PRESENTATION ★

1. Logan Thomas works at Adventure Travel Tours. He is working on a presentation about lightweight hiking to be presented to a group of interested clients. Logan recently found some new information to add to the presentation. He also wants to rearrange some slides and make a few other changes to improve the appearance of the presentation. The handouts of your completed presentation will be similar to those shown here.

   a. Open the file pp01_Triple Crown. Run the slide show.

   b. Enter your name in the subtitle on slide 1.

   c. Spell-check the presentation, making the appropriate corrections.

   d. Change the layout of slide 5 to Title Only.

   e. Move slide 6 before slide 5.

   f. Insert an appropriate photograph from the Clip Art gallery on slide 4. Size and position it appropriately.

   g. Insert a new slide using the Two Content layout after slide 4.

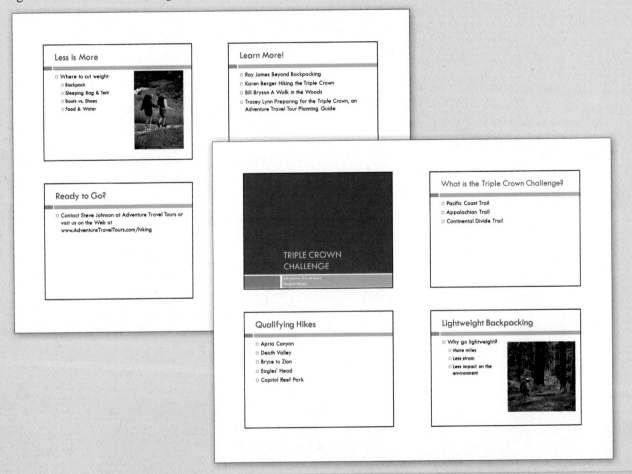

h. Enter the title **Less is More**. Insert an appropriate photograph on hiking from the Clip Art gallery in the right content placeholder. Move to slide 4 and select the second promoted bullet, "Where to cut weight:", and its subpoints. Cut this text and paste it in the left content placeholder of slide 5.

i. Change the layout of slide 7 to Title and Content layout. Add the following text in the text placeholder: **Contact Steve Johnson at Adventure Travel Tours or visit us on the Web at www. AdventureTravelTours.com/hiking**.

j. Run the slide show.

k. Save the presentation as Triple Crown Presentation. Print the slides in landscape orientation as handouts (four per page).

EMERGENCY DRIVING TECHNIQUES ★ ★

2. The Department of Public Safety holds monthly community outreach programs. Next month's topic is about how to handle special driving circumstances, such as driving in rain or snow. You are responsible for presenting the section on how to handle tire blowouts. You have organized the topics to be presented and located several clip art graphics that will complement the talk. Now you are ready to begin creating the presentation. Handouts of the completed presentation are shown here.

LAB EXERCISES

a. Open the PowerPoint presentation pp01_Handling Blowouts.

b. Run the spelling checker and correct any errors.

c. On slide 1, replace "Student Name" with your name.

Increase the title text to 54 pts.

Change title text color to Dark Red, Accent 1, Darker 50%.

d. On slide 5:

Promote bullet 4.

Demote the last bullet.

AutoFit the content text to the placeholder

e. On slide 6, insert a clip art image on the theme of tires and position it in the lower-right corner of the slide.

f. On slide 3, change the color of the clip art to Dark Red, Accent 6, Light. Apply the Bevel Rectangle picture style to the clip art image.

g. Save the presentation as Handling Blowouts.

h. Run the slide show.

i. Print the slides as handouts (six per page, horizontal) and close the presentation.

WRITING EFFECTIVE RESUMES ★ ★

3. You work for the career services center of a major university and are working on a presentation to help students create effective resumes and cover letters. You are close to finishing the presentation but need to clean it up and enhance it a bit before presenting it. The handouts of your completed presentation will be similar to those shown here.

a. Open the PowerPoint presentation pp01_Resume.

b. Run the spelling checker and correct any spelling errors.

c. On slide 1: Display in normal view.

Change title font size to 54 pt. Use the AutoFit option to fit the text into the placeholder.

Change subtitle font size to 20 pt.

Search the Clip Art gallery on the theme of success. Insert, size, and position an appropriate graphic.

Apply an appropriate picture style to the selected graphic and change its color.

d. On slide 2, replace "Student Name" with your name. Use picture styles and effects to improve the appearance of the picture.

e. On slides 3 and 4, search the Clip Art gallery on the theme of success. Insert, size, and position an appropriate graphic on each slide. Apply an appropriate picture styles to the graphics and change their colors.

f. On slide 5, capitalize the first word of each bulleted item.

g. On slide 6, split the slide content into two slides. Move the first bulleted item on the new slide (7) back to slide 6 so slide 7 begins with the "Other" bulleted item. Appropriately adjust the bullet level and font size of the moved item on slide 6.

h. On slide 10, reorganize the bulleted items so "Types of cover letters" is the first item.

WWW.MHHE.COM/OLEARY

i. To match the slide order with the way the topics are now introduced, move slide 13 before slide 11.

j. On slide 13: Break each bulleted item into two or three bullets each as appropriate.

Capitalize the first word of each bulleted item.

Remove any commas and periods at the end of the bullets.

k. Save the presentation as Resume1.

l. Run the slide show.

m. Print the slides as handouts (nine per page, horizontal, in landscape orientation) and close the presentation.

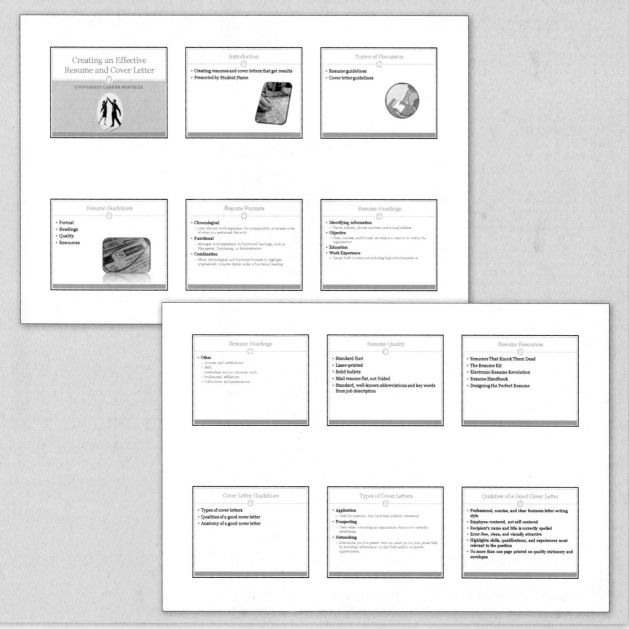

LAB EXERCISES

EMPLOYEE ORIENTATION ★ ★ ★

4. As the front desk manager of the Essex Inn, you want to make a presentation to your new employees about all of the amenities your hotel offers its guests as well as information on activities and dining in the area. The purpose of this presentation is to enable employees to answer the many questions that are asked by the guests about both the hotel and the town. The handouts of your completed presentation will be similar to those shown here.

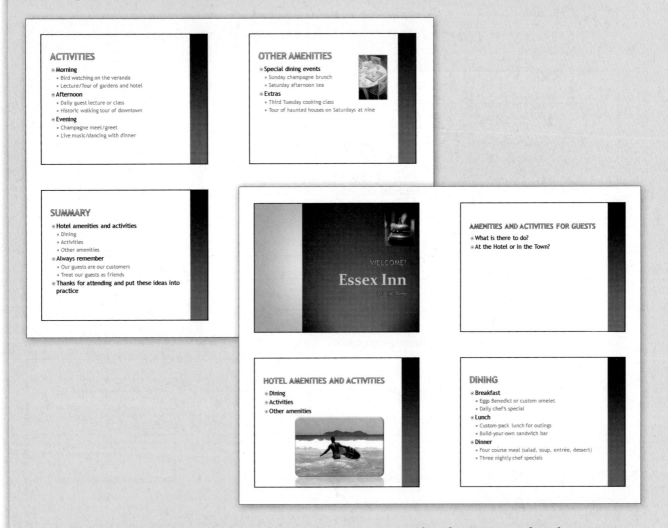

a. Open pp01_Essex Inn, which uses the Opulent content template from Microsoft Online.

b. On slide 1:

   Enter **Essex Inn** as the company name. Set the font to Constantia; apply Bold and Shadow. Change the font color to Ice Blue, Background 2, and size 66.

   Insert, size, and position a clip art image suitable as a hotel logo in place of the "your logo here" graphic.

   Insert a line after the title. Type your name on the line, and change the font size to Trebuchet MS and the font size to 20. Change the font color to White and apply italics.

c. On slide 2:

Enter **Amenities and Activities for Guests** as the title.

Change the font size of the title to 31.

Enter the sample bulleted text **What is there to do?** as the first bullet.

Enter **At the hotel or in the town?** as the second bullet.

Remove the remaining bulleted items.

d. Insert a new slide after slide 2. In this slide:

Set the layout to Title and Content.

Enter **Hotel Amenities and Activities** as the title.

Enter **Dining** as the first bullet.

Enter **Activities** as the second bullet.

Enter **Other amenities** as the third bullet.

Insert, size, and position a clip art image suitable for a hotel at the bottom center of the slide. Apply picture styles and effects.

e. Insert a new slide after slide 3. In this slide:

Set the layout to Title and Content.

Enter **Dining** as the title.

Enter **Breakfast** as the first bullet under Dining.

Enter **Eggs Benedict or custom omelet** and demote to appear as the first bullet under Breakfast.

Enter **Daily chef's special** as the second bullet under Breakfast.

Enter **Lunch** and promote to appear as the second bullet under Dining.

Enter **Custom-pack lunch for outings** and demote to appear as the first bullet under Lunch.

Enter **Build-your-own sandwich bar** as the second bullet under Lunch.

Enter **Dinner** and promote to appear as the third bullet under Dining.

Enter **Four course meal (salad, soup, entrée, dessert)** as the first bullet under Dinner.

Enter **Three nightly chef specials** as the second bullet under Dinner.

f. Insert a new slide after slide 4. In this slide:

Set the layout to Title and Content.

Enter **Activities** as the title.

Enter **Morning** as the first bullet under Activities.

Enter **Bird watching on the veranda** and demote to appear as the first bullet under Morning.

Enter **Lecture/Tour of gardens and hotel** as the second bullet under Morning.

Enter **Afternoon** and promote to appear as the second bullet under Activities.

Enter **Daily guest lecture or class** as the first bullet under Afternoon.

Enter **Historic walking tour of downtown** as the second bullet under Afternoon.

Enter **Evening** and promote to appear as the third bullet under Activities.

Enter **Champagne meet/greet** and demote to appear as the first bullet under Evening.

Enter **Live music/dancing with dinner** as the second bullet under Evening.

g. Insert a new slide after slide 5. In this slide:

Set the layout to Title and Content.

Enter **Other Amenities** as the title.

Enter **Special dining events** as the first bullet under Other Amenities.

Enter **Sunday champagne brunch** and demote to appear as the first bullet under Special Dining Events.

Enter **Saturday afternoon tea** as the second bullet under Special Dining Events.

Enter **Extras** and promote to appear as the second bullet for Other Amenities.

Enter **Third Tuesday cooking class** and demote to appear as the first bullet under Extras.

Enter **Tour of haunted houses on Saturdays at nine** as the second bullet under Extras.

Insert, size, and position a clip art image suitable for a hotel at the bottom center of the slide. Apply picture styles and effects.

h. Delete slides 7 through 13.

i. On the Summary slide 7.

Enter **Hotel amenities and activities** as the first bullet under Summary.

Enter **Dining** and demote to appear as the first bullet under Hotel amenities and activities.

Enter **Activities** as the second bullet under Hotel amenities and activities.

Enter **Other amenities** as the third bullet under Hotel amenities and activities.

Enter **Always remember** and promote to appear as the second bullet under Summary.

Enter **Our guests are our customers** and demote to appear as the first bullet under Always remember.

Enter **Treat our guests as friends** as the second bullet under Always remember.

Enter **Thanks for attending and put these ideas into practice** and promote to appear as the third bullet under Summary.

Delete any remaining bullet placeholders.

j. Save the presentation as Essex Inn Orientation.

k. Run the slide show.

l. Print the slides as handouts (four per page, horizontal, in landscape orientation).

WORKPLACE ISSUES ★ ★ ★

5. Tim is preparing for his lecture on "Workplace Issues" for his Introduction to Computers class. He uses PowerPoint to create presentations for each of his lectures. He has organized the topics to be presented, and located several clip art graphics that will complement the lecture. He is now ready to begin creating the presentation. Several slides of the completed presentation are shown here.

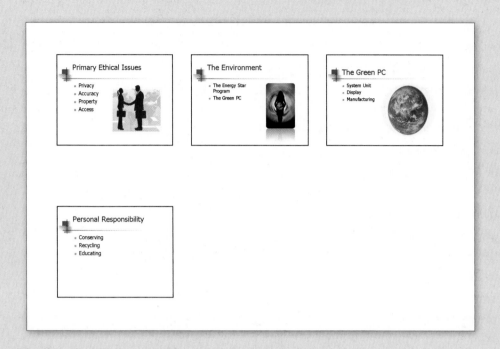

a. Open a new presentation using the Staff Training Presentation template. If you don't have access to the Internet, you can use the file pp01_Staff Training.

b. On slide 1:

Change the title to **Workplace Issues**. Change the font size to 48 and apply a bold effect.

Change the subtitle text to **Lecture 4**.

Add a line beneath the subtitle and type **Presented by Your Name**. Change the font size of this line to 24.

Insert, size, and position a clip art image suitable for the theme of an office meeting. Apply a picture style to the image.

c. On slide 2:

Enter **Topics of Discussion** as the title text.

Enter **Ergonomics** as bullet 1.

Enter **Ethics** as bullet 2.

Enter **Environment** as bullet 3.

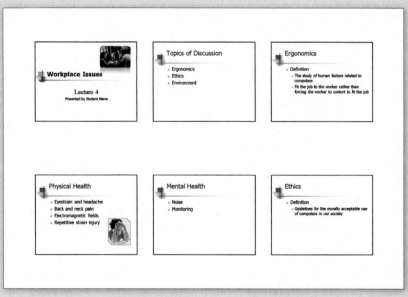

d. On slide 3:

Enter **Ergonomics** as the title.

Enter **Definition** as the first bullet.

Enter **Fit the job to the worker rather than forcing the worker to contort to fit the job** as the second bullet.

Enter **The study of human factors related to computers** as the third bullet.

e. Change the order of bullets 2 and 3 on slide 3.

Demote bullets 2 and 3.

f. On slide 4:

Change the title to **Mental Health**.

Include two bulleted items: **Noise** and **Monitoring**.

g. Change the title of slide 5 to **Physical Health** and include the following bulleted items:

Bullet 1: **Eyestrain and headache**

Bullet 2: **Back and neck pain**

Bullet 3: **Electromagnetic fields**

Bullet 4: **Repetitive strain injury**

Insert, size, and position a suitable clip art image. Use the picture formatting tools to customize the image to suit the presentation.

h. On slide 6:

Change the title to **Ethics**.

Include two bullets: **Definition** and **Guidelines for the morally acceptable use of computers in our society**.

Demote bullet 2.

i. Change the title of slide 7 to **Primary Ethical Issues**.

Enter **Privacy** as bullet 1.

Enter **Accuracy** as bullet 2.

Enter **Property** as bullet 3.

Enter **Access** as bullet 4.

Insert, size, and position a suitable clip art image. Use the picture formatting tools to customize the image to suit the presentation.

j. Insert a new Two Content layout slide between slides 7 and 8. On the new slide 8:

Enter **The Environment** as the title.

Enter **The Energy Star Program** as the first bullet.

Enter **The Green PC** as the second bullet.

In the right placeholder, insert, size, and position a suitable clip art image. Use the picture formatting tools to customize the image to suit the presentation.

k. Create a duplicate of slide 8. On the new slide 9:

Enter **The Green PC** as the title.

Enter **System Unit** as the first bullet.

Enter **Display** as the second bullet.

Enter **Manufacturing** as the third bullet.

In the right placeholder, insert, size, and position an appropriate clip art image.

l. On slide 10:

Enter **Personal Responsibility** as the title.

Enter **Conserving** as the first bullet.

Enter **Recycling** as the second bullet.

Enter **Educating** as the third bullet.

m. In Slide Sorter view, move slide 5 before slide 4.

n. Change the font of the words "Lecture 4" in the subtitle on the title slide to Times New Roman and the size to 44 pt.

o. Save the presentation as Workplace Issues.

p. Run the slide show. Revised PowerPoint_2010_Brief_Solutions

q. Print the slides as handouts (six per page in landscape orientation).

ON YOUR OWN

INTERNET POLICY PRESENTATION ★

1. You are working in the information technology department at International Sales Incorporated. Your manager has asked you to give a presentation on the corporation's Internet policy to the new-hire orientation class. Create your presentation with PowerPoint, using the information in the Word file pp01_Internet Policy as a resource. Use a template of your choice. When you are done, run the spelling checker, then save your presentation as Internet Policy and print it.

TELEPHONE TRAINING COURSE ★★

2. You are a trainer with Super Software, Inc. You received a memo from your manager alerting you that many of the support personnel are not using proper telephone protocol or obtaining the proper information from customers who call in. Your manager has asked you to conduct a training class that covers these topics. Using the Word document pp01_Memo data file as a resource, prepare the slides for your class. When you are done, save the presentation as Phone Etiquette and print the handouts.

LAB EXERCISES

VISUAL AIDS ★ ★

3. You are a trainer with Super Software, Inc. Your manager has asked you to prepare a presentation on various visual aids that may be used in presentations. Using the pp01_VisualAids data file as a resource, create an onscreen presentation using an appropriate template. Add clip art that illustrates the type of visual aid. Include your name on the title slide. When you are done, save the presentation as Presentation Aids and print the handouts.

WEB DESIGN PROPOSAL ★ ★ ★

4. Your company wants to create a Web site, but it is not sure whether to design its own or hire a Web design firm to do it. You have been asked to create a presentation to management relaying the pros and cons of each approach. To gather information, search the Web for the topic "Web design," and select some key points about designing a Web page from one of the "how-to" or "tips" categories. Use these points to create the first part of your presentation, and call it something like "Creating Our Own Web Page." Then search the Web for the topic "Web designers," and select two Web design firms. Pick some key points about each firm (for example, Web sites they have designed, design elements they typically use, and/or their design philosophy). Finally, include at least one slide that lists the pros and cons of each approach. Include your name on the title slide. When your presentation is complete, save it as Web Design and print the slides as handouts.

   You will expand on this presentation in On Your Own Exercise 4 of Lab 2.

CAREERS WITH ANIMALS ★ ★ ★

5. You have been volunteering at the Animal Rescue Foundation. The director has asked you to prepare a presentation on careers with animals to present to local schools in hopes that some students will be inspired to volunteer at the foundation. Using the Word document pp01_Animal Careers data file as a resource, create the presentation. Add photos or clip art where appropriate. When you are done, save the presentation as Careers with Animals and print the handouts.

Objectives

After completing this lab, you will know how to:

1 Find and replace text.

2 Create and enhance a table.

3 Insert pictures.

4 Modify graphic objects.

5 Create and enhance shapes.

6 Create a text box.

7 Change the theme.

8 Modify slide masters.

9 Add animation, sound, and transitions.

10 Control a slide show.

11 Add speaker notes.

12 Add and hide slide footers.

13 Customize print settings.

Animal Rescue Foundation

The Animal Rescue Foundation director was very impressed with your first draft of the presentation to recruit volunteers and asked to see the presentation onscreen. While viewing it together, you explained that you plan to make many more changes to improve the appearance of the presentation. For example, you plan to use a different color theme and to include more art and other graphic features to enhance the appearance of the slides. You also explained that you will add more action to the slides using the special effects included with PowerPoint to keep the audience's attention.

The director suggested that you include more information on ways that volunteers can help. Additionally, because the organization has such an excellent adoption rate, the director wants you to include a table to illustrate the success of the adoption program.

PowerPoint 2010 gives you the design and production capabilities to create a first-class onscreen presentation. These features include artist-designed layouts and color themes that give your presentation a professional appearance. In addition, you can add your own personal touches by modifying text attributes, incorporating art or graphics, and including animation to add impact, interest, and excitement to your presentation.

Displaying information in tables makes data easy to understand.

Pictures add interest and enhance the appearance of the slide.

Animations and transitions add action to a slide show.

The following concepts will be introduced in this lab:

1 Find and Replace To make editing easier, you can use the Find and Replace feature to find text in a presentation and replace it with other text.

2 Table A table is used to organize information into an easy-to-read format of horizontal rows and vertical columns.

3 Alignment Alignment controls the position of text entries within a space.

4 Theme A theme is a predefined set of formatting choices that can be applied to an entire document in one simple step.

5 Master A master is a special slide or page that stores information about the formatting for all slides or pages in a presentation.

6 Animations Animations are special effects that add action to text and graphics so they move around on the screen during a slide show.

Finding and Replacing Text

After meeting with the foundation director, you want to update the content to include the additional information on ways that volunteers can help the Animal Rescue Foundation.

- **Start PowerPoint 2010.**

- **Open the file pp02_Volunteer2**

- **If necessary, switch to Normal view.**

- **Replace Student Name in slide 1 with your name.**

- **Scroll the Slide pane to view the content of the revised presentation.**

Your screen should be similar to Figure 2.1

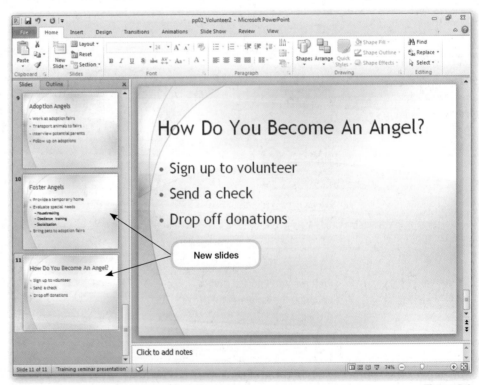

Figure 2.1

You added two new slides, 9 and 10, with more information about the Animal Angels volunteer organization, bringing the total number of slides in the presentation to 11. As you reread the content of the presentation, you decide to edit the text by finding the word "pet" and replacing it with the word "animal." To do this, you will use the Find and Replace feature.

Concept ① Find and Replace

To make editing easier, you can use the **Find and Replace** feature to find text in a presentation and replace it with other text. The Find feature will locate and identify any text string you specify in the presentation by highlighting it. When used along with the Replace feature, not only will the string be identified, but it will be replaced with the replacement text you specify if you choose. For example, suppose you created a lengthy document describing the type of clothing and equipment needed to set up a world-class home gym, and then you decided to change "sneakers" to "athletic shoes." Instead of deleting every occurrence of "sneakers" and typing "athletic shoes," you can use the Find and Replace feature to perform the task automatically.

The Replace feature also can be used to replace a specified font in a presentation with another. When using this feature, however, all text throughout the presentation that is in the specified font is automatically changed to the selected replacement font.

The Find and Replace feature is fast and accurate; however, use care when replacing so that you do not replace unintended matches.

FINDING TEXT

First, you will use the Find command to locate all occurrences of the word "pet" in the presentation. Because it is easier to read the text in the Slide pane, you will make that pane active before starting. If the Outline tab is active at the time you begin using Find and Replace, the located text will be highlighted in the Outline tab instead.

● **Make slide 1 active.**

● **If necessary, open the Home tab.**

● **Click 🔍 Find in the Editing group.**

Another Method
The keyboard shortcut is Ctrl + F.

Your screen should be similar to Figure 2.2

Figure 2.2

Finding and Replacing Text **PP2.5**

In the Find dialog box, you enter the text you want to locate in the Find what text box. The two options described in the following table allow you to refine the procedure that is used to conduct the search.

Option	Effect on Text
Match Case	Distinguishes between uppercase and lowercase characters. When selected, finds only those instances in which the capitalization matches the text you typed in the Find what box.
Find WholeWords Only	Distinguishes between whole and partial words. When selected, locates matches that are whole words and not part of a larger word. For example, finds "cat" only and not "catastrophe," too.

You want to find all occurrences of the complete word "pet." You will not use either option described above, because you want to locate all words regardless of case and because you want to find "pet" as well as "pets" in the presentation.

2

- Type **pet** in the Find what text box.

- Click Find Next .

- If necessary, move the dialog box so you can see the located text.

Your screen should be similar to Figure 2.3

Figure 2.3

PowerPoint begins searching beginning at the cursor location for all occurrences of the text to find and locates the first occurrence of the word "pet."

3

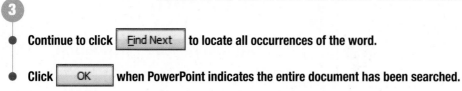

- Continue to click Find Next to locate all occurrences of the word.

- Click OK when PowerPoint indicates the entire document has been searched.

The word "pet" is used five times in the document. Using the Find command is a convenient way to quickly navigate through a document to locate and move to specified information.

REPLACING TEXT

You want to replace selected occurrences of the word "pet" with "animal" throughout the presentation. You will use the Replace feature to specify the text to enter as the replacement text.

1 Click [ab/ac Replace ▾] in the Editing group.

Your screen should be similar to Figure 2.4

Figure 2.4

The Find dialog box changes to the Replace dialog box, and the Find text is still specified in the Find what text box. You can now enter the replacement text in the Replace with text box. The replacement text must be entered exactly as you want it to appear in your presentation.

2

● Press Tab or click in the Replace with text box.

Having Trouble?

If necessary, type **pet** in the Find what text box.

Additional Information

After entering the text to find, do not press Enter or this will choose Find Next and the search will begin.

● Type **animal** in the Replace with text box.

● Click Find Next.

● If necessary, move the dialog box so you can see the located text.

● Click Replace.

Having Trouble?

Click Find Next to move to the next occurrence if the search does not advance automatically.

Your screen should be similar to Figure 2.5

Figure 2.5

The first located Find text is replaced with the replacement text, and the next occurrence of text in the Find what box is located. You could continue finding and replacing each occurrence. You will, however, replace all the remaining occurrences at one time. As you do, the replacement is entered in lowercase even when it replaces a word that begins with an uppercase character. You will correct this when you finish replacing.

- Click **Replace All** to continue.

- Click **OK** in response to the finished searching dialog box.

- Click **Close** to close the Replace dialog box.

- Edit the word "animals" to "Animals" in slide 3.

- Click somewhere outside the placeholder.

- Save the presentation as Volunteer2 to you solution file location.

Your screen should be similar to Figure 2.6

New file name

Why Are Animals Abandoned?

- Poor or deteriorating he
- Maintenance expenses
  - Veterinary bills
  - Food
- Change in lifestyle
- Behavioral problems
- Moving to a new location

Replacement text capitalization corrected

Click to add notes

Slide 3 of 11   "Training seminar presentation"   English (U.S.)

Figure 2.6

If you plan to change all occurrences, it is much faster to use **Replace All**. Exercise care when using Replace All, however, because the search text you specify might be part of another word and you may accidentally replace text you want to keep.

Creating a Simple Table

During your discussion with the director, he suggested that you add a slide containing data showing the success of the adoption program. The information in this slide will be presented using a table layout.

Concept 2 Table

A **table** is used to organize information into an easy-to-read format of horizontal rows and vertical columns. The intersection of a row and column creates a **cell** in which you can enter data or other information. Cells in a table are identified by a letter and number, called a **table reference**. Columns are identified from left to right beginning with the letter A, and rows are numbered from top to bottom beginning with the number 1. The table reference of the top-leftmost cell is A1 because it is in the first column (A) and first row (1) of the table. The third cell in column 2 is cell B3. The fourth cell in column 3 is C4.

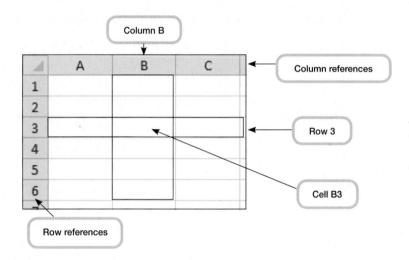

Tables are a very effective method for presenting information. The table layout organizes the information for readers and greatly reduces the number of words they have to read to interpret the data. Use tables whenever you can to make the information in your presentation easier to read.

The table you will create will display columns for the year and for the number of rescues and adoptions. The rows will display the data for the past four years. Your completed table will be similar to the one shown here.

Year	Rescues	Adoptions
2009	3759	3495
2010	3847	3784
2011	3982	3833
2012	4025	3943

CREATING A TABLE SLIDE

To include this information in the presentation, you will insert a new slide after slide 5. Because this slide will contain a table showing the adoption data, you want to use the Title and Content layout.

1

- Display slide 5.

- Open the [New Slide ▾] drop-down menu from the Slides group on the Home tab.

- Choose the Title and Content layout.

Your screen should be similar to Figure 2.7

Figure 2.7

Six icons appear inside the content placeholder, each representing a different type of content that can be inserted. Clicking an icon opens the appropriate feature to add the specified type of content.

INSERTING THE TABLE

First, you will add a slide title, and then you will create the table to display the number of adoptions and rescues.

1

- Enter the title **Success Rate** in the title placeholder.

- Click the [⊞] Insert Table icon in the center of the slide.

Your screen should be similar to Figure 2.8

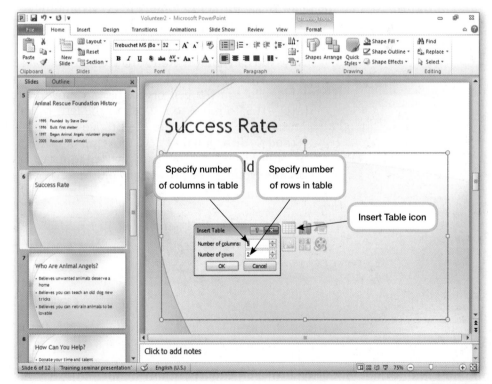

Figure 2.8

Creating a Simple Table   **PP2.11**

In the Insert Table dialog box, you specify the number of rows and columns for the table.

2

• **Specify 3 columns and 5 rows.**

Having Trouble?
You can type in the number or use the scroll buttons to increase or decrease the number.

• **Click** OK .

Your screen should be similar to Figure 2.9

Figure 2.9

A basic table consisting of three columns and five rows is displayed as a selected object. In addition, the Table Tools Design tab opens in anticipation that you will want to modify the design of the table.

ENTERING DATA IN A TABLE

Now you can enter the information into the table. The insertion point appears in the top-left corner cell, cell A1, ready for you to enter text. To move in a table, click on the cell or use [Tab] to move to the next cell to the right and [Shift] + [Tab] to move to the cell to the left. If you are in the last cell of a row, pressing [Tab] takes you to the first cell of the next row. You also can use the [↑] and [↓] directional keys to move up or down a row. When you enter a large amount of text in a table, using [Tab] to move is easier than using the mouse because your hands are already on the keyboard.

1

● Type **Year**

● Press **Tab** or click on the next cell to the right.

Your screen should be similar to Figure 2.10

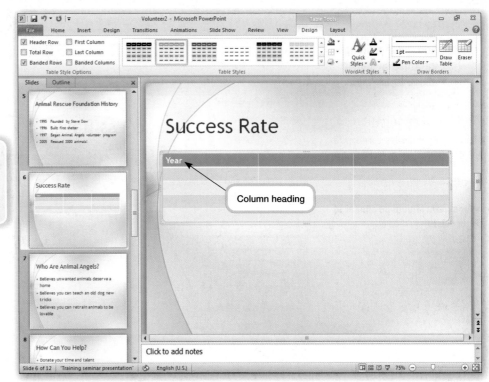

Figure 2.10

Next, you will complete the information for the table by entering the data shown below.

	Column A	Column B	Column C
Row 1	Year	Rescues	Adoptions
Row 2	2009	3759	3495
Row 3	2010	3847	3784
Row 4	2011	3982	3833
Row 5	2012	4025	3943

**Add the remaining
information shown
above to the table.**

Additional Information

You can also use the directional keys to
move from cell to cell in the table.

**Your screen should be similar to
Figure 2.11**

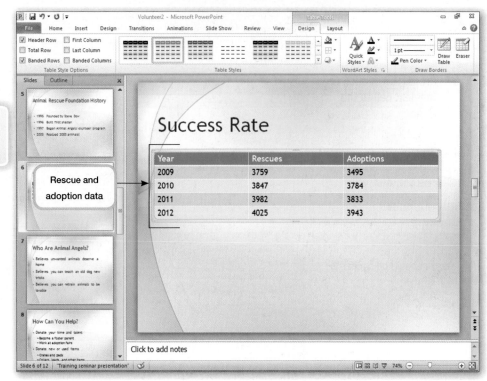

Figure 2.11

You are happy with the table but would like to increase the font size of the
text to make it more readable onscreen. The size of the font in a table can
be changed like any other text on a slide. However, selecting text in a table is
slightly different. The following table describes how to select different areas of
a table.

Area to Select	Procedure
Cell	Drag across the contents of the cell.
Row	Drag across the row or click in front of the row when the mouse pointer is a ➡.
Column	Drag down the column or click in front of the row when the mouse pointer is a ⬇.
Multiple cells, rows, or columns	Drag through the cells, rows, or columns when the mouse pointer is a ➧ or I.
	Or select the first cell, row, or column, and hold down ⇧Shift while clicking on another cell, row, or column.
Contents of next cell	Press Tab⇥.
Contents of previous cell	Press ⇧Shift + Tab⇥.
Entire table	Drag through all the cells or click anywhere inside the table and press Ctrl + A.

Select all the text in the table.

Open the Home tab.

Click **Increase Font Size in the Font group four times.**

Additional Information

Clicking increases the font size by units.

Your screen should be similar to Figure 2.12

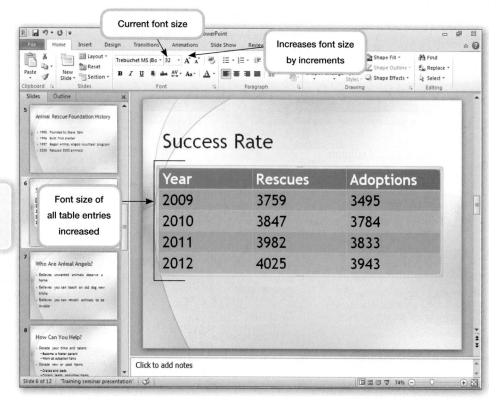

Figure 2.12

The font size has quickly been increased by four units, and at 32 points the text is much easier to read.

SIZING THE TABLE AND COLUMNS

You now want to increase the overall size of the table to better fill the space on the slide and then adjust the size of the columns to fit their contents.

1

Drag the lower-right corner sizing handle down to increase the table size as in Figure 2.13.

Additional Information

The mouse pointer will appear as ⬉ when you can drag the corner sizing handle and as ✛ while dragging.

Your screen should be similar to Figure 2.13

Figure 2.13

To adjust the individual column width or row height, you drag the row and column boundaries. The mouse pointer appears as a ✛ when you can size the column and ≑ when you can size the row. The mouse pointer appears as a ✛ when you can move the entire table.

2

● **Drag the right column boundary line of the year column to the left to reduce the column width as in Figure 2.14.**

Additional Information

You also can double-click on the boundary line to automatically size the width to the largest cell entry.

● **Drag the boundary lines of the other two columns to the left to reduce the column widths as in Figure 2.14.**

Your screen should be similar to Figure 2.14

Figure 2.14

Now the columns are more appropriately sized to the data they display and the overall table size is good. You decide it would look best to align the table in the center of the slide as well. You could do this manually by moving the object to center it. A more precise method is to use the built-in alignment feature.

3

- Open the Table Tools Layout tab.

- Click ▤ ▾ Align in the Arrange group to display the drop-down menu.

- Choose Align Center.

Your screen should be similar to Figure 2.15

Figure 2.15

ALIGNING TEXT IN CELLS

The next change you want to make is to center the text and data in the cells. To do this, you can change the alignment of the text entries.

Concept **3** Alignment

Alignment controls the position of text entries within a space. You can change the horizontal placement of an entry in a placeholder or a table cell by using one of the four horizontal alignment settings: left, center, right, and justified. You also can align text vertically in a table cell with the top, middle, or bottom of the cell space.

Horizontal Alignment	Effect on Text	Vertical Alignment	Effect on Text
Left	Aligns text against the left edge of the placeholder or cell, leaving the right edge of text, which wraps to another line, ragged.	Top	Aligns text at the top of the cell space.
Center	Centers each line of text between the left and right edges of the placeholder or cell.	Middle	Aligns text in the middle of the cell space.
Right	Aligns text against the right edge of the placeholder or cell, leaving the left edge of multiple lines ragged.	Bottom	Aligns text at the bottom of the cell space.
Justified	Aligns text evenly with both the right and left edges of the placeholder or cell.		

The commands to change horizontal alignment are on the Home tab in the Paragraph group. However, using the shortcuts shown below or the Mini toolbar is often much quicker.

Alignment	Keyboard Shortcut
Left	Ctrl + L
Center	Ctrl + E
Right	Ctrl + R
Justified	Ctrl + J

The data in the table is not centered within the cells. You want to center the cell entries both horizontally and vertically in their cell spaces.

①

- Select the entire contents of the table.

- Right-click on the selection and click ≣ Center in the Alignment group.

Another Method

You also could click ≣ Center in the Paragraph group of the Home tab.

- Click ▤ Center Vertically in the Alignment group.

Another Method

You can also open the ⊞▾ Align Text drop-down menu in the Paragraph group and choose Middle.

Centers vertically

Centers horizontally

All cell entries are centered horizontally and vertically within their cells

Figure 2.16

Your screen should be similar to Figure 2.16

CHANGING THE TABLE STYLE

Next, you will add a color and other formatting changes to the table. To quickly make these enhancements, you will apply a table style. Like picture styles, **table styles** are combinations of shading colors, borders, and visual effects such as shadows and reflections that can be applied in one simple step. You also can create your own table style effects by selecting specific style elements such as borders and shadows individually using the ▨ ▾ Shading, ⊞ ▾ Borders, and ◯ ▾ Effects commands from the Table Styles group on the Table Tools Design tab.

Open the Table Tools Design tab.

Click ⏷ More in the Table Styles group to display the Table Styles gallery.

Point to several table styles to see how they look in Live Preview.

Choose Medium Style 2, Accent 2 from the gallery.

Click in the table to clear the selection and see the new format.

Save the file.

Your screen should be similar to Figure 2.17

Figure 2.17

The selected table style has been applied to the table. The enhancements added to the table greatly improve its appearance, and the table now displays the information in an attractive and easy-to-read manner.

Inserting and Enhancing Pictures

Now you are ready to enhance the presentation by adding several more graphics. As you have seen, you can easily locate and add Clip Art graphics to slides. Next you want to add a picture to the presentation that you have saved as a file on your computer. You will insert the picture and then learn how to crop and enhance it using a picture style.

INSERTING A GRAPHIC FROM A FILE

You want to add the picture to the opening slide, but before you can begin, you need to reposition the placeholders to make more room for an image.

1

● Select slide 1.

● Select the title and subtitle placeholders and drag them down to position them as shown in Figure 2.18.

Having Trouble?

Click on the second placeholder while holding down Ctrl to select them both.

Your screen should be similar to Figure 2.18

Figure 2.18

You want to see how a digital photograph of a litter of puppies you recently received from one of the foster parents would look.

2

● Open the Insert tab.

● Click in the Picture Images group.

● Change the location to your data file location.

● If necessary, click and choose Large Icons to display thumbnails.

Having Trouble?

In Windows Vista, click Views and choose Large Icon.

Your screen should be similar to Figure 2.19

Figure 2.19

Inserting and Enhancing Pictures   **PP2.21**

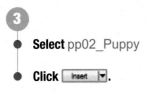
The Insert Picture dialog box is similar to the Open and Save dialog boxes, except that the only types of files listed are those with picture file extensions. A thumbnail preview of each picture is displayed above the file name.

3

● **Select** pp02_Puppy

● **Click** [Insert ▾].

Your screen should be similar to Figure 2.20

Figure 2.20

The picture is inserted in the center of the slide on top of the text. The Picture Tools Format tab is automatically displayed in the Ribbon, in anticipation that you may want to modify the graphic.

4 • Drag the bottom-right corner sizing handle inward to decrease its size to that shown in Figure 2.21.

Additional Information

To maintain an object's proportions while resizing it, hold down (Shift) while dragging the sizing handle.

Your screen should be similar to Figure 2.21

Figure 2.21

Although this is better, you decide it is not the right shape for the space. You decide that you can draw more attention to the dogs by cropping the picture on the slide.

CROPPING A GRAPHIC

Trimming or removing part of a picture is called **cropping**. Cropping removes the vertical or horizontal edges of a picture to help focus attention on a particular area. You will remove the upper part of the picture by cropping it to show the puppies only. This will make the picture smaller and rectangular shaped.

Figure 2.22

- **Click** [Crop] **from the Size group.**

- **Point to the upper-left corner of the photo, and when the mouse pointer changes to a [icon], drag down to just above the puppies.**

- **Click** [Crop] **from the Size group to turn off this feature.**

The upper part of the picture has been removed, leaving the puppies as the focus of attention. Next you want to increase the graphic's size and position it in the space above the title.

Your screen should be similar to Figure 2.22

2

● Size the picture as in Figure 2.23 (approximately 3 by 4.5 inches).

Additional Information

The Shape Height and Shape Width buttons in the Size group display the current shape's size as you drag.

● Open the [icon] Align drop-down menu in the Arrange group of the Picture Tools Format tab and choose Align Center.

● If necessary, position the graphic vertically on the slide as shown in Figure 2.23.

Your screen should be similar to Figure 2.23

Figure 2.23

ENHANCING A PICTURE

You decide to enhance the graphic on the title slide to match the picture effects that you applied to the question mark clip art image on slide 2. Repeating the same picture effects here will add consistency to the presentation. First you will select a picture style.

- Click ⊽ More in the Picture Styles group to display all the options in the Picture Styles gallery.

- Choose Beveled Oval, Black from the Picture Styles group.

- Click ☑ Picture Border ▾ and choose Blue, Accent 2 in the Theme Colors section of the gallery.

- Click ☐ Picture Effects ▾ and choose No Shadow from the Shadow group.

Your screen should be similar to Figure 2.24

Beveled Oval, Black style applied

Border changed to Blue, Accent 2

Figure 2.24

The addition of the picture of the puppies makes the title slide much more interesting and effective.

Inserting and Enhancing Shapes

At the end of the presentation, you want to add a concluding slide. This slide needs to be powerful, because it is your last chance to convince your audience to join Animal Angels.

ADDING A SHAPE

To create the concluding slide, you will duplicate slide 1 and then replace the picture with a graphic of a heart that you will create. To quickly add a shape, you will use one of the ready-made shapes supplied with PowerPoint. These shapes include rectangles and circles, lines, a variety of basic shapes, block arrows, flowchart symbols, stars and banners, action buttons, and callouts.

Additional Information

Most shapes also can be inserted from the Clip Organizer as well.

1

- Duplicate slide 1.

- Move slide 2 to the end of the presentation.

- Select the picture and press `Delete`.

- Click in the Drawing group of the Home tab.

Having Trouble?

If a small gallery of shapes is displayed in the Drawing group instead of, click ⊽ to open the Shapes gallery.

Another Method

You also can access the Shapes gallery using on the Insert tab.

Your screen should be similar to Figure 2.25

Additional Information

The selected shape will be added to the Recently Used Shapes section of the Shapes gallery.

Figure 2.25

Next, you need to select the shape you want from the Shapes gallery and then indicate where you want the shape inserted on the slide. When inserting a shape, the mouse pointer appears as $+$ when pointing to the slide. Then, to insert the shape, click on the slide and drag to increase the size.

2

- Click Heart in the Basic Shapes section.

- Click above the title on the slide and drag to insert and enlarge the heart.

Another Method

To maintain the height and width proportions of the shape, hold down [Shift] while you drag.

- Size and position the heart as in Figure 2.26.

Additional Information

A shape can be sized and moved just like any other object.

Your screen should be similar to Figure 2.26

Figure 2.26

The heart shape is inserted and the Drawing Tools Format tab is available.

ENHANCING A SHAPE

Next, you will enhance the heart graphic's appearance by selecting a shape style and adding a reflection. Just like the other styles in PowerPoint 2010, **shape styles** consist of combinations of fill colors, outline colors, and effects.

1

- Open the Drawing Tools Format tab.

- Click ⊽ More in the Shape Styles group to open the Shape Styles gallery.

- Choose Intense Effect—Green, Accent 1 from the Shape Styles gallery.

- Click 🟩 Shape Effects ⊽ and choose Half Reflection, 4 pt offset from the Reflection gallery.

Additional Information

The offset controls the amount of space between the object and the reflection.

Your screen should be similar to Figure 2.27

Figure 2.27

The addition of style and reflection effects greatly improves the appearance of the heart.

ADDING TEXT TO A SHAPE

Next, you will add text to the heart object. Text can be added to all shapes and becomes part of the shape; when the shape is moved, the text moves with it.

1

- Right-click on the heart to open the shortcut menu, and choose Edit Text.

- Type Open Your Heart

Having Trouble?

If the inserted text does not fit into the heart shape, increase the size of the heart.

Your screen should be similar to Figure 2.28

Figure 2.28

Inserting and Enhancing Shapes   **PP2.29**

Next, you want to improve the appearance of the text using character effects.

2

- Select the text in the heart.

- Click **B** Bold and **I** Italic on the Mini toolbar.

- Increase the font size to 24 points.

- Open the **A** Font Color gallery and choose Blue, Accent 2 in the Theme Colors section.

- Click outside the heart to deselect the shape.

Your screen should be similar to Figure 2.29

Figure 2.29

ROTATING THE OBJECT

Finally, you want to change the angle of the heart. You can rotate an object 90 degrees left or right, flip it vertically or horizontally, or specify an exact degree of rotation. You will change the angle of the heart to the right using the 🖈

rotate handle for the selected object, which allows you to rotate the object to any degree in any direction.

Additional Information

Holding down (Shift) while slowly dragging the rotate handle rotates the object in 15-degree increments.

Another Method

You also can use 🔄 in the Arrange group of the Drawing Tools Format tab to rotate an object.

- **Select the heart graphic.**

- **Drag the rotate handle to the right slightly.**

Additional Information

The mouse pointer appears as when positioned on the rotate handle, and Live Preview shows how the object will look as you rotate it.

Your screen should be similar to Figure 2.30

Figure 2.30

The graphic is a nice addition to the final slide of the presentation.

Working with Text Boxes

On slide 12, you want to add the foundation's contact information. To make it stand out on the slide, you will put it into a text box. A **text box** is a container for text or graphics. The text box can be moved, resized, and enhanced in other ways to make it stand out from the other text on the slide.

CREATING A TEXT BOX

First you create the text box, and then you add the content. When inserting a text box, the mouse pointer appears as ⌶ when pointing to the slide. Then, to create the text box, click on the slide and drag to increase the size.

1

- **Display slide 12.**

- **Open the Insert tab.**

- **Click** [A] **in the Text group.**

- **Click below the bullets and drag to the right.**

Your screen should be similar to Figure 2.31

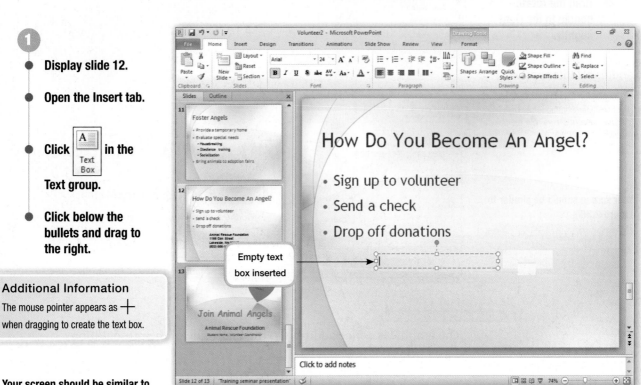

Figure 2.31

The text box is created and is a selected object. It is surrounded with a dashed border indicating you can enter, delete, select, and format the text inside the box.

ADDING TEXT TO A TEXT BOX

The text box displays a cursor, indicating that it is waiting for you to enter the text. As you type the text in the text box, it will increase in length automatically as needed to display the entire entry.

1

- Type the organization's name and address shown below in the text box. Press Enter to start a new line.

Animal Rescue Foundation

1166 Oak Street

Lakeside, NH 03112

(603) 555-1313

- Select all the text and increase the font size to 24 points and bold.

- If necessary, increase the width of the text box to display the name of the foundation on a single line.

Your screen should be similar to Figure 2.32

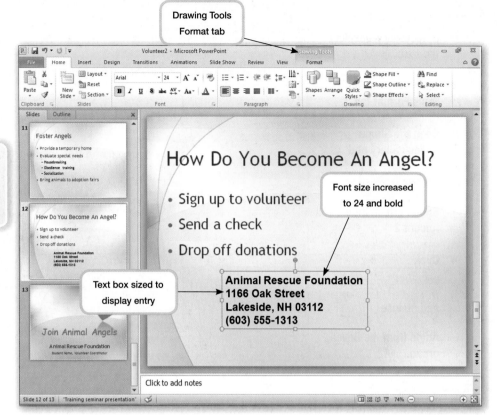

Figure 2.32

The text box is now more prominent and the content is easier to read.

ENHANCING THE TEXT BOX

Like any other object, the text box can be sized and moved anywhere on the slide. It also can be enhanced by adding styles and effects. You want to change the color and add a bevel effect around the box to define the space.

1

- If necessary, deselect the text.

- Open the Drawing Tools Format tab.

- Open the Shape Styles gallery and choose **Abc** Subtle Effect, Blue Accent 2.

- Click **Shape Effects ▾** and choose Angle from the Bevel group.

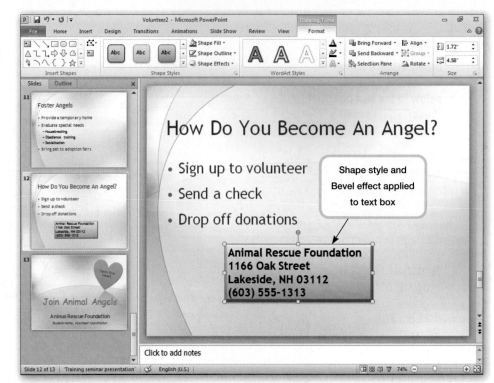

Figure 2.33

Your screen should be similar to Figure 2.33

Next, you will position the text within the text box and the box on the slide. You want to expand the margin on either side of the text to focus the attention on the text and not the box. By default, PowerPoint uses the AutoFit feature on text boxes, which automatically sizes the text box to fit around the text. You'll want to turn off the AutoFit feature so that you control the position of the text.

2

- Right-click within the text of the text box and choose Format Text Effects.

- Select Do Not AutoFit.

- Change the left and right internal margins to .3.

- Choose Middle Centered in the Vertical Alignment drop-down box.

- Close the Format Text Effects dialog box.

- Adjust the size of the text box to display the information as in Figure 2.34.

- Move the text box to the position shown in Figure 2.34.

- Deselect the text box.

- Save the presentation.

Your screen should be similar to Figure 2.34

NOTE If you are ending your session now exit PowerPoint 2010. When you begin again, open this file.

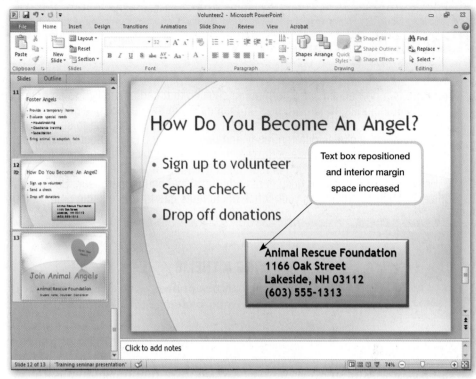

Figure 2.34

The information in the text box now stands out from the other information on the slide.

Changing the Presentation Design

When you first started this presentation, you used a PowerPoint template that included sample text as well as color and design elements. Now you are satisfied with the presentation's basic content and organization, but you would like to change its design style and appearance by applying a different document theme.

Concept [4] Theme

A **theme** is a predefined set of formatting choices that can be applied to an entire document in one simple step. PowerPoint includes 40 named, built-in themes. Each theme includes three subsets of components: colors, fonts, and effects. Each theme consists of 12 colors that are applied to specific elements in a document. Each font component includes different body and heading fonts. Each effects component includes different line and fill effects. You also can create your own custom themes by modifying an existing document theme and saving it as a custom theme. The default presentation uses the Office Theme.

Using themes gives your documents a professional and modern look. Because themes are shared across Office 2010 applications, all your Office documents can have the same uniform look.

APPLYING A THEME

A theme can be applied to the entire presentation or to selected slides. In this case, you want to change the design for the entire presentation.

1

- Display slide 1.

- Open the Design tab.

- Click ⏷ More in the Themes group to open the Themes gallery.

- Point to [Aa] Office Theme.

Your screen should be similar to Figure 2.35

Figure 2.35

The Themes gallery displays samples of the document themes. The This Presentation area displays a preview of the theme that is currently used in the presentation. This is the theme associated with the presentation template you used to start the presentation. The Built-In area displays examples of the themes that are available in PowerPoint. The Live Preview shows how the presentation would look if the Office Theme were used. As you can see, the slide colors, background designs, font styles, and overall layout of the slide are affected by the theme.

You will preview several other themes, and then use the Austin theme for the presentation.

2

● Preview several other themes.

● Choose the Austin theme.

Your screen should be similar to Figure 2.36

Figure 2.36

Additional Information

To apply a theme to selected slides, preselect the slides to apply the themes to in the Slide pane, and use the Apply to Selected Slides option from the theme's shortcut menu.

The Austin theme has been applied to all slides in the presentation. When a new theme is applied, the text styles, graphics, and colors that are included in the design replace the previous design settings. Consequently, the layout may need to be adjusted. For example, the photo on slide 1 will need to be repositioned and sized.

However, if you had made individual changes to a slide, such as changing the font of the title, these changes are not updated to the new theme design. In this case, the title font is still the Comic Sans MS that you selected; however, it has a smaller point size.

3

- Use the Slides tab to select each slide and check the layout.

- Make the adjustments shown in the table below to the indicated slides.

- Switch to Slide Sorter view to see how all your changes look.

- Reduce the zoom to display all the slides in the window.

Your screen should be similar to Figure 2.37

Figure 2.37

Slide	Adjustment
1	Increase the size of the graphic slightly. Realign the graphic to the center of the slide.
2	If needed, adjust the position of the text content placeholder so the bullets align with the title text. If needed, adjust the size of the graphic and reposition it slightly.
5	Select both content placeholders and move them slightly to the right to align the bullets with the title text.
6	Appropriately adjust the size and position of the table.
7	Reduce the width of the content placeholder so that more than one word wraps to a second line.
12	Adjust the position of the text box as needed.
13	If necessary, rotate, move, and resize the heart to fit the upper-right area of the slide.

CHANGING THE THEME COLORS

To make the presentation livelier, you decide to try changing the colors associated with the selected theme. Although each theme has an associated set of colors, you can change the colors by applying the colors from another theme to the selected theme.

1

- Display slide 1 in Normal view.

- Open the Design tab.

- Click Colors ▾ in the Themes group.

Your screen should be similar to Figure 2.38

Figure 2.38

Additional Information

The colors in the ▦ Colors ▾ button reflect the current theme colors.

The colors used in each of the themes are displayed in the Built-In drop-down list. Each theme's colors consist of eight coordinated colors that are applied to different slide elements. The Austin theme colors are selected because they are the set of colors associated with the Austin theme. You want to see how the colors used in the Oriel theme would look.

2

- Preview several other color themes.

- Select the Oriel theme colors.

Your screen should be similar to Figure 2.39

Figure 2.39

The slides are all converted to the colors used in the Oriel theme. You like the slightly softer colors associated with the Oriel theme. Using predefined theme colors gives your presentation a professional and consistent look.

CHANGING THE BACKGROUND STYLE

Although you like the color theme of the presentation now, you think it is a bit too dark. The quickest way to brighten up the look of a presentation is to change the background style. **Background styles** are a set of theme colors and textures that you can apply to the back of your slides.

The PowerPoint Background Styles gallery contains four background colors that can be combined with the three theme backgrounds, giving you twelve different background style options. In addition to the preselected background colors, you can also apply a picture, clip art, or watermark as a background style. When you apply one of these elements or use one of the built-in styles, you can make your presentation truly unique.

Click
Background Styles ▾
in the Background group of the Design tab.

Choose Style 2.

Your screen should be similar to Figure 2.40

Figure 2.40

Background Style 2 has been applied to all slides in the presentation. Whenever you change the background style or theme colors of a presentation, you should go back through the presentation and adjust font and graphic colors as necessary. For example, the picture border on slide 1 needs to be changed to make it stand out more from the background. Also you want to change the title text color on the opening and closing slides from orange to a deep red.

2

- Select the picture on slide 1 and change the border color to the Red, Accent 3 theme color (top row, seventh column).

- Click

  from the Picture Styles group.

- Select Weight and then choose 2¼ pt.

- Change the color of the title font on slides 1 and 13 to the Red, Accent 3 Theme color.

- Make slide 1 active.

- Save the presentation.

Your screen should be similar to Figure 2.41

Figure 2.41

Working with Master Slides

While viewing the slides, you think the slide appearance could be further improved by changing the bullet design on all slides. Although you can change each slide individually, you can make the change much faster to all the slides by changing the slide master.

Concept 5 Master

A **master** is part of a template that stores information about the formatting for the three key components of a presentation—slides, speaker notes, and handouts. Each component has a master associated with it. The masters are described below.

Slide master	Defines the format and layout of text and objects on a slide, text and object placeholder sizes, text styles, backgrounds, color themes, effects, and animation.
Handout master	Defines the format and placement of the slide image, text, headers, footers, and other elements that will appear on every handout.
Notes master	Defines the format and placement of the slide image, note text, headers, footers, and other elements that will appear on all speaker notes.

Any changes you make to a master affect all slides, handouts, or notes associated with that master. Each theme comes with its own slide master. When you apply a new theme to a presentation, all slides and masters are updated to those of the new theme. Using the master to modify or add elements to a presentation ensures consistency and saves time.

You can create slides that differ from the slide master by changing the format and placement of elements in the individual slide rather than on the slide master. For example, when you changed the font settings of the title on the title slide, the slide master was not affected. Only the individual slide changed, making it unique. If you have created a unique slide, the elements you changed on that slide retain their uniqueness, even if you later make changes to the slide master. That is the reason that the title font did not change when you changed the theme.

MODIFYING THE SLIDE MASTER

You will change the title text font color and the bullet style in the slide master so that all slides in the presentation will be changed.

1

● Open the View tab.

● Click [Slide Master icon] in the **Master Views group.**

Another Method

You also can hold down Shift and click ⊞ Normal View in the status bar to display Slide Master view.

Your screen should be similar to Figure 2.42

Figure 2.42

Additional Information

Every presentation contains at least one slide master. Each slide master contains one or more built-in or custom layouts.

The view has changed to Slide Master view, and a new tab, Slide Master, is displayed. Slide Master view consists of two panes: the slide thumbnail pane on the left containing slide thumbnails for the slide master and for each of the layouts associated with the slide master and the Slide pane on the right displaying the selected slide. In the slide thumbnail pane, the slide master is the larger slide image, and the associated layouts are positioned below the slide master. The slide master and all supporting layouts appear in the current theme, Austin, with the Oriel theme colors. Each slide layout displays a different layout arrangement. The thumbnail for the Title Slide Layout is selected, and the Slide pane displays the slide.

If you modify the slide master, all layouts beneath the slide master are also changed. If you modify a slide layout, although you are essentially also modifying the slide master, the changes effect only that layout under the slide master. You want to change the slide master so that your changes effect all the associated layouts.

Point to the thumbnails to see the ScreenTip.

Additional Information

The ScreenTip identifies the selected master or layout and the slides where it is used in the presentation.

Click on the Austin Slide Master thumbnail to select it.

Your screen should be similar to Figure 2.43

Figure 2.43

The Austin Slide Master consists of five area placeholders that control the appearance of all slides: title, content, date, slide number, and footer. The title and content areas display sample text to show you how changes you make in these areas will appear. You make changes to the slide master in the same way that you change any other slide. First you will change the font color for the title text throughout the presentation to match the dark red you applied to slides 1 and 13.

Click on the title area placeholder border to select it.

Having Trouble?

Do not select an individual item within the content area or the changes will be applied to that item only.

Open the Home tab.

Click A **to apply the selected color (Red, Accent 3 Theme color).**

Your screen should be similar to Figure 2.44

Figure 2.44

Next, you will modify the content area placeholder and change the current round bullet style to a picture bullet style.

4

- Click on the content area placeholder border to select it.

- Open the ☰ ▾ Bullets drop-down menu.

- Choose Bullets and Numbering.

- Click Picture....

Your screen should be similar to Figure 2.45

Figure 2.45

From the Picture Bullet dialog box, you select the bullet design you want to use from the bullet styles listed. You will use a round bullet design in a color that coordinates with the theme colors.

Figure 2.46

Working with Master Slides   **PP2.45**

The selected bullet style has been applied to all levels of items in the content area and to all layouts under the slide master that have bulleted items.

Now you want to see how the changes you have made to the slide master have affected the actual slides in the presentation.

- Click Slide Sorter view.

- Increase the magnification to 100%.

Your screen should be similar to Figure 2.47

Figure 2.47

You can now see that the change you made to the bullet style in the slide master is reflected in all slides in the presentation. Using the slide master allows you to quickly make global changes to your presentation.

You will run the slide show next to see how the changes you have made look full screen.

7

- Run the slide show beginning with slide 1.

- Click on each slide to advance through the presentation.

- Save the presentation.

Now that you are happy with the look of the presentation, you want to incorporate animation effects to change the way the text appears on the slides.

Animating the Presentation

You are pleased with the changes you have made to the presentation so far. However, you have several places in mind where using animation will make the presentation more interesting.

Concept 6 Animations

Animations are special effects that add action to text and graphics so they move around on the screen during a slide show. Animations provide additional emphasis for items or show the information on a slide in phases. There are two basic types of animations: object animations and transitions.

Object animations are used to display each bullet point, text, paragraph, or graphic independently of the other text or objects on the slide. You set up the way you want each element to appear (to fly in from the left, for instance) and whether you want the other elements already on the slide to dim or shimmer when a new element is added. For example, because your audience is used to reading from left to right, you could select animations that fly text in from the left. Then, when you want to emphasize a point, bring a bullet point in from the right. That change grabs the audience's attention.

Transitions control the way that the display changes as you move from one slide to the next during a presentation. You can select from many different transition choices. You may choose Dissolve for your title slide to give it an added flair. After that, you could use Wipe Right for all the slides until the next to the last, and then use Dissolve again to end the show. As with any special effect, use slide transitions carefully.

When you present a slide show, the content of your presentation should take center stage. You want the animation effects to help emphasize the main points in your presentation—not draw the audience's attention to the special effects.

ADDING TRANSITION EFFECTS

First, you want to add a transition effect to the slides. Although you can add transitions in Normal view, you will use Slide Sorter view so you can more easily preview the action on the slides.

1

- Switch to Slide Sorter view, if necessary.

- Select slide 1.

- Open the Transitions tab.

- Click ⏷ More in the Transition to This Slide group to open the Transitions gallery.

Your screen should be similar to Figure 2.48

Figure 2.48

There are three transition categories, Subtle, Exciting and Dynamic Content, with each containing variations on the category effect. You want to use a simple transition effect that will display as each slide appears. As you choose a transition effect next, watch the live preview of the effect on the selected slide.

Figure 2.49

2

- **Click** [Wipe icon] **Wipe in the Subtle category.**

- **Click** [Effect Options icon] **Effect Options in the Transition to This Slide group.**

- **Click** [From Left icon] **From Left.**

Having Trouble?

If you want to see the transition effect again, click [icon] below the slide in Slide Sorter view.

Another Method

You can also see the transition effect that is applied to a slide by selecting the slide and clicking [Preview icon] in the Preview group of the Transitions tab.

Your screen should be similar to Figure 2.49

Additional Information

You also can select transition effects from the Transitions gallery by scrolling the list in the Transition to This Slide group.

The selected slide displays the Wipe Left transition effect. This effect displays the next slide's content by wiping over the previous slide from the right with the new slide content. You want to use the same effect on slide 13. For the final slide, you want to use the default Wipe direction, which is from the right. You also want to try a similar effect on the other slides using the Push transition effect.

3

● Select slide 13.

● Click Wipe in
the Transition to This
Slide group.

● Select slides 2–12.

Having Trouble?

Select slide 2 and hold down ⇧Shift
while selecting slide 12.

● Choose [Push icon] Push
in the Transition to
This Slide group.

Your screen should be similar to
Figure 2.50

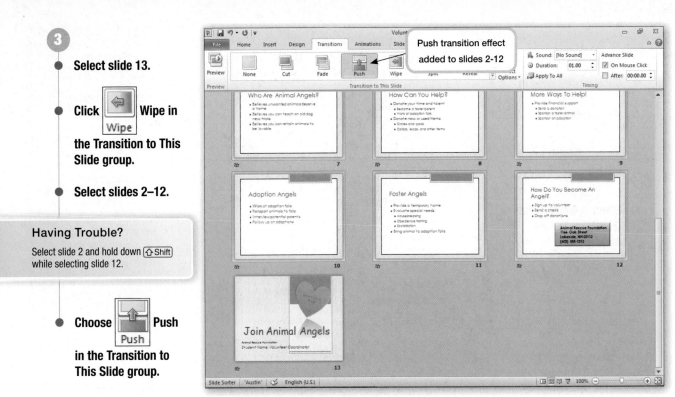

Figure 2.50

The transition animation effects associated with the selected slides were individually previewed beginning with slide 2, and each slide now displays a transition icon.

4

● Switch to Normal view.

● Save the presentation.

Notice an animation icon appears below each slide number in the Slides tab.

ANIMATING AN OBJECT

Next, you want to add an animation effect to the heart shape on the final slide. There are four different types of animation effects, described below. Animation effects can be used by themselves or in combination with other effects.

Type	Effect
Entrance	Makes an object appear on the slide using the selected effect.
Exit	Makes an object leave the slide using the selected effect.
Emphasis	Makes an object more noticeable by applying special effects to the object such as changing the text size and colors or adding bold or underlines.
Motion Path	Makes an object move in a selected pattern such as up, down, or in a circle.

1

- Display slide 13 in Normal view.

- Select the heart shape.

- Open the Animations tab.

- Point to several effects in the Animation group to see the Live Preview.

- Choose .

Your screen should be similar to Figure 2.51

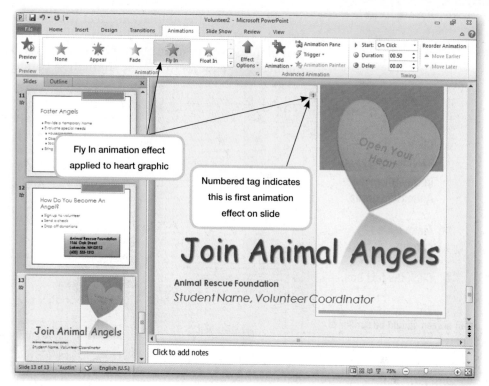

Figure 2.51

As you add animated items to a slide, each item is numbered. The number determines the order in which they display. A nonprinting numbered tag appears on the slide near each animated item that correlates to the effects in the list. This number does not appear during a slide show.

Next, you want to change the Fly In effect to come in from the left and to run slower.

2

- Click and choose From Left.

- In the Duration box in the Timing group, increase the duration to 1.00.

- Click in Preview the Preview group to preview the new animation settings.

Your screen should be similar to Figure 2.52

Figure 2.52

Animating the Presentation   **PP2.51**

You like the way the animation effect livens up the final slide of the presentation, so you decide to apply the same effect to the text box on slide 12. Since you plan to use the same animation settings for both slides, the easiest way to duplicate an effect is to use the Animation Painter.

3

- **Click**
  ⭐ **Animation Painter**
  in the Advanced Animation group.

- **Make slide 12 current.**

- **Click the text box.**

Your screen should be similar to Figure 2.53

Figure 2.53

The Fly In animation effect is applied to the text box and previewed for you.

ADDING SOUND EFFECTS

Now that you have added animations to your presentation, you decide to give the animation on slide 13 extra emphasis by adding sound to the animation effect. To add the more advanced animation effects, you need to display the Animation pane.

- Select the heart on slide 13.

- Click in the Advanced Animation group.

- Click ▶ Play in the Animation pane.

Your screen should be similar to Figure 2.54

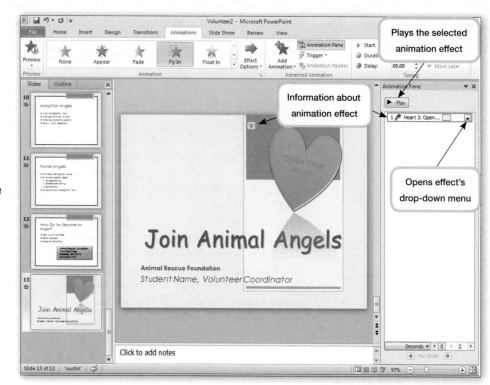

Figure 2.54

Additional Information

You will learn more about using the Animation pane in later labs.

This pane shows information about each animation effect on a slide. This includes the type of effect, the order of multiple effects in relation to one another, the name of the object affected, and the duration of the effect. It also is used to manage the animations and to add advanced effects to existing animations. You will use it to add a sound to the Fly In effect.

2

- Open the `1 ★ Heart 1: Open... ▼` drop-down menu and choose Effect Options.

- From the Sound drop-down list choose Chime.

- Click OK .

Additional Information

You must have a speaker and a sound card to hear the sound.

- Run the slide show beginning with the current slide.

- Click on the slide to start the animation.

- Press Esc to end the slide show.

The slide transition effect is followed by the heart fly-in animation and the sound effect being played as it will when the slide show is run. You had to click the mouse button to start the heart animation, because this is the default setting to start an animation.

ANIMATING A SLIDE MASTER

The next effect you want to add to the slides is an animation effect that will display each bullet or numbered item progressively on a slide. When the animation is applied to a slide, the slide initially shows only the title. The bulleted text appears as the presentation proceeds. You want to add this effect to all the slides that have bulleted items (slides 2–5 and 7–12). However, you do not want slide 5, which contains the foundation's history, to display with an animation because you want the history to appear all at the same time.

To apply the animation to the bulleted items, you could add the effect to each slide individually. However, when there are many slides, it is faster to add the effect to the slide master so all slides based on the selected slide layout display the effect. You will move to slide 2, the first slide in the presentation to use bullets, and apply the animation effects to the associated slide layout under the slide master.

- **Make slide 2 current.**

- **Change to Slide Master view.**

- **Point to the slide layout thumbnail to see the slide layout name and confirm that the correct slides will be affected (Title and Content Layout: used by slide(s) 2–4, 6–9, 12).**

Having Trouble?

If this is not your selected slide master, change the selection to this master.

- **Select the content placeholder.**

- **Open the Animations tab.**

- **Scroll the Animation gallery to see the second row of effects.**

- **Click** **.**

- **Click** **and choose From Right.**

Your screen should be similar to Figure 2.55

Figure 2.55

Animation icons appear next to each bulleted item in the content placeholder, and the Animation pane displays the information about the animation. The preview demonstrated how this effect will appear on the slide. Although the slide master preview does not show it, each bullet will appear individually on the slide. You can confirm this because a number tab appears next to each bullet in the content area indicating that the effect will be applied to each line.

You also want to add a second animation effect to give more emphasis to the bulleted items. You will add the Darken animation effect and change the Start timing setting associated with the effect. The Start settings control the method used to advance the animation for each bullet item while you run the slide show. The default Start setting, On Click, means you need to click the mouse to start each animation effect. You want the Darken effect to begin automatically after the first animation effect is finished.

2

- Select the content placeholder again.

- Click **Add Animation** in the Advanced Animation group.

- Choose **Darken** from the Emphasis category.

- Click **Start:** in the Timing group and choose After Previous.

- Click **▶ Play** to view the effect.

Figure 2.56

Your screen should be similar to Figure 2.56

The preview showed that the Darken effect correctly started after the Wipe effect ended. You are concerned, however, that the timing for the Wipe effect is too fast and the Darken emphasis is too subtle. You will lengthen the duration for the Wipe effect and change the Darken emphasis to another.

3

- Click on 1 ⭐ Content Place... ☐ in the Animation pane to select it.

- Increase the Duration setting in the Timing group to 3.00.

- Click on ⭐ Content Place... in the Animation pane to select it.

- Choose **Bold Reveal** from the Animation gallery.

- Click ▶ Play.

Figure 2.57

Your screen should be similar to Figure 2.57

The changes in the animation effects are shown in the Animation pane and have been applied to slides 2–4, 6–9, and 12. To check how the animation effects actually appear in a slide, you will return to Normal view and preview the animations.

Additional Information

The bar in each effect in the Animation pane indicates the length of the duration.

4

- Change to Normal view and preview the animation on slide 2.

The preview demonstrates how the Wipe effect and then the Bold Reveal emphasis appears one-by-one on each bullet. Since you like the way the animation looks, you want to apply it to all the other bulleted slides except 5.

5

- Change to Slide Master view.

- Select the content placeholder.

- Click ⭐ Animation Painter in the Advanced Animation group of the Animations tab.

- Select the Title and Text Layout: used by slide(s) 10–11 slide master (second to last layout in Slide pane).

- Click the content placeholder.

Your screen should be similar to Figure 2.58

Figure 2.58

The same animation effects that are on the Title and Content Layout (slides 2–4, 6–9, and 12) have been quickly copied to the Title and Text Layout (slides 10–11). If a new slide were inserted using one of these layouts, it would have the same animation effects. However, if the layout for a slide containing animations were changed to another layout, it would then have the animation effects (if any) associated with that layout.

Now slides 1 and 5 are the only slides that are not animated. You will change back to Normal view and check the animation effects in several slides.

6

- Return to Normal view.

- Preview the animation on slides 10 and 11.

- Move to slide 5 and verify that there are no animations associated with it.

- Play the animation on slide 6.

You noticed on slide 11 that the animation effects were applied individually to first-level bullets, and any sub-bullets were included with the first-level bullets. This seems appropriate. The animation effect on slide 6 was applied to the table as a whole. This is because the slide was created using the Title and Content layout and the table is considered a single bulleted item.

REMOVING ANIMATION EFFECTS

You want to remove the animation from slide 6. However, because the animation is associated with the slide master, removing it would remove it from all slides using that layout. Instead, you will change the slide layout to another layout that does not have an animation associated with it. Then you will add some other animation effects to this slide and apply these same effects to slide 5.

1

- Change the slide layout of slide 6 to the Title Only layout.

- Center the table in the slide space.

- Select the title placeholder and apply the Fly In from Left animation.

- Change the Start setting to With Previous.

- Select the table, click **Add Animation** and choose the Random Bars animation.

- Copy the title placeholder animation to the title placeholder of slide 5.

- Copy the table animation from slide 6 to both content placeholders on slide 5.

- Preview the animations on slide 5.

Your screen should be similar to Figure 2.59

Figure 2.59

You like the title animation; however, you decide to remove the animations associated with the two content placeholders.

● **Select both content placeholders.**

Having Trouble?

Hold down ⇧Shift while clicking on each placeholder to select them both.

● **Choose** **from the Animations gallery.**

● **Play the animation on this slide.**

Your screen should be similar to Figure 2.60

Figure 2.60

Be careful when using animations, as sometimes too many animation effects distract from the slide content. You think your animation changes will add interest without making the presentation appear too lively. To see how the transitions and animations work together, you will run the slide show next.

3

● **Close the Animation pane.**

● **Save the presentation.**

As you run the slide show to see the animation effects, you will also practice preparing for the presentation. As much as you would like to control a presentation completely, the presence of an audience usually causes the presentation to change course. PowerPoint has several ways to control a slide show during the presentation.

NAVIGATING IN A SLIDE SHOW

Running the slide show and practicing how to control the slide show help you to have a smooth presentation. For example, if someone has a question about a previous slide, you can go backward and redisplay it. You will try out some of the features you can use while running the slide show.

1

- Start the slide show from the beginning.

- Click to advance to slide 2.

- Click 4 times to display the four bullets.

Your screen should be similar to Figure 2.61

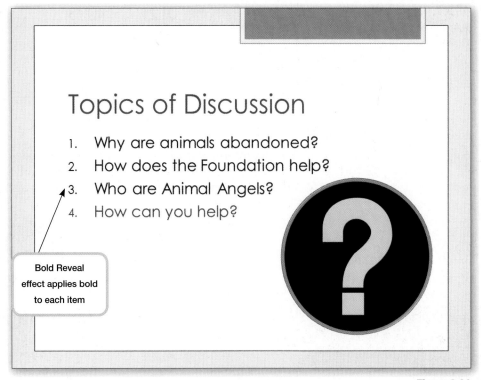

Figure 2.61

Another Method

You can also use the mouse wheel to move forward or backward through a presentation.

The first slide appeared using the Wipe From Left transition effect associated with the slide. The second slide appeared using the Push transition effect. Each bulleted item on slide 2 appeared when you clicked using the Wipe animation effect, and the Bold Reveal animation effect started automatically as soon as the last bullet appeared.

When an animation is applied to the content area of a slide, the content items are displayed only when you click or use any of the procedures to advance to the next slide. This is because the default setting to start an animation is On Click. This allows the presenter to focus the audience's attention and to control the pace of the presentation. The Bold Reveal associated with slide 2 started automatically because you changed the Start setting to After Previous.

2

● Continue to click or press [Spacebar] until the title of slide 8, "How Can You Help?", appears.

● Press [Backspace] (5 times).

Additional Information

You can return to the first slide in the presentation by holding down both mouse buttons for two seconds.

Your screen should be similar to Figure 2.62

Success Rate

Year	Rescues	Adoptions
2009	3759	3495
2010	3847	3784
2011	3982	3844
2012	4025	3943

Pressing [Backspace] moves backward through presentation

Figure 2.62

You returned the onscreen presentation to slide 6, but now, because the audience has already viewed slide 7, you want to advance to slide 8. To go to a specific slide number, you type the slide number and press [Enter].

3

● Type **8** and press [Enter].

Another Method

You also can choose Go to Slide from the shortcut menu and select a slide to display.

● Click two times to display the bulleted items.

● Click again to display slide 9.

Your screen should be similar to Figure 2.63

More Ways To Help!

Typing a slide number moves directly to that slide

Figure 2.63

Slide 9, More Ways To Help!, is displayed.

Sometimes a question from an audience member can interrupt the flow of the presentation. If this happens to you, you can black out the screen to focus attention on your response.

4

● Press b or B.

Additional Information

You also can white out the screen by pressing W.

The screen goes to black while you address the topic. When you are ready to resume the presentation, you can bring the slide back.

5

● Click, or press b.

● Click to display the bulleted items on slide 9.

ADDING FREEHAND ANNOTATIONS

During your presentation, you may want to point to an important word, underline an important point, or draw checkmarks next to items that you have covered. To do this, you can use the mouse pointer during the presentation. When you move the mouse, the mouse pointer appears and the Slide Show toolbar is displayed in the lower-left corner of the screen. The mouse pointer in its current shape can be used to point to items on the slide. You also can use it to draw on the screen by changing the mouse pointer to a ballpoint pen, felt-tip pen, or highlighter, which activates the associated freehand annotation feature.

1

● Move the mouse on your desktop to display the mouse pointer and the Slide Show toolbar.

● Click in the Slide Show toolbar to display the Pointer Options menu.

Another Method

You also can select Pointer Options from the shortcut menu.

Your screen should be similar to Figure 2.64

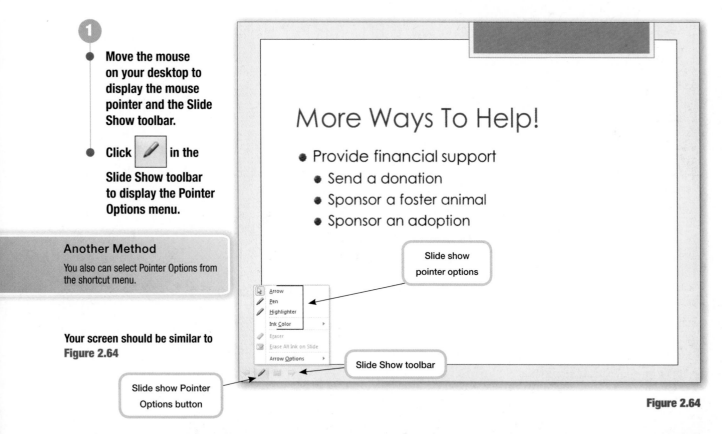

Figure 2.64

The mouse pointer and arrow options are described in the following table.

Pointer Options	Effect
Arrow	Displays the mouse pointer as an arrow.
Pen	Changes the mouse pointer to a diamond shape and turns on ballpoint pen annotation.
Highlighter	Changes the mouse pointer to a bar shape and turns on highlighter.
Ink Color	Displays a color palette to select a color for the annotation tool.
Eraser	Erases selected annotations.
Erase All Ink on Slide	Removes all annotations from the slide.
Arrow Options	(These options apply only if Arrow is selected.)
Automatic	Hides the mouse pointer if it is not moved for 15 seconds. It reappears when you move the mouse. This is the default setting.
Visible	Displays the mouse pointer as an arrow and does not hide it.
Hidden	Hides the mouse pointer until another pointer option is selected.

You will try out several of the freehand annotation features to see how they work. To draw, you select the pen style and then drag the pen pointer in the direction you want to draw.

● **Choose Pen.**

Another Method

You also can use Ctrl + P to display the Pen.

● **Move the dot pointer to near the word "Send" and then drag the dot pointer until a circle is drawn around the word "Send".**

● **Select Ink Color from the Pointer Options menu and choose Light Blue from the Standard Colors bar.**

Additional Information

The Automatic ink color setting determines the default color to use for annotations based upon the slide theme colors.

● **Draw three lines under the word "Help!".**

● **Choose Highlighter from the Pointer Options menu and highlight the word "donation".**

Additional Information

The mouse pointer changes shape depending upon the selected annotation tool.

Your screen should be similar to Figure 2.65

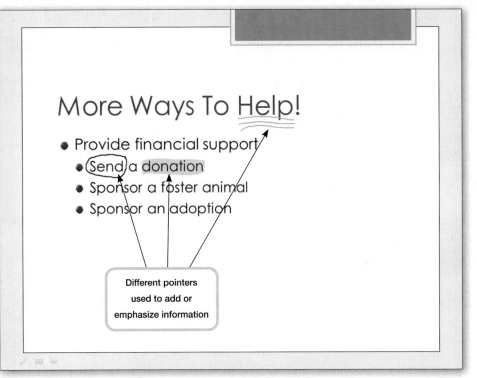

Figure 2.65

The freehand annotation feature allows you to point out and emphasize important information on a slide during the presentation.

③

● Practice using the freehand annotator to draw any shapes you want on the slide.

● To erase the annotations, choose Erase All Ink on Slide from the Pointer Options menu.

Another Method

The keyboard shortcut to erase annotations is E.

● To turn off freehand annotation, choose Arrow from the Pointer Options menu.

Another Method

You also can use Ctrl + A to display the arrow.

The freehand annotation feature allows you to point out and emphasize important information on a slide during the presentation.

Another feature that you can use to emphasize information on a slide is to change the mouse pointer to a laser pointer.

④

● Click to display the four bulleted items on slide 10.

● Press Ctrl and hold down the left mouse button to turn the mouse pointer into a laser light.

Additional Information

You can control the color of the laser light by clicking Set Up Slideshow on the Slide Show tab. You can then click the Laser pointer color drop-down list to choose a different color.

● Use the laser pointer to point to the first bulleted item on the slide.

Adoption Angels

● Work at adoption fairs
● Transport animals to fairs
● Interview potential parents
● Follow up on adoptions

Laser pointer

Your screen should be similar to Figure 2.66

Figure 2.66

The laser pointer is much brighter than the regular mouse pointer; however, it is not as convenient because you have to hold Ctrl while using the feature.

If you do not erase annotations before ending the presentation, you are prompted to keep or discard the annotations when you end the slide show. If you keep the annotations, they are saved to the slides and will appear as part of the slide during a presentation.

Adding Speaker Notes

When making your presentation, there are some critical points you want to be sure to discuss. To help you remember the important points, you can add notes to a slide and then print the **notes pages**. These pages display the notes below a small version of the slide they accompany. You can create notes pages for some or all of the slides in a presentation. You decide to add speaker notes on slide 9 to remind you to suggest foster care donations.

1

- Press ⎋Esc to end the slide show.

- Display slide 9 in Normal view.

- Increase the size of the Notes pane to that shown in Figure 2.67.

> **Having Trouble?**
>
> Adjust the size of the notes pane by dragging the pane splitter bar.

- Click in the Notes pane and type the following:

  Suggested foster animal donations per month

  Cat: $10

  Dog: $15/small $20/medium $25/large

> **Having Trouble?**
>
> Press ⭾Tab to separate the dollar amounts.

Your screen should be similar to Figure 2.67

Figure 2.67

You will preview the notes page to check its appearance before it is printed.

- Open the View tab.

- Click in the Presentation Views group.

Your screen should be similar to Figure 2.68

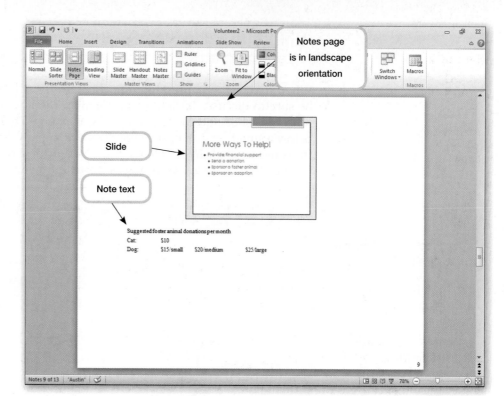

Figure 2.68

The notes pages display the note you added below the slide that the note accompanies. The notes page is in landscape orientation because the orientation for handouts was set to landscape (end of Lab 1). The page orientation setting affects both handouts and notes pages and is saved with the file.

To make the speaker notes easier to read in a dimly lit room while you are making the presentation, you will increase the font size of the note text.

3

- Click on the note text to select the placeholder.

- Select the note text.

- Use the Mini toolbar to increase the font size to 20.

- Click outside the note text border.

Your screen should be similar to Figure 2.69

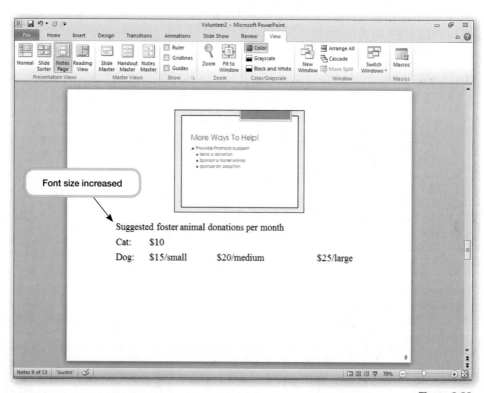

Figure 2.69

Adding Headers and Footers

Currently, the only information that appears in the footer of the notes page is the page number. You want to include additional information in the header and footer of the notes and handouts. The header and footer typically display information inside the margin space at the top and bottom of each printed page. Additionally, slides also may include header and footer information.

ADDING A HEADER TO A NOTES PAGE

You want to include the date and your name in the header of the notes pages.

1

- Open the Insert tab.

- Click in the Text group.

- If necessary, open the Notes and Handouts tab.

Your screen should be similar to Figure 2.70

Figure 2.70

On notes and handouts, you can include header text and a page number. The Preview box identifies the four areas where this information will appear and identifies the currently selected areas, in this case page number, in bold.

● Choose **Date and Time** to turn on this option and, if necessary, choose **Update Automatically**.

● Choose **Header** and enter your name in the Header text box.

● Click � Apply to All ⎤.

Your screen should be similar to Figure 2.71

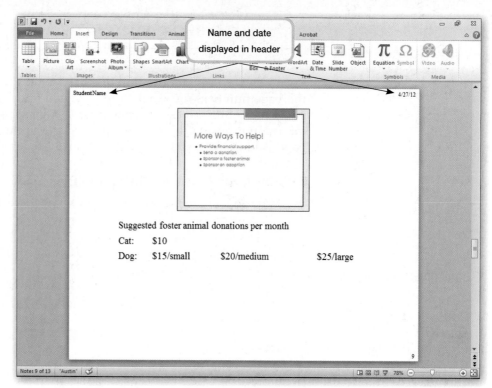

Figure 2.71

The information is displayed in the header as specified.

ADDING SLIDE FOOTER TEXT

You also would like to include the name of the foundation and slide number in a footer on the slides. The slide master controls the placement and display of the footer information but does not control the information that appears in those areas.

- Switch to Slide Sorter view.

- Click in the Text group.

- If necessary, open the Slide tab.

Your screen should be similar to Figure 2.72

Figure 2.72

Slides can display the date and time, slide number, or footer text. The Preview box shows the location of the placeholders for each of these elements on the selected slide. When specified, this information can be displayed on all slides or selected slides only. You also can turn off the display of this information in title slides only. You would like to add the foundation name in the footer and the slide number to all slides, except the title slides.

2

- **Choose the Slide Number option.**

- **Choose the Footer option.**

- **Type Animal Rescue Foundation in the Footer text box.**

- **Choose the Don't Show on Title Slide option.**

- **Click** Apply to All .

Additional Information

The Apply command button applies the settings to the current slide or selected slides only.

- **Double-click slide 3.**

- **Save the presentation.**

Your screen should be similar to Figure 2.73

Figure 2.73

Additional Information

You can also delete the footer and slide number placeholders from individual slides to remove this information.

The text you entered is displayed in the Footer area placeholder, and the slide number appears in the blue bar. No footer information is displayed on the first or last slides in the presentation because they use the Title Slide layout.

You have created both slides and a notes page for the presentation. Now you want to print the notes page and some of the slides. Customizing the print settings by selecting specific slides to print and scaling the size of the slides to fill the page are a few of the ways to make your printed output look more professional.

PRINTING NOTES PAGES

First you will print the notes page for the slide on which you entered note text.

1

- Make slide 9 current.

- Open the File tab and choose Print.

- If necessary, select the printer.

- Choose Print Current Slide as the slide to print.

- Choose Notes Pages as the layout.

- Change the orientation to Portrait Orientation.

- If necessary, change the color setting to Grayscale.

Your screen should be similar to Figure 2.74

> Preview of notes page in grayscale and portrait orientation

Figure 2.74

The notes page is displayed in grayscale and in portrait orientation, as it will appear when printed.

2

- Click .

Additional Information

To print multiple Notes pages, enter the slide number of each slide (separated by commas) you want to print in the Slides text box.

PRINTING SELECTED SLIDES

Next you will print a few selected slides to be used as handouts. You will change the orientation to portrait and scale the slides to fit the paper size.

1

- Open the File tab and choose Print.

- In the Slides text box, type **1,6,12,13**

Additional Information

The print setting automatically changes to Custom Range.

- Specify Handouts 4 Slides Horizontal as the layout.

- Choose Scale to Fit Paper from the Layout drop-down menu.

- If necessary, change the color setting to Grayscale.

Your screen should be similar to Figure 2.75

Figure 2.75

The four selected slides are displayed in portrait orientation, and the slide images were sized as large as possible to fill the page.

2

- **Print the handout.**

- **Open the File tab and if necessary, choose Info.**

- **In the Properties pane, enter** your name **in the Author text box.**

- **In the Tags text box, enter** Volunteer, Recruit

- **Save the completed presentation.**

- **Exit PowerPoint.**

The view you are in when you save the file is the view that will be displayed when the file is opened.

FOCUS ON CAREERS

EXPLORE YOUR CAREER OPTIONS

Communications Specialist

Are you interested in technology? Could you explain technology in words and pictures? Communications specialists, also known as public relations specialists, assist sales and marketing management with communications media and advertising materials that represent the company's products and services to customers. In high-tech industries, you will take information from scientists and engineers and use PowerPoint to transform the data into eye-catching presentations that communicate effectively. You also may create brochures, develop Web sites, create videos, and write speeches. If you thrive in a fast-paced and high-energy environment and work well under the pressure of deadlines, then this job may be for you. Typically a bachelor's degree in journalism, advertising, or communications is desirable. Typical salaries range from $38,400 to $98,000, depending on the industry. To learn more about this career, visit the Web site for the Bureau of Labor Statistics of the U.S. Department of Labor.

Find and Replace (PP2.5)

To make editing easier, you can use the Find and Replace feature to find text in a presentation and replace it with other text as directed.

Table (PP2.10)

A table is used to organize information into an easy-to-read format of horizontal rows and vertical columns.

Alignment (PP2.18)

Alignment controls how text entries are positioned within a space.

Theme (PP2.36)

A theme is a predefined set of formatting choices that can be applied to an entire document in one simple step.

Master (PP2.42)

A master is a special slide or page that stores information about the formatting for all slides in a presentation.

Animations (PP2.47)

Animations are special effects that add action to text and graphics so they move around on the screen during a slide show.

KEY TERMS

alignment PP2.18
animation PP2.47
background styles PP2.40
cell PP2.10
cropping PP2.23
Find and Replace PP2.5
master PP2.42
notes pages PP2.67
object animations PP2.47

rotate handle PP2.30
shape styles PP2.28
table PP2.10
table reference PP2.10
table styles PP2.19
text box PP2.31
theme PP2.36
transition PP2.47

COMMAND SUMMARY

Command	Shortcut	Action
Home tab		
Paragraph group		
Align Left	Ctrl + F	Aligns text to the left
Align Center	Ctrl + E	Centers text
Align Right	Ctrl + R	Aligns text to the right
Justify	Ctrl + F	Aligns text to both the left and right margins
Align Text		Sets vertical alignment of text
Drawing group		
Shapes		Inserts a shape
Editing group		
Find	Ctrl + F	Finds specified text
Replace	Ctrl + H	Replaces located text with replacement text
Insert tab		
Images group		
Picture		Inserts picture from a file
Illustrations group		
Shapes		Inserts a shape
Text group		
Text Box		Inserts text box or adds text to selected shape
Header & Footer		Inserts a header and footer
Design tab		
Themes group		
More		Opens gallery of document themes

COMMAND SUMMARY (CONTINUED)

Command	Shortcut	Action
■ Colors ▾		Changes the color for the current theme
Transitions tab		
Preview group		
Preview		Displays the transition effect
Transition to This Slide group		
Effect Options ▾		Opens a gallery of effect options
▼		Opens gallery of transition effects
Animations tab		
Preview group		
Preview		Displays the transition effect
Animation group		
Effect Options ▾		Opens a gallery of effect options
▼		Opens a gallery of animation effects
Advanced Animation group		
★ Preview		Adds animation effect to selected object
📝 Animation Pane		Opens the Animation pane
★ Animation Painter		Copies animation effect to another object
Timing group		
Start: ▾		Sets the trigger for the animation
⏱ Duration: 00.50 ▴▾		Controls the amount of time for the animation to complete
View tab		
Presentation Views group		
Notes Page		Displays current slide in Notes view to edit the speaker notes
Slide Master		Opens Slide Master view to change the design and layout of the master slides

COMMAND SUMMARY (CONTINUED)

Command	Shortcut	Action
Drawing Tools Format tab		
Shapes Styles group		
⏷ More		Opens the Shape Styles gallery to select a visual style to apply to a shape
Shape Effects ▾		Applies a visual effect to a shape
Arrange group		
⬁▾		Rotates or flips the selected object
Picture Tools Format tab		
Adjust group		
Color ▾		Recolors picture
Picture Styles		
⏷ More		Opens Picture Styles gallery to select an overall visual style for picture
Picture Effects ▾		Applies a visual effect to picture
Arrange group		
▤▾ Align		Aligns edges of multiple selected objects
Size group		
Crop		Crops off unwanted section of a picture
Table Tools Design tab		
Table Styles group		
⏷ More		Opens the Table Styles gallery to choose a visual style for a table
⬥▾ Shading		Colors background behind selected text or paragraph
⬚▾ Border		Applies a border style
⬧▾ Effects		Applies a visual effect to the table such as shadows and reflections
Table Tools Layout group		
Alignment group		
▤ Center		Centers the text within a cell
▤ Center Vertically		Centers the text vertically within a cell
Arrangement group		
▤▾ Align		Aligns edges of multiple selected objects

LAB EXERCISES

MATCHING

Match the item on the left with the correct description on the right.

1. rotate handle   ____ a. consists of 12 colors that are applied to specific elements in a document

2. color theme   ____ b. organizes information into an easy-to-read format of horizontal rows and vertical columns

3. table   ____ c. allows you to spin an object to any degree in any direction

4. object animation   ____ d. controls the way the display changes as you move from one slide to the next

5. animation   ____ e. predefined set of formatting choices that can be applied to an entire document

6. theme   ____ f. the intersection of a row and column

7. transition   ____ g. motion, such as clip art that flies in from the left

8. Animation Painter   ____ h. special effects that add action to text and graphics

9. master   ____ i. quickly copies an animation effect and applies it to a different object

10. cell   ____ j. slide that stores information about the formatting for all slides or pages in a presentation

TRUE/FALSE

Circle the correct answer to the following questions.

1. A master is a special slide or page on which the formatting for all slides or pages in your presentation is defined.   **True**   **False**

2. You can print 12 slides per page using notes pages.   **True**   **False**

3. Columns in a table are identified by letters.   **True**   **False**

4. When you create a footer, it is automatically applied to every slide in the presentation.   **True**   **False**

5. Masters are professionally created slide designs that can be applied to your presentation.   **True**   **False**

6. A theme can be applied to selected slides in a presentation.   **True**   **False**

7. Find and Replace makes it difficult to locate specific words or phrases.   **True**   **False**

8. Tables contain rows and columns.   **True**   **False**

9. Alignment controls the position of text entries in a placeholder.   **True**   **False**

10. When adding text to a text box in PowerPoint, the text box will lengthen automatically to display the entire entity.   **True**   **False**

FILL-IN

Complete the following statements by filling in the blanks with the correct terms.

1. _____ provides access to a combination of different formatting options such as edges, gradients, line styles, shadows, and three-dimensional effects.

2. Cells in a table are identified by a letter and number, called a _____.

3. Object _____ are used to display each bullet point, text, paragraph, or graphic independently of the other text or objects on the slide.

4. A _____ is a container for text or graphics.

5. The _____ slide is a special slide that stores information about the formatting for all slides or pages in a presentation.

6. _____ add action to text and graphics so they move on the screen.

7. _____ controls the position of text entries within a space.

8. The _____ tool allows you to change the shape of a graphic.

9. A _____ is part of a template that stores information about the formatting for the three key components of a presentation—slides, speaker notes, and handouts.

10. You can align text _____ in a table cell with the top, middle, or bottom of the cell space.

LAB EXERCISES

MULTIPLE CHOICE

Circle the letter of the correct response to the questions below.

1. A(n) _____ is a predefined set of formatting choices that can be applied to an entire document in one simple step.
   a. theme
   b. animation
   c. slide layout
   d. master

2. Each _____ theme consists of eight coordinated colors that are applied to different slide elements.
   a. color
   b. document
   c. master
   d. slide layout

3. _____ control the way that the display changes as you move from one slide to the next during a presentation.
   a. Graphics
   b. Transitions
   c. Animations
   d. Slide masters

4. If you want to display information in columns and rows, you would create a _____.
   a. slide layout
   b. shape
   c. table
   d. text box

5. You can change the horizontal placement of an entry in a placeholder or a table cell by using one of the four horizontal alignment settings: left, center, right, and _____.
   a. located
   b. marginalized
   c. highlighted
   d. justified

6. To substitute one word for another in a presentation, you would use the _____ feature.
   a. Find and Replace
   b. Duplicate
   c. Copy
   d. Locate and Move

7. If you wanted to add a company logo on each slide in your presentation, you would place it on the _____.
   a. master
   b. notes page
   c. handout
   d. outline slide

8. To help you remember the important points during a presentation, you can add comments to slides and print _____.
   a. notes pages
   b. handouts
   c. slide handouts
   d. preview handouts

9. The _____ defines the format and placement of the slide image, note text, headers, footers, and other elements that will appear on all speaker notes.
   a. handouts master
   b. title master
   c. slide master
   d. notes master

10. _____ add action to text and graphics so they move around on the screen.
    a. Animations
    b. Slides
    c. Transitions
    d. Masters

STEP-BY-STEP

ENHANCING A STAFF TRAINING PRESENTATION ★

1. You are working on the staff training presentation for the Sleepy Time Inn. You have already created the introductory portion of the presentation and need to reorganize the topics and make the presentation more visually appealing. Three slides from your modified presentation will be similar to those shown here.

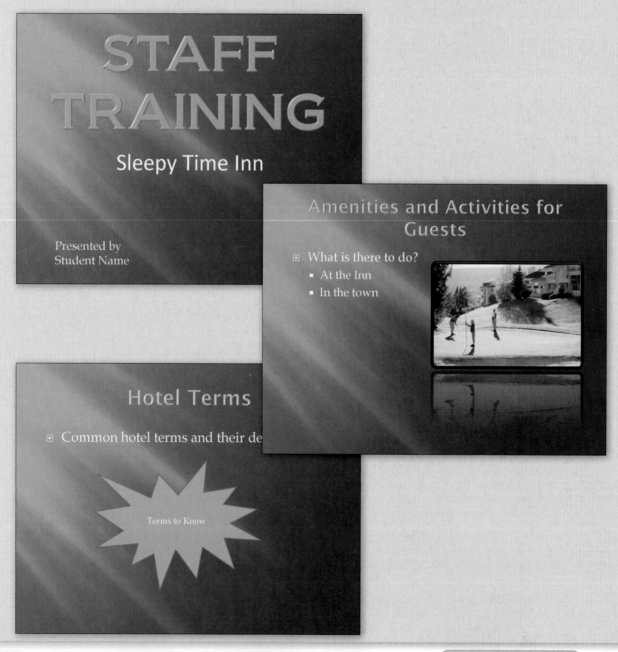

a. Open the file pp02_Sleepy Time Staff Training.

b. Run the slide show to see the progress so far.

c. Spell-check the presentation, making the appropriate corrections.

d. Find and replace any occurrence of "city" with the word **town**.

e. In slide 1:

Insert a text box below the subtitle.

Type **Presented by Your Name**.

Set the font size to 24 and position the text box appropriately on the slide.

Add the following speaker note: **Be sure to introduce yourself and play the name game**.

f. In slide 4:

Add a shape of your choice to emphasize the text on the inserted shape.

Enter and format the text **Terms to Know**.

Position and size the shape appropriately. Add an animation effect of your choice to the shape.

g. In slide 5:

Set the Picture Style to Reflected Bevel, Black.

Set the Picture Effect to Half Reflection, 4 pt offset.

h. Move slide 4 after slide 12.

i. Change the design of the slides to one of your choice from the Themes gallery. Check all slides and make any needed adjustments.

j. Duplicate slide 1 and move it to the end of the presentation. Delete the speaker note from slide 15.

k. Add a transition effect of your choice to all slides. Add an animation effect and sound to the first slide.

l. Add your name to the File properties. Save the file as Sleepy Time Training.

m. Print slides 1, 4, 12, and 15 as handouts (four slides horizontal in portrait orientation).

EMERGENCY DRIVING TECHNIQUES ★

 2. To complete this problem, you must have completed Step-by-Step Exercise 2 in Lab 1. You have completed the first draft of the presentation on tire blowouts, but you still have some information to add. Additionally, you want to make the presentation look better using many of the presentation features. Several slides of the modified presentation are shown here.

a. Open the presentation Handling Blowouts, which was saved at the end of Step-by-Step Exercise 2 in Lab 1. If necessary, switch to Normal view.

b. In Slide Master view, make the following adjustments to the Title Slide Layout:

Delete the page number placeholder.

Change the font of the title and subtitle to Tahoma or a similar font. Add a shadow.

Decrease the title text to 54 pts.

Change title text color to Dark Red, Accent 1, Darker 50%.

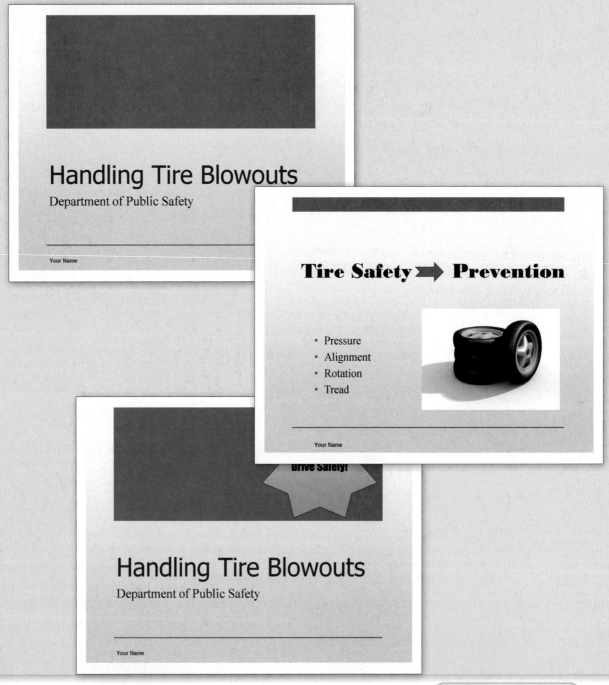

c. On slide 6, replace the = in the title with a right-facing block arrow AutoShape. Add a Fly In from the Left animation to the AutoShape. Modify slide title text as necessary to fit on one line.

d. Select slide 1. On the Home tab, click Reset in the slides group to see the changes you made to the Title Slide Layout in slide master view.

e. Duplicate the title slide and move it to the end of the presentation. Add a drawing object to this slide that includes the text **Drive Safely!**. Modify the shape style.

e. Select an animation scheme of your choice to add transition effects to all the slides. Run the slide show.

f. Add the following note to slide 7 in a point size of 18:

> **Underinflation is the leading cause of tire failure.**
>
> **Maximum inflation pressure on tire is not recommended pressure.**

g. Add the following note to slide 10 in a point size of 18:

> **Penny test–tread should come to top of the head of Lincoln.**

h. Add file documentation and save the completed presentation as Blowouts2.

i. Print the notes page for slide 7. Print slides 1, 6, and 11 as handouts with three slides per page.

ENHANCING THE ASU PRESENTATION ★★

3. Bonnie is the Assistant Director of New Admissions at Arizona State University. Part of her job is to make presentations at community colleges and local high schools about the university. She has already created the introductory portion of the presentation and needs to reorganize the topics and make the presentation more visually appealing. Several slides of the modified presentation are shown here.

a. Open the file pp02_ASU Presentation.

b. Run the slide show to see what Bonnie has done so far.

c. Spell-check the presentation, making the appropriate corrections.

d. Move slide 5 before slide 4.

e. Use the Find and Replace feature to locate all occurrences of "Arizona State University" and replace them with "ASU" on all slides except the first and second slides.

f. Enter your name as the subtitle in slide 1. Insert the picture pp02_PalmWalk on the title slide. Size the picture and position the placeholders on the slide appropriately.

g. Demote all the bulleted items on slides 8 and 9 except the first item.

h. Change the document theme to one of your choice. Change the color theme to a color of your choice. If necessary, reposition graphics and change font sizes.

i. Modify the text color of the all titles in the presentation using the slide master.

j. Duplicate slide 1 and move the duplicate to the end of the presentation. Replace your name with **Apply Now!**.

k. Bonnie would like to add some picture of the building at the end of presentation. Switch to Slide Sorter view and select slides 12, 13, and 14. Apply the Two Content layout. Insert the picture pp02_Student Services in slide 12, the picture pp02_Library in slide 13, and the picture pp02_Fine Arts in slide 14. (Hint: Use the Insert/Picture command to insert the picture and then drag the inserted picture into the clip art placeholder.)

l. Add a custom animation and sound to the picture on the title slide.

m. Apply random transitions to all slides in the presentation.

n. Apply the Fly In From Right build effect to all slides with bullet items.

o. Run the slide show.

p. Add file documentation and save the presentation as ASU Presentation1. Print slides 1, 2, and 12–15 as handouts (six per page).

4. To complete this problem, you must have completed Step-by-Step Exercise 1 in Lab 1. Logan's work on the Triple Crown Presentation was well received by his supervisor. She would like to see some additional information included in the presentation, including a table of upcoming qualifying hikes. Four slides from your updated presentation will be similar to those shown here.

LAB EXERCISES

a. Open the file Triple Crown Presentation.

b. Change the document theme to one of your choice. Change the color theme to a color of your choice. If necessary, reposition graphics and change font sizes.

c. Using the slide master, change the text color of the titles and subtitles. Change the bullet styles.

d. Use the Find and Replace command to replace any occurrence of "Paria Canyon" with **Emerald Pools**.

e. Replace slide 3 with a new Title and Content slide. In this slide:

Enter the title **Qualifying Hikes**.

Create a table with five columns and four rows.

Enter the following information in the table:

Hike	Location	Distance	Date	Guide
Death Valley	California	35 miles	August 29, 2012	Logan Thomas
Paria Canyon	Page, AZ	40 miles	September 12, 2012	Logan Thomas
Bryce to Zion	Utah	95 miles	October 15, 2012	Tracey Lynn

Adjust the column and row size as needed.

Center the cell entries both horizontally and vertically in their cell spaces.

Change the table style to one of your choice.

Position the table appropriately.

f. Add a footer that does not display the date and time but does display your name and the slide number on all slides except the title slide.

g. Add the Float In animation to the graphics on slides 4 and 5. Add an animation effect of your choice to all slides that include bullets. Add a transition effect of your choice to all slides.

h. Duplicate slide 1 and place the copy at the end of the presentation. In this slide:

Change the title to **Adventure is Waiting!**.

Add the slide footer. (Hint: Use Copy and Paste to copy your name and the slide number to the final slide.)

Add a shape of your choice to the final slide with the text: **Call us Today!**.

i. Add the following information to the file properties:

Author: **Your Name**

Title: **Triple Crown Presentation**

j. Save the file as Triple Crown Presentation2.

k. Print slides 1, 3, 5, and 8 as a handout with four slides, horizontal, on one page.

5. To complete this problem, you must have completed Step-by-Step Exercise 5 in Lab 1. Tim has completed the first draft of the presentation for his class lecture on workplace issues, but he still has some information he wants to add to the presentation. Additionally, he wants to make the presentation look better using many of the PowerPoint design and slide show presentation features. Several slides of the modified presentation are shown here.

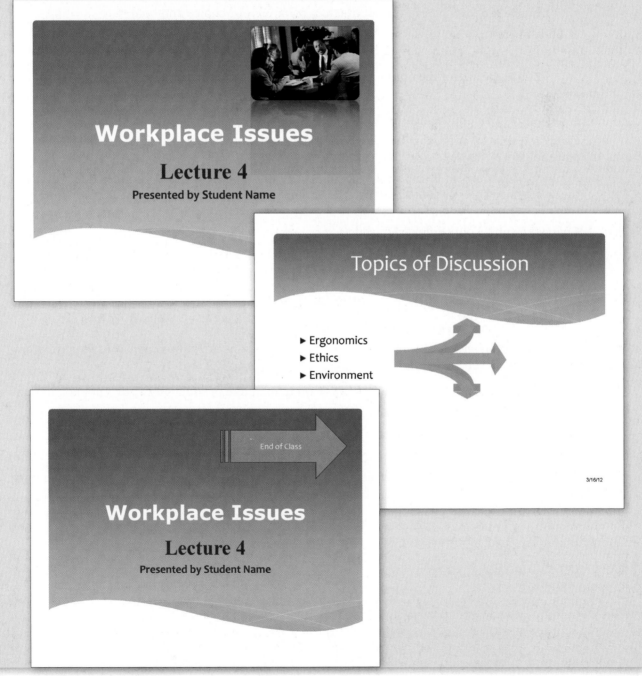

LAB EXERCISES

a. Open the presentation Workplace Issues, which was saved at the end of Step-by-Step Exercise 5 in Lab 1. If necessary, switch to Normal view.

b. Change the design template to Waveform. Change the color scheme to a color of your choice. Modify fonts as appropriate.

c. Change to Slide Sorter view and check the slide layouts. Make the following adjustments:

   Title Slide Layout (in Slide Master view):

   Delete the date area and number area placeholders.

   Change the text color of the subtitle to a color of your choice and bold it.

   Slide master:

   Change the bullet style to a picture style of your choice.

   Reduce the size of the object area placeholder and center it on the slide.

   Slide 1:

   Change the font of the title to Verdana or a similar font. Apply the shadow effect.

d. Check the slide layouts again in Slide Sorter view and fix the placement and size of the placeholders as needed.

e. Apply the Two Content layout to slide 2. Insert the clip art pp02_Arrows into the slide. Modify the AutoShape color to coordinate with the colors in your color scheme. Add a custom animation and sound to the clip art.

f. Change the angle of the clip art in slide 4.

g. Duplicate the title slide and move it to the end of the presentation. Delete the graphic and add a drawing object to this slide that includes the text **End of Class**. Format the object and text appropriately.

h. Add transition effects to all the slides. Run the slide show.

i. Add the following notes to slide 3 in a point size of 18:

   Computers used to be more expensive—focus was to make people adjust to fit computers

   Now, people are more expensive—focus is on ergonomics

   Objective—design computers and use them to increase productivity and avoid health risks

   Physical as well as mental risks

j. Add a bullet format to the notes on slide 3.

k. Add file documentation and save the completed presentation as Workplace Issues2.

l. Print the notes page for slide 3. Print slides 1, 2, 6, and 11 as handouts with four slides per page.

ON YOUR OWN

CLUTTER CONTROL ★

1. You work for a business that designs and builds custom closet solutions. You have been asked to prepare a presentation for new clients that will help them prepare for the construction phase. Clients need to organize and categorize their items before the crews arrive on-site; your presentation will serve as an organization guide. Research ideas on reducing clutter on the Web. Add transitions, animations, and a document theme that will catch the viewer's attention. Include your name and the current date in a slide footer. When you are done, save the presentation as Custom Closets, and print the presentation as handouts, nine per page.

PROMOTING A TRIP ★ ★

2. Your travel club is planning a trip next summer. You want to visit Rome and Venice, and you want to prepare a presentation on cost and key tourist attractions to help convince your club to add those cities to the itinerary. Research these two cities on the Web to determine flight costs, train costs between cities, hotel costs, and key tourist attractions. Start a new presentation and add appropriate text content. Include a table. Add transitions, graphics, animations, and a document theme that will catch the viewer's attention. Include your name and the current date in the slide footer. When you are done, save the presentation as Travel Italy and print the handouts.

ENHANCING THE CAREERS WITH ANIMALS PRESENTATION ★ ★ ★

3. To add interest to the Careers with Animals presentation that you created in Lab 1, On Your Own Exercise 5, select a document theme and color theme of your choice. Add clip art, animation, sound, and transitions that will hold your audience's interest. Add speaker notes with a header that displays your name. Include your name and the current date in a slide footer. When you are done, add appropriate documentation to the file, save the presentation as Careers with Animals2, print the presentation as handouts, and print the notes pages for only the slides containing notes.

ENHANCING THE INTERNET POLICY PRESENTATION ★ ★ ★

4. After completing the Internet Policy presentation you created in Lab 1, On Your Own Exercise 1, you decide it could use a bit more sprucing up. You want to add some information about personal computing security. Do some research on the Web to find some helpful tips on protecting personal privacy and safeguarding your computer. Enter this information in one or two slides. Add some animated clip art pictures and transitions to help liven up the presentation. Make these and any other changes that you think would enhance the presentation. Add a table and format it appropriately. Include speaker notes for at least one slide. Add appropriate documentation to the file. When you are done, save it as Internet Policy2; print the presentation as handouts, nine per page; and print the notes pages (with a header displaying your name and the current date) for only the slides containing notes.

LAB EXERCISES

ENHANCING THE WEB DESIGN PRESENTATION ★ ★ ★

5. After completing the Web Design presentation in Lab 1, On Your Own Exercise 4, you decide it needs a bit more sprucing up. First of all, it would be more impressive as an onscreen presentation with a custom design. Also, the pros and cons information would look better as a table, and a few animated clip art pictures, nonstandard bullets, builds, and transitions wouldn't hurt. Make these and any other changes that you think would enhance the presentation. Include speaker notes for at least one slide. Include your name and the current date in a slide footer. When you are done, add appropriate documentation to the file and save it as Web Design2. Print the presentation as handouts and print the notes pages for only the slides containing notes.

CASE STUDY

Animal Rescue Foundation

The director of the Animal Rescue Foundation has reviewed the PowerPoint presentation you created and has asked you to include an adoption success rate chart that was created using Excel. Additionally, the director has provided a list of dates for the upcoming volunteer orientation meetings that he feels would be good content for another slide.

Frequently you will find that you want to include information that was created using a word processing, spreadsheet, or database application in your slide show. As you will see, you can easily share information between applications, saving you both time and effort by eliminating the need to re-create information that is available in another application. You will learn how to share information between applications while you create the new slides. The new slides containing information from Word and Excel are shown here.

NOTE **The Working Together section assumes that you already know how to use Microsoft Word and Excel 2010 and that you have completed PowerPoint Lab 2.**

Information can be easily copied from a file created in another application, such as Word or Excel, and pasted into a PowerPoint slide as a linked or embedded object.

The orientation meeting information was already prepared in a document using Word 2010. As you have learned, all the Microsoft Office system applications have a common user interface, such as similar Ribbons and commands. In addition to these obvious features, the applications have been designed to work together, making it easy to share and exchange information between applications.

Rather than retype the list of orientation meeting dates provided by the director, you will copy the list from the Word document into the presentation. You also can use the same commands and procedures to copy information from PowerPoint or other Office applications into Word.

COPYING FROM WORD TO A POWERPOINT SLIDE

First, you need to modify the PowerPoint presentation to include a new slide for the orientation meeting dates.

- **Start PowerPoint 2010.**

- **Open the presentation** Volunteer2 **(saved at the end of Lab 2).**

Having Trouble?

If this file is not available, open ppwt1_Volunteer2. Be sure to change Student Name on the first slide to your name

- **Insert a new slide using the Title Only layout after slide 12.**

Your screen should be similar to Figure 1

Figure 1

To copy information from the Word document file into the PowerPoint presentation, you need to open the Word document.

2

- Start Word 2010.

- Open the document ppwt1_Orientation Meetings

- If necessary, maximize the window, hide the rulers, and set the magnification to 100%.

Having Trouble?

Click ☒ View Ruler at the top of the vertical scroll bar to view/hide the ruler.

Your screen should be similar to Figure 2

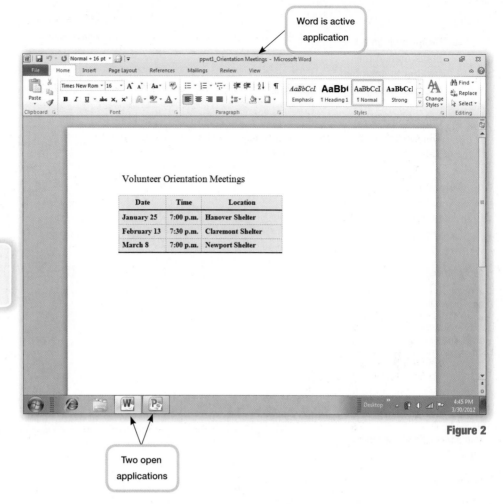

Figure 2

There are now two open applications, Word and PowerPoint. PowerPoint is open in a window behind the Word application window. Both application buttons are displayed in the taskbar. There are also two open files, ppwt1_ Orientation Meetings in Word and Volunteer2 in PowerPoint. Word is the active application, and ppwt1_Orientation Meetings is the active file. To make it easier to work with two applications, you will display the windows next to each other to view both on the screen at the same time.

③

- **Right-click on a blank area of the taskbar to open the shortcut menu.**

- **Choose Show Windows Side by Side.**

- **If necessary, click in the Word window to make it the active window.**

Your screen should be similar to Figure 3

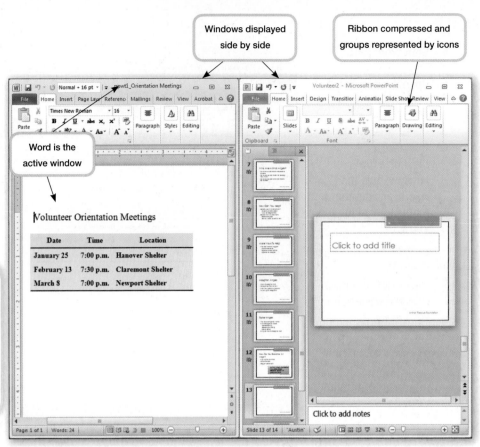

Figure 3

The active window is the window that displays the cursor and does not have a dimmed title bar. It is the window in which you can work. Because the windows are side by side and there is less horizontal space in each window, the Ribbon groups are compressed. To access commands in these groups, simply click on the group button and the commands appear in a drop-down list.

First, you will copy the title from the Word document into the title placeholder of the slide. While using the Word and PowerPoint applications, you have learned how to use cut, copy, and paste to move or copy information within the same document. You can also perform these same operations between documents in the same application and between documents in different applications. The information is pasted in a format that the application can edit, if possible.

4

- Select the title "Volunteer Orientation Meetings."

- Click [icon] ▾ Copy on the Home tab in Word.

- Click on the PowerPoint window to make it the active window.

- Right-click in the title placeholder in the Slide pane in PowerPoint.

- Choose [A icon] Keep Text Only in the Paste Options area of the shortcut menu to apply the slide formatting to the title.

Another Method

You also could use drag and drop to copy the text to the slide.

- Click on the slide to deselect the placeholder.

Your screen should be similar to Figure 4

Additional Information

You could also click [Reset icon] Reset in the Slides group of the Home tab to quickly convert all the text on the slide to match the presentation's theme.

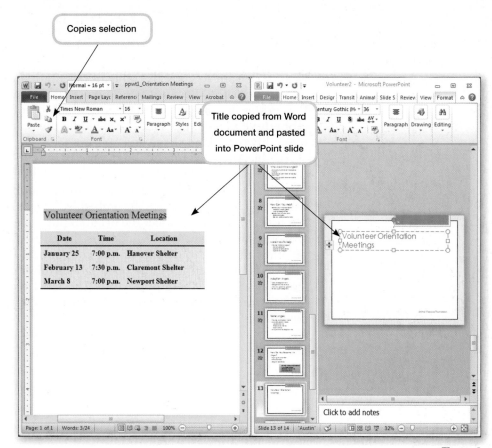

Copies selection

Title copied from Word document and pasted into PowerPoint slide

Figure 4

The title has been copied into the slide and can be edited and manipulated within PowerPoint. Because you used the Keep Text Only paste option, the formats associated with the slide master were applied to the copied text.

Embedding a Word Table in a PowerPoint Slide

Next, you want to copy the table of orientation dates and place it below the title in the slide. Because you know that you are going to want to change the formatting of the table to match the look of your presentation, you will **embed** the table in the slide. Embedding the object will give you the freedom to modify the table's shape and appearance.

An object that is embedded is stored in the file in which it is inserted, called the **destination file**, and becomes part of that file. The embedded object can then be edited using features from the source program, the program in which it was created. Since the embedded object is part of the destination file, modifying it does not affect the original file, called the **source file**.

Notice that because the window is tiled, the Ribbon is smaller and there is not enough space to display all the commands. Depending on how small the Ribbon is, the groups on the open tab shrink horizontally and show a single icon that displays the group name. The most commonly used commands or features are left open. Clicking the icon opens the group and displays the commands.

1

- Make the Word window active.

- Click within the table and open the Layout tab.

- Click ⬚ Select ▾ in the Table group and choose Select Table.

Another Method

You can also click the ⊞ Table Selection Handle or drag to select the entire table.

- Open the Home tab and click 📋 ▾ Copy.

- Click on the PowerPoint window.

- Open the Paste drop-down menu and choose 📋 Embed.

Having Trouble?

See "Copying and Moving Selections," in the Introduction to Microsoft Office for more information on the Paste Options feature.

Your screen should be similar to Figure 5

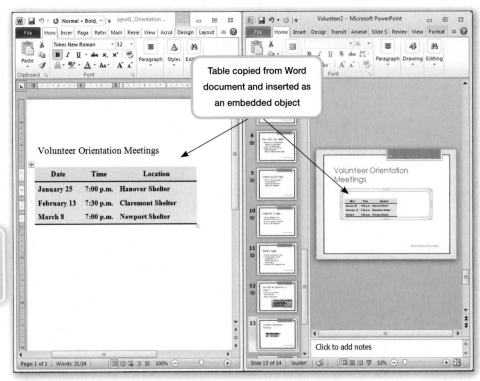

Figure 5

The table, including the table formatting, is copied into the slide as an embedded object that can be manipulated. The object container is larger than the table it holds.

EDITING AN EMBEDDED OBJECT

As you look at the table, you decide to change the size and appearance of the table. To do this, you will edit the embedded object using the source program.

- **Choose Undo Show Side by Side from the taskbar shortcut menu.**

Additional Information

If you use Windows 7, you can click on the title bar of the PowerPoint window and simply drag it to the top of the screen to maximize it.

- **If necessary, maximize the PowerPoint window.**

- **Double-click the table.**

Your screen should be similar to Figure 6

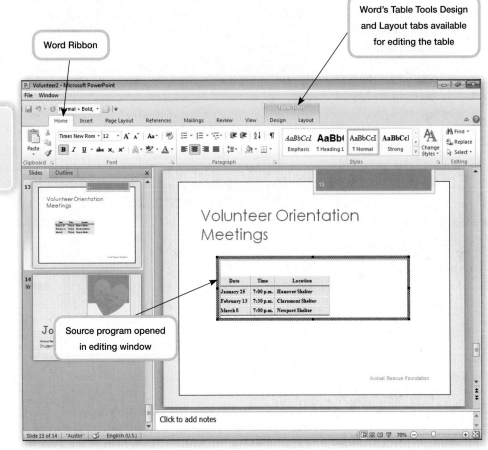

Word Ribbon

Word's Table Tools Design and Layout tabs available for editing the table

Source program opened in editing window

Figure 6

Additional Information

You must have the source program on your system to be able to open and edit an embedded object.

The source program, in this case Word 2010, is opened. The Word Ribbon replaces the PowerPoint Ribbon. The embedded object is displayed in an editing window. If your table does not display gridlines, this is because this feature is not on in your application. First, you will increase the size of the embedded object so that you can increase the size of the table within it.

Additional Information

If you want to see gridlines in your table, open the Layout tab and click

.

Drag the bottom-center sizing handle down to increase the object's size as in Figure 7.

Your screen should be similar to Figure 7

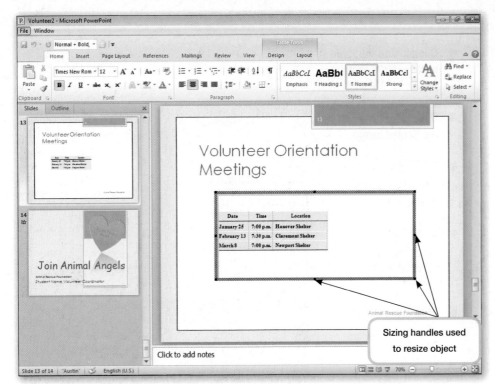

Figure 7

Now that the embedded object's container is larger, you can resize and reposition the table within the container.

3

- Click inside the table and open the Layout tab.

- Click Properties in the Tables group.

- Click Positioning... in the Properties dialog box.

- In the Vertical area, open the Position drop-down menu and choose Top.

- Click OK and then click OK.

Figure 8

Having Trouble?

If the entire table is not visible, click in the table and press Shift + Tab until the first column is visible. You can also use the scroll wheel to adjust it vertically.

- Drag the bottom-right corner sizing handle of the table to increase the size of the table in the object's container.

Having Trouble?

If you can't see the table's bottom-right corner sizing handle, try clicking in the table and scrolling up and down until it appears.

Having Trouble?

If the table gets too large to fit in the container, click Undo to reset it and try again.

Your screen should be similar to Figure 8

Next, you will use the Word commands to edit the object. You want to apply a different table design style, change the appearance of the text in the table.

4

● Open the Design tab.

● Click ▾ More in the Table Styles group.

● Choose Light List, Accent 1 from the Table Styles gallery (third column, eighth row).

● Drag to select the table and open the Layout tab.

● In the Alignment group, choose ▤ Align Center Left.

● With the table still selected, open the Home tab and click **A⁺** Grow Font once to increase the font size to 14.

● Drag to select the first row of table headings and click **A⁺** Grow Font two more times to increase the font size of the three headings to 18.

● Click anywhere outside the object twice to close the source program and deselect the object.

Your screen should be similar to Figure 9

Figure 9

The embedded object in the PowerPoint slide is updated to reflect the changes you made in the Word table.

4

● Click in the taskbar to switch to the Word application.

● **Deselect the table and notice that the source file has not been affected by the changes you made to the embedded object.**

● **Exit Word.**

Linking between Applications

Next, you want to copy the chart of the rescue and adoption data into the presentation. You will insert the chart object into the slide as a **linked object**, which is another way to insert information created in one application into a document created by another application. With a linked object, the actual data is stored in the source file (the document in which it was created). A graphic representation or picture of the data is displayed in the destination file (the document in which the object is inserted). A connection between the information in the destination file and the source file is established by creating a link. The link contains references to the location of the source file and the selection within the document that is linked to the destination file.

When changes are made in the source file that affect the linked object, the changes are automatically reflected in the destination file when it is opened. This connection is called a **live link**. When you create linked objects, the date and time on your machine should be accurate. This is because the program refers to the date of the source file to determine whether updates are needed when you open the destination file.

LINKING AN EXCEL CHART TO A POWERPOINT PRESENTATION

The chart of the rescue and adoption data will be inserted into another new slide following slide 6.

1

- Insert a new slide following slide 6 using the Title Only layout.

- Start Excel 2010 and open the workbook ppwt1_RescueData from your data files.

- Display the application windows side by side.

Your screen should be similar to Figure 10

Figure 10

The worksheet contains the rescue and adoption data for the past four years as well as a bar chart of the data. Again, you have two open applications, PowerPoint and Excel. Next you will copy the second title line from the worksheet into the slide title placeholder.

2

- Click on cell **B2** to select it.

- Click [icon] ▾ Copy in the Home tab.

- Make the PowerPoint window active.

- Right-click the title placeholder in the slide and choose [A] Keep Text Only from the Paste Options area of the shortcut menu.

- Press [Backspace] five times to remove the extra blank lines below the title and the extra space at the end of the title.

- Click on the slide to deselect the placeholder.

Your screen should be similar to Figure 11

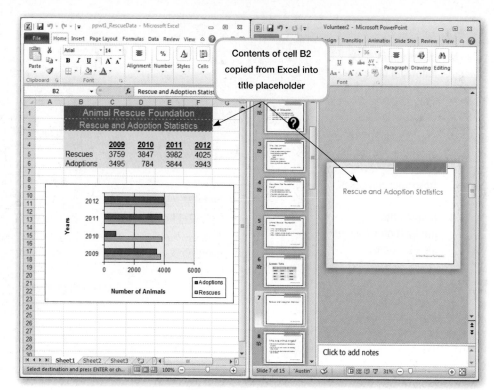

Figure 11

Now you are ready to copy the chart. By making the chart a linked object, it will be updated automatically if the source file is edited.

- **Make the Excel window active.**

- **Press** Esc **to deselect B2 and the click on the chart object in the worksheet to select it.**

Having Trouble?

Click on the chart to select it when the ScreenTip displays "Chart Area."

- **Click** **Copy.**

- **Click on the slide.**

- **Open the** **drop-down menu and choose Paste Special.**

Your screen should be similar to Figure 12

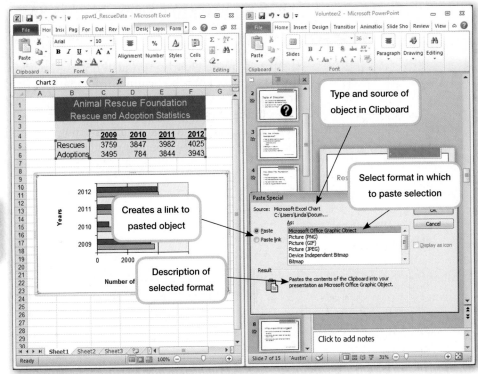

Figure 12

The Paste Special dialog box displays the type of object contained in the Clipboard and its location in the Source area. From the As list box, you select the type of format in which you want the object pasted into the destination file. The Result area describes the effect of your selections. In this case, you want to insert the chart as a linked object to Microsoft Excel.

- **Choose Paste link.**

- **Click** OK **.**

- **Appropriately size and center the linked object on the slide.**

Your screen should be similar to Figure 13

Figure 13

The chart object was inserted as a picture, and a link was created to the chart in the source file.

UPDATING A LINKED OBJECT

While looking at the chart in the slide, you decide to change the chart type from a bar chart to a column chart. You believe that a column chart will show the trends more clearly. You also notice the adoption data for 2010 looks very low. After checking the original information, you see that the wrong value was entered in the worksheet and that it should be 3784.

To make these changes, you need to switch back to the Excel application. Double-clicking on a linked object quickly switches to the open source file. If the source file is not open, it opens the file for you. If the application is not started, it both starts the application and opens the source file.

1

● **Double-click the chart object in the slide.**

Another Method

You can also right-click the edge of the object and select Linked Worksheet Object/Edit.

● **Make the Excel window active.**

● **Maximize the Rescue Data workbook within Excel.**

● **Click on the chart object to select it, if necessary.**

● **Open the Design tab and click** .

Another Method

You could also right-click one of the columns and choose Change Series Chart Type.

● **Choose Column.**

● **Choose** 3-D **Clustered Column (first row, fourth item)**

● **Click** OK .

● **Change the value in cell D6 to 3784 and press** Enter .

Your screen should be similar to Figure 14

Figure 14

The chart in both applications has changed to a column chart, and the chart data series has been updated to reflect the change in data. This is because any changes you make in the chart in Excel will be automatically reflected in the linked chart in the slide.

2

- Undo the side-by-side window display.

- Save the revised Excel workbook.

- Exit Excel.

- If necessary, maximize the PowerPoint window.

Linking documents is a very handy feature, particularly in documents whose information is updated frequently. If you include a linked object in a document, make sure the source file name and location do not change. Otherwise the link will not operate correctly.

Printing Selected Slides

Next, you will print the two new slides.

1

- Open the File tab and choose Print.

- If necessary, select the printer.

- Enter 7,14 in the Slides text box to specify the slides to print.

- Specify Handouts (2 slides) as the type of output.

- Change the color setting to Grayscale.

- If necessary, click the Edit Header & Footer link and change the header to display your name.

- Print the page.

- Save the PowerPoint presentation as Volunteer3 Linked and exit PowerPoint.

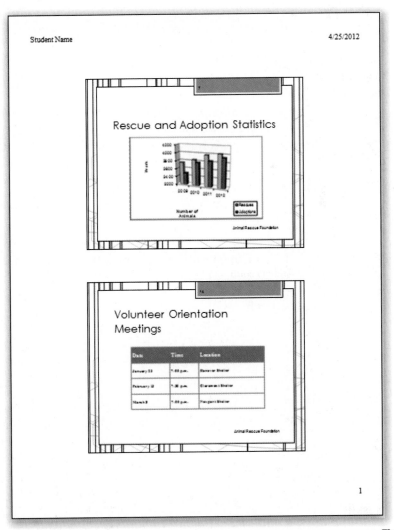

Figure 15

Your screen should be similar to Figure 15

Your printed output will be similar to that shown here.

KEY TERMS

destination file PPWT1.6	live link PPWT1.12
embed PPWT1.6	source file PPWT1.6
linked object PPWT1.12	

COMMAND SUMMARY

Command	Shortcut	Action
Home tab		
Clipboard group		
Embed		Embeds an object from another application
/Paste Special/Paste Link		Inserts an object as a linked object
Paste	Paste	Inserts the copied text or object
A	Keep Text Only	Keeps the format associated with the destination format.
Slides group		
Reset	Reset	Converts all the slides content to match the presentation's theme.

STEP-BY-STEP

EMBEDDING A TABLE OF MASSAGE PRICES ★

1. At the Hollywood Spa and Fitness Center, you have been working on a presentation on massage therapy. Now that the presentation is almost complete, you just need to add some information to the presentation about prices. Your manager has already given you this information in a Word document. You will copy and embed this information into a new slide. The completed slide is shown below.

   a. Start Word and open the file ppwt1_MassagePrices.

   b. Start PowerPoint and open the Massage Therapy2 presentation.

   c. Add a new slide after slide 9 using the Title Only layout.

   d. Copy the title from the Word document into the slide title placeholder. Use the Keep Text Only option.

   e. Copy the table into the slide as an embedded object. Exit Word.

   f. Size and position the object on the slide appropriately.

   g. Edit the table to change the font color to an appropriate font color.

   h. Change the fill color of the table to match the slide design.

   i. If necessary, change the footer to display your name.

   j. Save the presentation as Massage Therapy.

   k. Print the new slide.

Massage Price List

Swedish Massage	**$65 per hour**
Reflexology	**$65 per hour**
Shiatsu and Acupressure	**$75 per hour**
Sports Massage Therapy	**Make appointment for evaluation**

Student Name

LAB EXERCISES

EMBEDDING A TABLE OF BLOWOUT INDICATORS ★ ★

2. To complete this problem, you must have completed Step-by-Step Exercise 2 in Lab 2. The Blowouts section for the Department of Safety presentation is almost complete. You just need to add some information to the presentation about the indicators of a flat tire. This information is already in a Word document as a table. You will copy and embed it into a new slide. The completed slide is shown below.

   a. Start Word and open the ppwt1_BlowoutSigns file.

   b. Start PowerPoint and open the Blowouts2 presentation. If this file is not available, you can use ppwt1_Blowouts2.

   c. Add a new slide after slide 3 using the Title Only layout.

   d. Copy the title from the Word document into the slide title placeholder.

   e. Copy the table into the slide as an embedded object. Exit Word.

   f. Size and position the object on the slide appropriately.

   g. Change the design of the table to suit your presentation.

   h. Change the fonts and font sizes of the table headings.

   i. If necessary, change the footer to display your name.

   j. Save the presentation as Blowouts3.

   k. Print the new slide.

3. To complete this problem, you must have completed Step-by-Step Exercise 4 in Lab 2. Logan has found some interesting data on the increase in Americans hiking and wants to include this information in his lecture presentation. The completed slide is shown below.

   a. Start PowerPoint and open the Triple Crown Presentation2 file. If this file is not available, you can use ppwt1_Triple Crown Presentation2. Save the presentation as Triple Crown Presentation3.

   b. Start Excel and open the ppwt1_Forest Use worksheet. Save the worksheet as Forest Use Linked.

   c. Add a new slide after slide 6 using the Title Only layout.

   d. Copy the worksheet cell A1 and paste it in the title placeholder using the Keep Text Only.

   e. Change the look of the presentation by apply the Hardcover theme and the Austin color theme.

   f. Copy the worksheet range A2 through B6 as a linked object into slide 7. Size and position it appropriately.

   g. Format the linked data so that it blends appropriately with the presentation.

   h. Add an appropriate Shape Outline to the linked object's container in the slide.

   i. You notice that the percentage for hiking seems low. After checking the original source, you see you entered the value incorrectly. In Excel, change the value in cell B5 to 42%.

   j. Copy the text in cell A8 and paste it into the Notes for slide 7.

   k. Exit Excel.

   l. If necessary, change the footer to display your name.

   m. Save the changes to the presentation as Triple Crown Presentation3.

   n. Print the new slide.

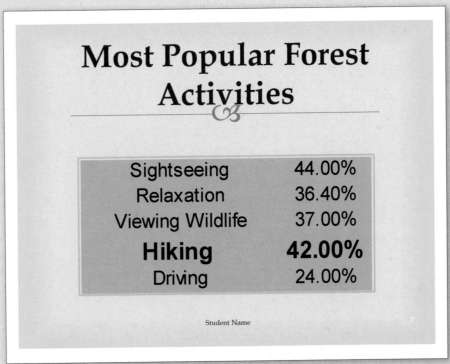

POWERPOINT 2010 COMMAND SUMMARY

COMMAND	SHORTCUT	ACTION
Quick Access Toolbar		
💾 Save	Ctrl + S	Saves presentation
↩ Undo	Ctrl + Z	Reverses last action
File Tab		
💾 Save As Save	Ctrl + S	Saves presentation
💾 Save As	F12	Saves presentation using new file name and/or location
📂 Open	Ctrl + O	Opens existing presentation
📄 Close		Closes presentation
Info		Document properties
New	Ctrl + N	Opens New Presentation dialog box
Print	Ctrl + P	Opens print settings and a preview pane
✖ Exit		Closes PowerPoint
Home Tab		
Clipboard Group		
📋 Paste	Ctrl + V	Pastes item from Clipboard
📋 Paste / 📋		Embeds an object from another application
📋 Paste /Paste Special/Paste Link		Inserts an object as a linked object
✂ Cut	Ctrl + X	Cuts selection to Clipboard
📋 Copy	Ctrl + C	Copies selection to Clipboard
Slides Group		
🗔 New Slide	Ctrl + M	Inserts new slide with selected layout
🗔 Layout		Changes layout of a slide
📋 Paste /Paste		Inserts the copied text or object

POWERPOINT 2010 COMMAND SUMMARY

COMMAND	SHORTCUT	ACTION
[A] /Keep Text Only		Keeps the format associated with the destination format.
Reset /Reset		Converts all the slides content to match the presentation's theme.
Font Group		
Trebuchet MS (He ▾) Font		Changes font type
44 ▾ Size		Changes font size
A˄ Increase Font Size	Ctrl + Shift + >	Increases font size of selected text
A˅ Decreases font size		
I Italicizes text		
U Underlines text		
S Applies a shadow effect		
A ▾ Changes font color		
Paragraph Group		
☰ ▾ Bullets/Bullets		Formats bulleted list
☰ ▾ Numbering/Bulleted		Formats numbered lists
Align Text		Sets vertical alignment of text
Align Left	Ctrl + F	Aligns text to the left
Align Center	Ctrl + E	Centers text
Align Right	Ctrl + R	Aligns text to the right
Justify	Ctrl + F	Aligns text to both the left and right margins
Drawing Group		
Shapes		Inserts a shape
Editing Group		
Find	Ctrl + F	Finds specified text

POWERPOINT 2010 COMMAND SUMMARY

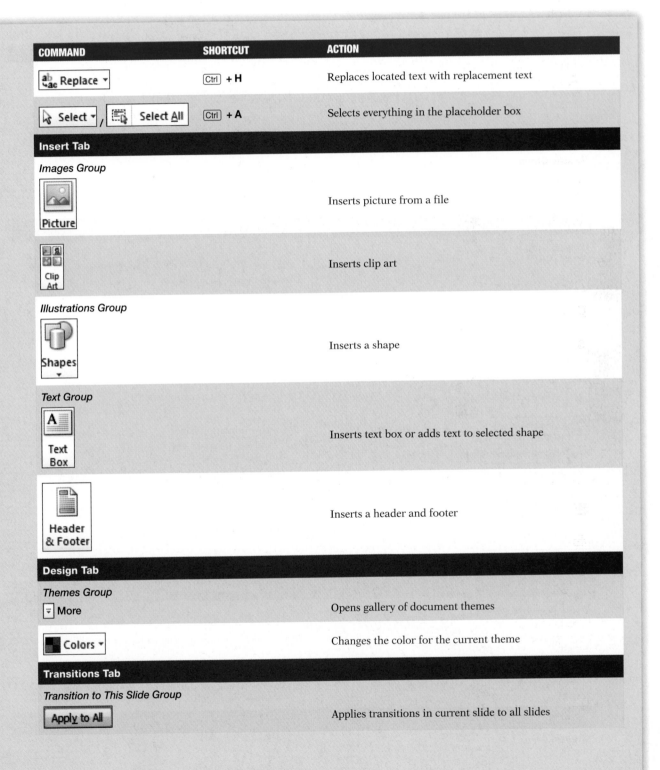

COMMAND	SHORTCUT	ACTION
Replace ▾	Ctrl + H	Replaces located text with replacement text
Select ▾ / Select All	Ctrl + A	Selects everything in the placeholder box

Insert Tab

Images Group

Picture		Inserts picture from a file
Clip Art		Inserts clip art

Illustrations Group

Shapes		Inserts a shape

Text Group

Text Box		Inserts text box or adds text to selected shape
Header & Footer		Inserts a header and footer

Design Tab

Themes Group

▾ More		Opens gallery of document themes
Colors ▾		Changes the color for the current theme

Transitions Tab

Transition to This Slide Group

Apply to All		Applies transitions in current slide to all slides

POWERPOINT 2010 COMMAND SUMMARY

COMMAND	SHORTCUT	ACTION
Effect Options ▾		Opens a gallery of effect options
▾		Opens a gallery of transition effects
Preview Group		
Preview		Displays the transition effect
Animations Tab		
Preview Group		
Preview		Displays the transition effect
Animation Group		
Effect Options ▾		Opens a gallery of effect options
▾		Opens a gallery of animation effects
Animation Pane		Opens the Animation pane
Advanced Animation Group		
Animation Painter		Copies animation effect to another object
Timing Group		
Start:		Sets the trigger for the animation
Duration: 00.50		Controls the amount of time for the animation to complete
Slide Show Tab		
Start Slide Show Group		
From Beginning	F5	Displays presentation starting with the first slide
From Current Slide	Shift + F5	Displays presentation starting with the current slide
Review Tab		
Proofing Group		
Spelling	F7	Spell-checks presentation

POWERPOINT 2010 COMMAND SUMMARY

COMMAND	SHORTCUT	ACTION
View Tab		
Presentation Views Group		
Normal		Switches to Normal view
Slide Sorter		Switches to Slide Sorter view
Notes Page		Displays current slide in Notes view to edit the speaker notes
Master Views Group		
Slide Master		Opens Slide Master view to change the design and layout of the master slides
Picture Tools Format Tab		
Adjust Group		
9 Slides Horizontal Handouts (9 slides per page)		Modifies the color of the picture
Picture Styles Group		
More		Applies an overall visual style to picture
Picture Border		Applies a border style to picture
Picture Effects		Applies a visual effect to picture
Picture Layout		Changes layout of a drawing
Arrange Group		
		Opens a gallery of alignment options
Size Group		
Crop		Crops off unwanted section of a picture
Drawing Tools Format Tab		
Shapes Styles Group		
More		Opens the Shape Styles gallery to select a visual style to apply to a shape
Shape Effects		Applies a visual effect to a shape

POWERPOINT 2010 COMMAND SUMMARY

COMMAND	SHORTCUT	ACTION
Arrange Group		
⬛		Rotates or flips the selected object
Table Tools Design Tab		
Table Styles Group		
⬛ More		Opens gallery of table designs
⬛ Shading		Colors background behind selected text or paragraph
⬛ Border		Applies a border style
⬛ Effects		Applies a visual effect to the table, such as shadows and reflections
Table Tools Layout Tab		
Table Group		
⬛ Properties		Edit table properties within the embedded object
Alignment Group		
⬛		Centers the text within a cell
⬛		Centers the text vertically within a cell
Arrangement Group		
⬛		Opens a gallery of alignment options

b

Backstage view: Contains commands that allow you to work with your document, unlike the Ribbon that allows you to work in your document; contains commands that apply to the entire document.

Buttons: Graphical elements that perform the associated action when you click on them using the mouse.

c

Clipboard: Where a selection is stored when it is cut or copied.

Commands: Options that carry out a selected action.

Context menu: Also called a shortcut menu; opened by right-clicking on an item on the screen.

Contextual tabs: Also called on-demand tabs; tabs that are displayed only as needed. For example, when you are working with a picture, the Picture Tools tab appears.

Cursor: The blinking vertical bar that marks your location in the document and indicates where text you type will appear; also called the insertion point.

d

Database: A collection of related data.

Default: The standard options used by Office 2010.

Destination: The new location into which a selection that is moved from its original location is inserted.

Dialog box launcher: A button that is displayed in the lower-right corner of a tab group if more commands are available; clicking opens a dialog box or task pane of additional options.

Document window: The large center area of the program window where open application files are displayed.

e

Edit: To revise a document by changing the parts that need to be modified.

Enhanced ScreenTip: Displayed by pointing to a button in the Ribbon; shows the name of the button and the keyboard shortcut.

f

Field: The smallest unit of information about a record; a column in a table.

Font: Type style; also called typeface.

Font size: Size of typeface, given in points.

Format: The appearance of a document.

g

Groups: Part of a tab that contains related items.

h

Hyperlink: Connection to information located in a separate location, such as on a Web site.

i

Insertion point: Also called the cursor; the blinking vertical bar that marks your location in a document and indicates where text you type will appear.

k

Keyboard shortcut: A combination of keys that can be used to execute a command in place of clicking a button.

Keyword: A descriptive word that is associated with the file and can be used to locate a file using a search.

l

Live Preview: A feature that shows you how selected text in a document will appear if a formatting option is chosen.

m

Metadata: Details about the document that describe or identify it, such as title, author name, subject, and keywords; also called document properties.

Mini toolbar: Appears automatically when you select text; displays command buttons for often-used commands from the Font and Paragraph groups that are used to format a document.

o

Office Clipboard: Can store up to 24 items that have been cut or copied.

On-demand tabs: Also called contextual tabs; tabs that are displayed only as needed.

p

Paste Preview: Shows how a Paste Option will affect a selection.

Properties: Shown in a panel along the right side of the Info tab, divided into four groups; information such as author, keywords, document size, number of words, and number of pages.

q

Quick Access Toolbar: Located to the right of the Window button; provides quick access to frequently used commands such as Save, Undo, and Redo.

r

Records: The information about one person, thing, or place; contained in a row of a table.

Ribbon: Below the title bar; provides a centralized location of commands that are used to work in your document.

s

ScreenTip: Also called a tooltip; appears with the command name and the keyboard shortcut.

Scroll bar: Horizontal or vertical, it is used with a mouse to bring additional information into view in a window.

Selection cursor: Cursor that allows you to select an object.

Shortcut menu: A context-sensitive menu, meaning it displays only those commands relevant to the item or screen location; also called a context menu, it is opened by right-clicking on an item on the screen.

Slide: An individual page of a presentation.

Slide shows: Onscreen electronic presentations.

Source: The original location of a selection that is inserted in a new location.

Status bar: At the bottom of the application window; displays information about the open file and features that help you view the file.

t

Tables: A database object consisting of columns and rows.

Tabs: Used to divide the Ribbon into major activity areas.

Tag: A descriptive word that is associated with the file and can be used to locate a file using a search; also called a keyword.

Task pane: A list of additional options opened by clicking the dialog box launcher; also called a dialog box.

Text effects: Enhancements such as bold, italic, and color that are applied to selected text.

Tooltip: Also called a ScreenTip; appears displaying a command name and the keyboard shortcut.

Typeface: A set of characters with a specific design; also commonly referred to as a font.

u

User interface: A set of graphical elements that are designed to help you interact with the program and provide instructions for the actions you want to perform.

v

View buttons: Used to change how the information in the document window is displayed.

w

Worksheet: An electronic spreadsheet, or worksheet, that is used to organize, manipulate, and graph numeric data.

z

Zoom slider: Located at the far right end of the status bar; used to change the amount of information displayed in the document window by "zooming in" to get a close-up view or "zooming out" to see more of the document at a reduced view.

a

Alignment: Controls the position of text entries within a space.

Animation: Special effects that add action to text and graphics so they move around on the screen during a slide show.

AutoCorrect: A feature that makes some basic assumptions about the text you are typing and, based on those assumptions, automatically corrects the entry.

b

Background styles: A set of theme colors and textures that you can apply to the background of your slides.

c

Cell: The intersection of a row and a column in a table.

Character formatting: Applies changes such as color and size to the selected characters only.

Clip art: Simple drawings; available in the Clip Organizer, a Microsoft Office tool that arranges and catalogs clip art and other media files stored on the computer's hard disk.

Cropping: Trimming or removing part of a graphic.

Current slide: The slide that will be affected by any changes you make.

Custom dictionary: The dictionary you can create to hold words you commonly use, such as proper names and technical terms, that are not included in the spelling checker's main dictionary.

d

Default settings: The most commonly used settings, automatically used in a new blank presentation file.

Demote: Indenting a bulleted point to the right, making it a lower or subordinate topic in the outline hierarchy.

Destination file: The file into which an object is embedded.

Document theme: A predefined set of formatting choices that can be applied to an entire document in one simple step.

Drawing object: A graphic consisting of shapes such as lines and boxes.

e

Embedded object: Graphics that were created from another program and are inserted in a slide. An embedded object becomes part of the presentation file and can be opened and edited using the program in which it was created.

f

Find and Replace: A feature used to find text in a presentation and replace it with other text.

g

Graphic: A nontext element or object, such as a drawing or picture, that can be added to a slide.

k

Keyword: Descriptive words or phrases associated with a graphic or figure that give information about the properties of the object.

l

Layout: Defines the position and format for objects and text that will be added to a slide. A layout contains placeholders for the different items such as bulleted text, titles, charts, and so on.

Linked object: A way to insert information created in one application into a document created by another application. With a linked object, the actual data is stored in the source file.

Live link: Connection that allows changes made in the source file that affect the linked object to be automatically reflected in the destination file when it is opened.

m

Main dictionary: The dictionary that is supplied with the spelling checker program.

Master: A special slide or page that stores information about the formatting for all slides or pages in a presentation.

Metadata: Additional data saved by PowerPoint as part of the presentation, may include author's name and other personal information.

n

Notes pages: Pages that display notes below a small version of the slide they accompany.

Notes pane: View that includes space for you to enter notes that apply to the current slide.

o

Object animations: Used to display each bullet point, text, paragraph, or graphic independently of the other text or objects on the slide.

Outline tab: Displays the text content of each slide in outline format.

p

Paragraph formatting: Formatting features that affect an entire paragraph.

Picture: An image such as a graphic illustration or a scanned photograph, created in another program.

Picture style: Effects added to a picture, such as borders and shadows.

Placeholder: Boxes with dotted borders that are used to contain content such as text, graphics and other objects.

Placeholder text: Messages inside placeholders that prompt you to enter text.

Promote: Removes the indentation before a line. Promoting a line moves it to the left, or up a level in the outline hierarchy.

r

Rotate handle: Allows you to rotate the selected object to any degree in any direction.

s

Sans serif font: A font without a flair at the base of each letter, such as Arial or Helvetica.

Serif font: A font that has a flair at the base of each letter, such as Roman or Times New Roman.

Shape styles: Combinations of fill colors, outline colors, and effects used to enhance the appearance of a shape.

Sizing handles: The four circles and squares that appear at the corners and sides of a selected placeholder's border.

Slide: An individual "page" of your presentation.

Slide indicator: Identifies the number of the slide that is displayed in the workspace, along with the total number of slides in the presentation.

Slide pane: View that displays the selected slide.

Slide show: Displays each slide full screen and in order.

Slides tab: View that displays a miniature version, or thumbnail, of each slide.

Source file: The original file used to create an embedded object.

Source program: The program in which an object was created.

Spelling checker: Locates all misspelled words, duplicate words, and capitalization irregularities as you create and edit a presentation, and proposes possible corrections.

Style: A combination of formatting options that can be applied in one easy step.

t

Table: Used to organize information into an easy-to-read format of horizontal rows and vertical columns.

Table reference: A letter and number used to identify cells in a table. Columns are identified from left to right beginning with the letter A, and rows are numbered from top to bottom beginning with the number 1.

Table styles: Combinations of shading colors, borders, and visual effects such as shadows and reflections that can be applied to a table.

Template: A file containing predefined settings that can be used as a pattern to create many common types of presentations.

Text box: A container for text or graphics.

Text effects: Enhancements to the text such as color and shadow.

Thumbnail: A miniature version of a slide, picture, or object.

Transition: Controls the way that the display changes as you move from one slide to the next during a presentation.

v

View: A way of looking at a presentation that provides the means to interact with the presentation.

Instructional conventions, IO.12–IO.13
Interface features, IO.14–IO.15
Italic, PP1.51, PP1.53

j

.jpg, PP1.34, PP1.54
Justified, PP2.18

k

Keyboard directional keys, IO.31, IO.35
Keyboard shortcuts, IO.16
Keyword, IO.51, PP1.56

l

Laser pointer, PP2.66
Last slide in presentation, PP1.12
Layout, PP1.41–PP1.43
Left alignment, PP2.18
Linked object, PPWT1.12
Linking Excel chart to PowerPoint presentation,
    PPWT1.12–PPWT1.17
Live link, PPWT1.12
Live Preview, IO.40, PP1.49, PP1.60, PP2.36

m

Magnification, IO.33
Main dictionary, PP1.16
Major concepts. See Concept
Master, PP2.42
Master slide. See Slide master
Master Views group, PPCS.4
.mdb, IO.54
Metadata, IO.51
Microsoft Help system, IO.60–IO.65
Middle alignment, PP2.18
Mini toolbar, IO.39, IO.41–IO.43, PP1.48, PP1.50
Minimize button, IO.14
Minimize/expand ribbon, IO.24
Motion Path, PP2.50
Mouse actions, IO.31, IO.37
Mouse pointer, IO.14
Move, IO.47–IO.48
    bulleted item, PP1.24
    numbered list, PP1.31–PP1.32
    placeholder, PP1.45
    selection, PP1.20
    slide, PP1.22, PP1.40–PP1.41
    between slides, PP1.11–PP1.13

n

Navigation keys, IO.31, IO.35
    slide, PP1.12
    Slide Show view, PP1.62
New Slide drop-down menu, PP2.11
New tab, IO.26
Next slide, PP1.12
Normal view, PP1.6
Notes master, PP2.42
Notes pages, PP2.67–PP2.68
    header, PP2.69–PP2.70
    print, PP2.73
Notes pane, PP1.5, PP1.6

Number of bullets per slide, PP1.28
Number of words per line, PP1.28
Numbered list
    create, PP1.30–PP1.31
    demote, PP1.33
    move, PP1.31–PP1.32
    promote, PP1.33

o

Object, PP1.6
Object animations, PP2.47
Office 2010 programs, IO.2
Office clipboard, IO.45
Office help, IO.60–IO.65
Office.com templates, PP1.10
On-demand tabs, IO.20
OneNote 2010, IO.2
Open dialog box, IO.28
Open options, IO.29
Opening a file, IO.28–IO.30
Opening a presentation template, PP1.9–PP1.11
Orientation, PP1.67, PP1.68, PP2.68
Outline tab, PP1.6, PP1.13–PP1.15
Outlook 2010, IO.2
Overview (application programs). See Application
    programs (overview)

p

Page orientation, PP1.67, PP1.68, PP2.68
Paragraph, PP1.47
Paragraph dialog box, IO.23
Paragraph formatting, PP1.47
Paragraph group, PP1.74, PP2.79, PPCS.2
Paste, IO.45, IO.46, IO.48
Paste Options, IO.46
Paste Preview, IO.46
Paste Special dialog box, PPWT1.15
.pcx, PP1.54
Pen, PP2.64, PP2.65
Photograph, PP1.54
Picture, PP1.54, PP2.20–PP2.26
    crop, PP2.23–PP2.24
    enhance, PP2.25, PP2.26
    insert, PP2.20
Picture Border, PP1.59, PP1.61, PP2.26
Picture bullet designs, PP2.45
Picture Bullet dialog box, PP2.45
Picture Effects, PP1.59, PP1.61, PP2.26
Picture Layout, PP1.59
Picture style, PP1.59, PP1.60, PP2.25, PP2.26
Picture Styles gallery, PP1.59
Picture Styles group, PP1.75, PP2.81, PPCS.4
Picture Tools Format tab, PP1.58, PP1.74–PP1.75,
    PP2.22, PP2.81, PPCS.4
Placeholder, PP1.6
    AutoFit, PP1.28
    change, PP1.43–PP1.44
    move, PP1.45
    size, PP1.44
    two content layout, PP1.43–PP1.44
Placeholder text, PP1.6
Plan, PP1.4
.potm, IO.54
.potx, IO.54
Power failure, IO.53
PowerPoint 2010, IO.10–IO.11

Speaker notes, PP2.67–PP2.68. *See also* Notes pages
Spelling checker, PP1.16–PP1.17, PP1.37–PP1.38
Spelling corrections, PP1.16–PP1.18, PP1.37–PP1.38
Spelling dialog box, PP1.37
Spelling indicator, PP1.16, PP1.38
Splitting text between slides, PP1.28–PP1.30
Start Slide Show group, PP1.74, PPCS.3
Starting an Office 2010 application, IO.14–IO.15
Status bar, IO.14, IO.15, PP1.5
Style, PP1.59
Subscript, PP1.51
Superscript, PP1.51
System clipboard, IO.45, IO.47

t

Table, PP2.9–PP2.20
   aligning text in cells, PP2.17–PP2.19
   create table slide, PP2.10–PP2.11
   enter data, PP2.12–PP2.15
   insert, PP2.11–PP2.12
   overview, PP2.10
   selection options, PP2.14
   sizing, PP2.15–PP2.16
   style, PP2.19–PP2.20
Table group, PPCS.5, PPWT1.18
Table reference, PP2.10
Table style, PP2.19–PP2.20
Table Styles group, PP2.19, PP2.81, PPCS.5, PPWT1.18
Table Tools Design tab, PP2.19, PP2.81, PPCS.5, PPWT1.18
Table Tools Layout tab, PPCS.5, PPWT1.18
Tabs, IO.18, IO.19–IO.20
Tag, IO.51
Task pane, IO.24
Template, PP1.5, PP1.9–PP1.11
Terminology. *See* Concept; Glossary
Text
   edit, IO.36, IO.37
   enter, IO.34–IO.35
   format, IO.40–IO.43
   select, IO.37–IO.40
Text box, PP2.31–PP2.35
Text effects, IO.40, PP1.50–PP1.53
Text group, PP2.80, PPCS.3
Theme, PP2.36–PP2.40
Theme color, PP2.38–PP2.40
Themes gallery, PP2.36
Themes group, PP2.80, PPCS.3
.thmx, IO.54
Thumbnail, PP1.6
.tif, PP1.34
Title, IO.51

Title bar, IO.14
Title slide, PP1.6
Tooltip, IO.16
Top alignment, PP2.18
Transition, PP2.47–PP2.50
Transition to This Slide group, PP2.80, PPCS.3
Transitions tab, PPCS.3
Two Content layout, PP1.43
Typeface, IO.40

U

Underline, PP1.51, PP1.52
Undo, IO.43–IO.45
Undo drop-down menu, IO.44

V

Version compatibility, IO.55
Vertical alignment, PP2.18
View, PP1.6, PP2.75
View buttons, IO.15, PP1.5
View selector, IO.14
View tab, IO.67, PP1.74, PP2.80, PPCS.4
Visio 2010, IO.2

W

Wavy red line, PP1.16
White out the screen, PP2.63
Window, IO.14–IO.15, PP1.5
Window button, IO.14
Window title bar, PP1.35
Wipe Left transition effect, PP2.49
Word 2010, IO.2–IO.4

X

.xls, IO.54
.xlsm, IO.54
.xlsx, IO.54
.xltx, IO.54
.xml, PP1.34
.xps, IO.54

Z

Zoom, IO.33–IO.34
Zoom dialog box, IO.33, IO.34
Zoom group, IO.67
Zoom slider, IO.14, IO.15, IO.33

Credits